extraordinary
uses for *Ordinary* things

1,120 Secrets for Better Cleaning, Fixing, Healing, & Gardening

Ingenious Ways to Use Everyday Items that **Save Time** and **Money**

Reader's Digest

Pleasantville, New York / Montreal

Project Staff

Editor
Don Earnest

Designers
Richard Kershner
Michele Laseau
Elizabeth Tunnicliffe

Production Associate
Erick Swindell

Contributing Writers
Kim Gayton Elliott
Beth Kalet
Deliliah Smittle

Contributing Proofreader
Marilyn Knowlton

Contributing Indexer
Nan Badget

Reader's Digest Books

Editor in Chief
Neil Wertheimer

Managing Editor
Suzanne G. Beason

Creative Director
Michele Laseau

Production Technology Director
Doug Croll

Manufacturing Manager
John L. Cassidy

Marketing Director
Dawn Nelson

President and Publisher, Trade Publishing
Harold Clarke

President,
U.S. Books & Home Entertainment
Dawn Zier

Reader's Digest Association, Inc.

President, North America
Global Editor in Chief
Eric Schrier

Address any comments about
Extraordinary Uses for Ordinary Things to:

The Reader's Digest Association, Inc.
Editor in Chief, Books and Music
Reader's Digest Road
Pleasantville, NY 10570-7000

To order copies of *Extraordinary Uses for Ordinary Things*,
call 1-800-846-2100.
Visit our website at **rd.com**

Printed in the United States of America
3 5 7 9 10 8 6 4 2

To Our Readers:

The information in this book has been carefully researched, and all efforts have been made to ensure its accuracy and safety. Reader's Digest Association, Inc., does not assume any responsibility for any injuries suffered or damages or losses incurred as a result of following the instructions in this book. Before taking any action based on information in this book, study the information carefully and make sure that you understand it fully. Observe all warnings and test any new or unusual repair or cleaning method before applying it broadly, or on a highly visible area or valuable item. The mention of any brand or product in this book does not imply an endorsement. All prices and product names mentioned are subject to change and should be considered general examples rather than specific recommendations.

Do the
Extraordinary
With the Ordinary

Welcome to the cleverest collection
of time- and money-saving advice you've ever seen!
Inside you'll find more than 1,100 ingenious tips
like these that harness the amazing power
of everyday pantry items.

What's the secret to fluffy omelets?

Just whip in a half teaspoon of baking soda for every three eggs you use.

Are your wrapping paper rolls a raggedy mess?

Tuck the rolls into tubes made from cutting the legs off old pantyhose.

Need to safely store small holiday ornaments?

Use egg cartons; they have a protective lid and readily stack in a larger box.

What's an easy way to make your toilet bowl gleam?

Drop a denture tablet in the bowl, wait 20 minutes, and then flush.

Got an ink stain on your carpet?

Apply a paste made with a little milk and cornstarch, let dry well, then vacuum.

Got a tough tomato stain on your shirt?

Just spray some WD-40 on it, wait a couple of minutes, then wash as usual.

Can't get that old wallpaper off the wall?

Saturate it using a solution of 1 capful of fabric softener in 4 cups of water.

Want a sparkling windshield fast?

Clean it with club soda. Carbonation speeds the process and removes droppings and grime.

Want a good flea and tick repellant for your dog?

Fill a spray bottle with equal parts white vinegar and water, apply it to his coat, and rub it in well.

extraordinary
uses for Ordinary things

What's Inside

Extraordinary!

SPECIAL ∧ SECTION

Extraordinary Uses for **60 Everyday Items** page 90

Hundreds of tips guaranteed to simplify your day and save you a fortune!

The Happiest Grocery Trip of Your Life

Are you reading this standing in line at the grocery store checkout? Yes? Good. We cordially invite you to spend the next 10 minutes with us. Trust us, you'll enjoy this.

Politely remove your cart from the line. Walk to the Cleaning Supplies aisle. Observe the window cleaners. Lines and lines of blue, purple, yellow concoctions. Special formulations, boosted power, floral scents—the labels are intriguing. Now look at the prices. Ouch! Up to $5.99 a bottle? Too much! If there is one in your shopping cart already, put it back. Then walk with us, to the condiments aisle.

There on the bottom is a jug of distilled white vinegar. A couple of teaspoons of vinegar, mixed in some water, cleans windows every bit as good as those fancy brand-name products—and at pennies to the dollar! And this same vinegar can unclog pipes, shine your silverware, and remove berry stains from your hands. In fact, we know of 188 ingenious uses for vinegar. They are all inside here, starting on page 66. So go ahead and buy the gallon jug.

Next, roll your cart back to the produce section. Find the lemons. Yes, lemons. Oh, magical lemons! These little squirts will clean marble, deodorize sinks, whiten clothes, soothe poison ivy, and keep rice from sticking. In this book you'll find more than three dozen ingenious uses for lemons. So find a three-pound bag and toss it in!

This is getting fun. Ready for a real good one? Head to the Baking Supplies section. Locate the baking soda. Still under $1 a box! But what amazing power for just a few pennies' worth! Baking soda can fluff omelets, clean cutting boards, remove crayon marks from walls, fill in as a tooth cleaner and antiperspirant, and serve as a plant food. And that's barely a start. Yes, take some home!

OK, you can check out now. Or not. You first might want to head to the Baby Supplies aisle for wipes, powder, and oil—dozens of clever, surprising uses for those. Or the pharmacy area for some toothpaste, dental floss, and mouthwash—you'd be amazed how many handy uses there are for each that have nothing to do with dental hygiene. Or get some club soda, mayonnaise, or yogurt—all have purposes beyond their usual role as mere food.

Back in line? Be sure to throw this special report into your cart as well. After all, by skipping all those costly brand-name products, we just saved you a small fortune! Imagine how much you'll save on your next grocery-shopping trip, having read *Extraordinary Uses for Ordinary Things!*

—— THE EDITORS

Power up dish-washing liquid by adding BAKING SODA.

Use PLASTIC STORAGE LIDS to keep frozen hamburgers separated.

Prevent grease splatters by adding SALT to the hot oil.

Remove tarnish from silverware with SOUR MILK.

Amazing Kitchen Rescues

Prepping, cooking, cleaning, storing— the kitchen is by far the busiest room in the house. Here are our favorite tricks for being a meal master—tricks that you can conjure up from your own kitchen staples.

Did you know that secreted away in your own kitchen cabinets are a wide variety of ordinary products that make your cooking, cleaning, and other kitchen tasks a lot more hassle free and even fun to do?

You can use them to speed food preparation, make meals cook easier and faster, prepare fancy desserts, and create environmentally safe, powerful cleansers. They can even be used to prolong the storage life of perishable foods, handle minor cuts and burns, and repel insects. And these produces are truly ordinary everyday things—toothpicks, plastic bags, recycled squeeze bottles and plastic lids, aluminum foil, baking soda, coffee filters, even apples, to name a few.

Other products that are ordinarily found in your bathroom or garage— mouthwash and WD-40, for example—can do double duty as spot removers and disinfecting agents in your kitchen.

Now is the time to stop wasting money on those expensive commercial cleansers, prepared foods, and condiments, and learn how to save both time and cash with the simple, proven fixes on the following pages.

Unexpected tricks to help the family cook

You'd be surprised at the number of ways that ordinary items from the refrigerator or a cabinet shelf can help you prepare better meals and do it more easily. Here are some examples.

> Want a juicy roast chicken? If your roasted chicken tends to emerge from the oven as dry as a snow boot on a summer's day, don't fret. There's an easy solution. The next time you roast a chicken, stuff an apple inside the bird before placing it in the roasting pan. When it's done cooking, toss the fruit in the trash, and get ready to sit down to a delicious—and juicy—main course.

> To keep your rice from sticking together in a gloppy mass, add a spoonful of lemon juice to the boiling water when cooking. When the rice is done, let it cool for a few minutes; then fluff with a fork before serving.

> To microwave potatoes faster, stick four toothpick "legs" in one side. The suspended potato will cook much faster because the microwaves will reach the bottom as well as the top and sides.

> To eliminate stinky fish smell, try this trick. Put a dollop of peanut butter in the pan with the frying fish. The peanut butter absorbs the odor instead of your furnishings.

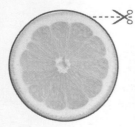

> Prevent your potatoes from turning brown, which tends to happen during boiling—especially when you're having company for dinner. Again, lemon juice is the answer. Just squeeze a teaspoon of fresh lemon juice into the cooking water. Do the same for cauliflower, which also tends to brown.

> To rein in splatters when frying, poke a few holes in the bottom of a clean recycled aluminum pie pan and place it upside down over the food in your frying pan. Use a pair of tongs or a fork to lift the pie pan and don't forget to wear a cooking glove.

> Another way to prevent grease splatters: Add a few dashes of salt to the pan before beginning to fry foods that can splatter. You'll cook without pain, and you won't have to clean grease off your cooktop.

> Keep a pot from boiling over and making a mess. Just stick a toothpick, laid flat, between the lid and pot. The little space will allow enough steam to escape to prevent the pot from boiling over. This also works with a casserole dish that's cooking in the oven.

> To keep sausages from rolling around in the frying pan, the answer again is toothpicks. Just insert them between pairs of sausages. It also makes turning them over easy, and they'll cook more evenly and only need to be turned over once.

> To microwave bacon mess-free, layer two paper towels on the bottom of your microwave and lay slices of bacon side by side on them. Cover with two more paper towels. Run your microwave on High at 1-minute intervals, checking for crispness. It should take 3 to 4 minutes. The towels absorb the grease; just toss them for easy cleanup.

> What's the secret to making fluffier omelets? For every three eggs used, add 1/2 teaspoon of baking soda. Shhhh! Don't let it get around.

> To make soggy lettuce crisp, all you need is a little lemon juice. Add the juice of half a lemon to a bowl of cold water. Then put the soggy lettuce in it and refrigerate for 1 hour. Make sure to dry the leaves completely before putting them into salads or sandwiches.

> Need an extra-large salad bowl? You've invited half the neighborhood over for dinner, but don't have a bowl big

4 hassle-free ways to travel with food

Here are some unexpected tricks that can make carrying food with you on a trip a lot easier.

1 Worried about checking into a hotel after the kitchen has closed? You won't have to resort to the cold, overpriced snacks in the mini-bar if you remember to pack a couple of cheese sandwiches wrapped in aluminum foil. Just use the free clothes iron found in most hotel rooms to press both sides of the wrapped sandwich, and you'll have a tasty hot snack.

2 Has your doctor put you on a low-sodium diet or do you need potassium salt for restaurant meals? Or do you want to take salt and pepper to season your brown-bag lunch? Straws provide an easy way to carry small amounts of dry seasonings. Fold one end over and tape it shut, fill it, and fold and tape the other end. If moisture is a concern, use plastic straws.

3 Need to bring home-made food for Baby on the road? Use a disposable margarine tub for a container that won't break in your baby bag. It's also a handy food bowl, and you won't have to wrap it up and bring it home for cleaning.

4 And what about Fido? Lightweight, disposable margarine tubs also make perfect pet food containers—and double as food and water bowls. And those valuable dog cookies won't get crushed if you put them in a plastic tub.

enough to toss that much salad. Don't panic. Just line the kitchen sink with aluminum foil and toss away!

> If you're short on mixing bowls when you're cooking for a crowd, use a plastic bag instead. Place all the dry ingredients to be mixed in the bag, gather it up, and gently shake. If the ingredients are wet, use your hands to mix them by squeezing the outside of the bag.

> To easily remove a garlic clove from marinade, stick a toothpick through the clove so you can just lift it out when you are ready to serve the food.

> When freezing hamburgers for later use, plastic lids can be very helpful. Season the meat and shape it into patties. Place each patty on a plastic lid. Then stack them up, place in a plastic bag, and freeze. When the grill is fired up, you'll have no trouble separating your pre-formed hamburgers.

> Stew too salty? Salting to taste is one thing, but it is possible to overdo it. When you find yourself getting heavy-handed with the saltshaker, simply drop a few apple (or potato) wedges in your pot. After cooking for another 10 minutes or so, remove the wedges—along with the excess salt.

> To keep bread fresher longer— especially if you live in a high-humidity area—store it in a paper bag rather than a plastic one. The paper's ability to "breathe" will keep the bread's crust crisp while allowing the center of the loaf to stay soft and moist.

> To keep frozen bread from getting soggy, place a paper towel in each bag of bread to be frozen. When you're ready to eat that frozen loaf, the paper towel absorbs the moisture as the bread thaws. This is an especially helpful idea if you like to buy bread in bulk from the discount store and freeze it.

Helpful tricks for the home dessert chef

There's no denying that urge to pop something sweet and aromatic in the oven on a chilly day. But often problems come up that make the process more of a hassle than it should be. And just as often the solution is already in your cabinet.

> For a perfect piecrust, keep the edges from burning by covering them with strips of aluminum foil. The foil prevents the edges from getting overdone while the rest of your pie gets perfectly browned.

> To make a teddy bear birthday cake, a Valentine's Day heart cake, a Christmas tree cake, or whatever shaped cake the occasion may call for, just form a double thickness of heavy-duty aluminum foil into the desired shape inside a large cake pan.

> Making a graham cracker crust? Don't spend hard-earned grocery dollars on a box of pre-crushed crackers or a ready-to-fill cracker crust. It's a snap to crush graham crackers yourself. Just roughly crumble several graham crackers into a plastic bag. Lay the bag on the kitchen counter and go over it several times with a rolling pin. In no time, you'll have as many crumbs as you need, plus the remainder of a box of crackers to snack on as well.

> To soften hardened brown sugar, chip off a piece, wrap it in aluminum foil, and bake it in the oven at 300°F (150°C) for five minutes.

> Another way to fluff up hardened brown sugar: If you have more time, simply place an apple wedge in a self-sealing plastic bag with the chunk of hardened brown sugar. Tightly seal the bag and put it in a dry place for a day or two. Your sugar will once again be soft enough to use.

> To grease a cake pan or cookie sheet, place a sandwich bag over your hand, scoop up a small amount of shortening or butter from the tub, and start greasing. You can leave the bag in the canister of shortening for next time.

> For dusting your cake pans or muffin cups, put flour into a large salt-shaker. Keep it neat and keep it handy in the cupboard, especially if you have an aggressively helpful junior chef!

> For cinnamon toast in a hurry, a large saltshaker is also the answer. Just mix sugar and cinnamon in the shaker. Once you've found the proportions you like, you can make cinnamon toast easily and consistently every time. Your cinnamon-sugar shaker is also perfect for sprinkling a little flavor on cereal.

> No pastry bag handy? No problem. Form a piece of heavy-duty aluminum foil into a tube and fill it with free-flowing frosting. Bonus: There's no

Easy instant centerpieces

Here are couple of easy ways you can make a quick centerpiece for your table with the help of some ordinary things that you probably already have around the house.

1 Secure a pillar candle or a few votive candles to an **aluminum pie pan** by melting some wax from the bottom of the candles onto the pan. Add a thin layer of **water or sand,** and put in several **rose petals or seashells.**

2 Add a cozy, country feel to your table setting by creating a natural candleholder. Use an apple corer to carve a hole three-quarters of the way down into a pair of **large apples,** insert a tall decorative candle into each hole, surround the apples with a few **leaves, branches, or flowers,** and voilà! You have a lovely centerpiece.

BONUS TIP: Don't let loose candles spoil the romantic mood or cause a fire at your next candlelight dinner. If the candles don't fit snugly into the holder, wrap layers of tape around their bottom edges until they fit just right.

pastry bag to clean—simply toss out the foil when you're done.

> **Another quick pastry bag:** Place the decorating frosting into a self-sealing plastic bag. Squish out the air and zip it shut. Snip off a corner of the bag to the size you want—start conservatively—and you are ready to begin squeezing. Works with deviled-egg mix, too.

> **To decorate a cake** with fine curlicues of chocolate, reach for the vegetable peeler. A peeler is also handy when you need cheese slivers that are thinner than you can cut with a knife.

> **For fail-safe cake decorating,** cut a piece of wax paper the same size as your cake, using the cake pan as a guide. Then pipe the name and the message onto the paper.

Then supporting the paper with a piece of cardboard, put it in the freezer. After just half an hour it should be easy to handle. Loosen the frosting and slide it off onto the cake using a spatula. Everyone will think that you're a cake-decorating professional!

> **To keep cakes fresh longer,** store them in an airtight container or sealed plastic bag with half an apple. It helps the cake maintain moisture much longer than merely popping it into the fridge.

> **Another cake preserver:** Store the cake in an airtight container with a couple of sugar cubes, and it will stay fresh for days longer. Store a few lumps of sugar with cheese the same way to prevent the cheese from molding.

> **To create a gelatin or mousse centerpiece** for your next birthday party or barbecue, don't buy a fancy mold; just use a large margarine tub as the mold. The flexible tubs are easy to squeeze to release the dessert.

> **For fun individual gelatin dessert molds,** use smaller margarine tubs and put a surprise gummy or mini-marshmallow face on the top, which will show

Extraordinary!

Butter too hard to cut?

If you're in a hurry and don't have time to soften the butter to room temperature, shave off what you need with a vegetable peeler. You'll have soft butter in moments. Note: This is handy when your recipe will not allow you to use melted butter.

through from the bottom when the mold is inverted.

> **To keep ice cream smooth—**and free of those annoying, yucky ice crystals that form once the container has been opened—rewrap the container completely in plastic wrap before you return it to the freezer. Or put the container inside a large seal-sealing plastic bag.

> **To soften hardened marshmallows,** warm (don't boil) some water in a pan. Put the marshmallows in a sealable plastic bag, seal, and place in the pan. The warmth will soften them up in no time, and you'll be ready to make s'mores.

> **Melt chocolate without a mess!** Warm some water in a pan (again, do not boil). Seal the chocolate in a freezer bag and place it in the pan. In a few moments, you'll have melted chocolate, ready to bake or use for decoration.

To pipe the chocolate onto a cake, just leave the bag sealed and snip off a bottom corner of the bag. When you are done, just toss the bag; no messy bowl or pot to wash.

> **To color cookie dough** without staining your hands, place your prepared dough in a bag, add the drops of food coloring, and squish around until the color is uniform. Use the dough now or stick it in the freezer ready to roll out when the occasion arises.

Fast fixes for kitchen problems

There's nothing quite as frustrating as trying to find the end of the plastic food wrap roll, having to trot across the house for a broom when you need it now, or trying to pry apart stuck drinking glasses. But with these easy fixes—using such common items as toothpicks and rubber bands—you'll never have to get steamed in the kitchen again.

> **Can't open a jar?** Grab a piece of sandpaper and place it grit side down on the lid. The sandpaper should improve your grip enough to do the job.

> **Filling narrow-mouthed spice jars** can also make a big mess. Roll a piece of wax paper into a funnel shape and pour spices into your jars without spilling a single mustard seed. In a pinch, you can even funnel liquids by using a couple of layers of wax paper offset so the seams in the layers don't line up.

> **Other made-do funnels:** That handiest of kitchen tools, the funnel, can also be replicated easily with a small sandwich bag. Fill the bag with the contents you need funneled. Snip off a corner and transfer into the needed container. Then just toss the bag when the funneling is done.

Or make a couple of disposable funnels from an envelope. Seal the envelope, cut it in half diagonally, and snip off one corner on each half. Now you have two funnels for pouring spices into your smaller jars.

> **Need an instant colander?** Just grab a clean aluminum pie pan and a small nail, and start poking holes. Then bend the pan to fit comfortably over a deep bowl. Rinse your new colander clean, place it over the bowl, and carefully pour out your pasta.

> **Keep your spoon from slipping** into the mixing bowl by wrapping a rubber band around the top of the handle. Now you won't have to fish it out of the messy batter.

> **Securing your casserole lids** is another great use for rubber bands. If you have lovingly prepared a casserole for a potluck dinner, secure the lid to the base with a couple of wide rubber bands and you won't have to worry about carrying it safely in the car.

> **Keep your cutting board from moving** around when you're chopping up veggies. Give the board some traction by putting a rubber band around each end.

> **Can't find your turkey baster?** A cleaned squeeze bottle makes a dandy substitute. Simply squeeze out some air, and then use it to suck up the fat from your roasts and soups. You can even effectively use it to distribute marinades and drippings over meat.

> **To stop cooking oil drips,** a cleaned, recycled squirt bottle is also the answer. Fill it with olive oil or another favorite cooking oil. It's a lot easier to handle than a jar or bottle, and you can pour precisely the right amount of oil over your salads or into your frying pan without having to worry about drips or spills.

> **For easy-to-use condiments,** consider using recycled squirt bottles as well. Indeed they're great for storing any foodstuffs that are typically sold in jars—such as mayonnaise, salad dressing, jelly and jams, or honey. In addition to having fewer sticky or messy jars in your refrigerator, you'll also be lightening the load in your dishwasher by eliminating the

need for knives or spoons. Make sure you give the bottles a thorough cleaning before using.

> **Kitchen scissors losing their edge?** To sharpen them, take a piece of leftover aluminum foil, smooth it out, then fold it over a few times. Next, cut the folded foil into strips. Seven or eight cuts should be enough to put a sharp edge back on the scissors

> **Got a waffle-eating waffle iron?** Nonstick surfaces don't last forever. You can't fix the problem permanently, but to get it to work today, put a layer of wax paper in between the plates of the waffle iron for a few minutes while it heats up. The wax will be transferred to the plates, temporarily helping waffles pop out again.

> **Can't find the beginning of a plastic wrap roll?** Try this time-saving trick: Put a piece of transparent tape on your finger, sticky-side out, and dab your finger on the roll until you find the edge. Then use the short piece of tape to lift the edge and pull gently.

> **To remove a jar label or price sticker,** just soak the label with vegetable oil. It will slide right off without leaving a sticky residue.

> **Stacked drinking glasses stuck together?** It seems like nothing you can do will separate them. But the solution is simple: Pour a little vegetable oil around the rim of the bottom glass and the glasses will pull apart with ease.

> **To mend a cracked plate** from your grandmother's old china set, try using milk. Place the plate in a pan, cover it with milk (fresh or reconstituted powdered milk), and bring to a boil. As soon as it starts to boil, lower the heat and simmer for about 45 minutes. The protein in the milk will miraculously meld most fine cracks.

> **Tired of cleaning the cheese grater?** Pasta is always better with a dash of freshly grated Parmesan. But

4 ways to cope with kids and food

Children and food are a natural duo. Here are some ways that you can use ordinary things from your kitchen cabinet to make that combination work more smoothly.

1 Sandwich-bag kitchen gloves
There's nothing more welcome than helping hands in the kitchen. But when they're little hands that tend to get dirty and leave prints all over the place, then something must be done. Before they start "helping" you make those chocolate chip cookies, place small sandwich bags over their hands. These instant gloves are disposable for easy cleanup.

2 Plastic lid coasters
Entertaining a crowd of kids and want to make sure your tabletops survive? (Or at least give them a fighting chance!) Give kids plastic lids to use as coasters. Write their names on the coasters so they won't get their drinks mixed up.

3 Paper towel place mat
Your darling grandchildren are coming for an extended visit, and though they are adorable, they're a disaster at mealtime. Paper towels can help you weather the storm. Use a paper towel as a place mat. It will catch spills and crumbs during the meal and makes cleaning up easy.

4 Clever lunch box tubs
Give kids some lunch box variety. As a break from the usual sandwich, put some fruit salad, rice mix, or other interesting fare in one or two recycled margarine tubs for your child's lunch. The tubs are easy to open and will keep the food from getting crushed.

who wants to bother washing the grater after each use? Instead, stick the grater into a sealable plastic bag along with the cheese wedge and keep them in the fridge together.

> **Keep that cookbook from getting splattered**—especially if it's one you've borrowed to try a new recipe. Cover the book with a clear plastic bag. You'll be able to read the directions, while the book stays clean.

Surprising ways to ease your kitchen cleanup

Spills, stains, tarnish, and hard-to-remove grease and food are all an inevitable part of life in the kitchen. But with some fixes you may not have thought of, you can easily clean up the mess. At the same time, you can detox your cleaning supplies, stretch your budget, and save space in your cupboard by making your own simple, safe kitchen-cleaning supplies.

> For a more powerful dish-washing liquid, try adding 2 tablespoons baking soda to the usual amount of liquid you use. Then watch it cut through grease like a hot knife!

> For a cheap, effective scouring mix that can be safely used on all of your metal cookware, simply combine equal parts salt and flour and add just enough vinegar to make a paste. Work the paste around the cooking surface and the outside of the utensil, then rinse off with warm water and dry thoroughly with a soft dish towel.

> Stubborn baked-on food and grease? Before washing, sprinkle salt over the stuck-on food. Dampen it with a sprinkling of water and let it sit until the salt causes the baked-on food to come loose, then wash it away with soapy water.

> To get burnt-on stains off enamel pans, you don't have to scrub until you run out of elbow grease. Soak the pan overnight in saltwater. Then boil the saltwater in the pan the next day. The stains should lift right off.

> Stuff stuck on your nonstick pan? We all know that food often sticks to so-called nonstick pans. And, of course, using steel wool to get it off is a no-no. The quick solution: scrape off the gunk with a plastic lid.

> Clean your can opener by "opening" a paper towel. Close the wheel on the edge of a paper towel, close the handles, and turn the crank. The paper towel will clean off the gunk as the wheel cuts through it.

> Keep cast-iron pots rust-free. After they're clean, place a paper towel in each to absorb any moisture. Store lids separately from the pots, separated by a lining of paper towels. No more ugly surprises when you reach for the pot again.

> To brighten copper pots and pans—or decorative copper molds—don't pay big bucks for smelly cleaners. Shine them with ketchup. That's right: plain old everyday ketchup. It's cheaper than commercial tarnish removers—a lot cheaper if you use the store brand—and you don't have to wear protective gloves to apply it.

Just coat the surface of the copper with a thin layer of ketchup. Let it sit for five to thirty minutes, depending on how badly tarnished the pan is. Acids in the ketchup will react with the tarnish and remove it, leaving your pan gleaming. Rinse the pan and dry immediately.

> To remove especially stubborn tarnish, make a paste by mixing lemon juice with salt. Coat the affected area of the pan and leave it on for five minutes or so. Then wash in warm water, rinse, and buff dry. That should restore the pan's shine.

The same mixture will brighten dull brass or stainless steel pans, and metal kitchen sinks, too. And you can substitute baking soda or cream of tartar for the salt.

> Need to polish your silverware? Don't buy expensive, messy silver polish. Make your tarnished silverware look like new with a little help from some sour milk.

Now we know that most people don't keep sour milk on hand if they can help it. But you can easily make some by adding a little vinegar to fresh milk (add 1 tablespoon of vinegar for each cup of milk, and stir).

Then simply soak the silver in the milk for half an hour to loosen the tarnish. Finish by washing in warm, soapy water and buffing with a soft cloth.

> Another way to polish silverware: Try an ion exchange, a molecular reaction in which aluminum acts as a catalyst. All you have to do is line a pan with a sheet of aluminum foil, fill it with cold water, and carefully stir in 2 teaspoons of salt.

Drop your tarnished silverware into the solution, let it sit for two to three minutes, then rinse off and dry.

> To keep silverware untarnished, store your freshly cleaned silver on top of a sheet of aluminum foil.

> For long-term storage of silverware, first tightly cover each piece in cellophane wrap—be sure to squeeze out as much air as possible—then wrap in foil and seal the ends.

> To protect kitchen cabinet tops that don't extend to the ceiling, put a layer of wax paper on top to catch dust and grease particles. You can even cover the top of your refrigerator with waxed paper. Every month or two, just carefully fold up the old dusty wax paper, discard it, and put down a fresh layer.

> To shine chrome fixtures, you don't need pricey commercial cleaners. A nongel-type toothpaste works just as

Don't have a scrub pad?

When a regular scrub pad isn't handy, crumple up a handful of aluminum foil and use it to scrub your pots. You can even use foil that you were going to toss.

Extraordinary!

well. Just smear on the toothpaste, straight from the tube, and polish the area with a soft dry cloth.

> Never have a broom when you need it? Don't run to the hall closet every time you need to sweep. Instead, use a screw to attach a magnet about halfway down the broom handle. Then store the broom by sticking the magnet to the side of your refrigerator between the fridge and the wall, where it will remain hidden until you are ready to use it.

Quick ways to blast kitchen stains—with WD-40!

The next time you visit the hardware store, buy an extra can of WD-40, yes WD-40, to keep in your kitchen—it's an amazing stain remover. Just remember to open the windows if you are using a lot of it because this product is famous for its fumes.

Remove tea stains from countertops by spraying a little WD-40 on a sponge or damp cloth and just wipe the stain away.

For an obstinate tomato stain on your favorite apron or other garment, just spray some WD-40 directly on the spot, wait a couple of minutes, and then wash as usual.

Spray a carpet stain on your kitchen or dining room with WD-40, wait a minute or two, and then use your regular carpet cleaner—or gently cleanse with a sponge and warm, soapy water until the stain disappears completely.

To remove tough scuff marks on a vinyl or tile floor, spray them with WD-40. It won't harm the surface, and you won't have to scrub nearly as much.

6 nontoxic bug blasters for the kitchen

You can make your kitchen a no-fly zone for insect pests with non-toxic repellents and traps that you can make from everyday kitchen staples.

1 To get rid of **fruit flies** hovering in the kitchen, get out a fine-misting spray bottle and fill it with rubbing alcohol. Spraying the little flies knocks them out and makes them fall to the floor, where you can sweep them up.

2 Make your own **pest strips** by covering empty paper-towel or toilet-paper rolls with transparent tape, sticky side out. Hang them in the kitchen or wherever else you need them.

3 Keep your kitchen free of flies with a homemade **flytrap** that uses no toxic chemicals. In a small saucepan, simmer 2 cups of milk, 1/4 pound (115 grams) of raw sugar, and 2 ounces (55 grams) of ground pepper for about 10 minutes, stirring occasionally. Pour into shallow dishes or bowls and set them around the kitchen, patio, or anywhere the flies are a problem. The pestiferous bugs will flock to the bowls and drown!

4 To **ant-proof** your kitchen, give it the lemon treatment. First squirt some lemon juice on door thresholds and windowsills. Then squeeze lemon juice into any holes or cracks where the ants are getting in. Finally, scatter small slices of lemon peel around the outdoor entrance. The ants will get the message that they aren't welcome.

5 For **roaches and fleas**, lemons are also effective. Simply mix the juice of 4 lemons (along with the rinds) with 1/2 gallon (2 liters) of water and wash your floors with it; then watch the fleas and roaches flee. They hate the smell.

6 If you have **roaches**, don't call an exterminator to spray noxious pesticides. Instead, scatter a mixture of equal parts sugar and baking powder over the infested area. The sugar will attract the roaches, and the baking powder will kill them. Replace it frequently with a fresh mixture to prevent future infestations.

Appliances clean and simple

Appliances. We can't live without them, but—it's as if they have a secret life of their own—they seem to attract dirt and funky odors even when you don't use them. How do they do it? How do you deal with it?

> Has ice cream or meat juice leaked in your freezer? You don't have to defrost the freezer to clean them up. Spilled, sticky foods frozen to the bottom of your freezer don't stand a chance against glycerin. Unstick the spill and wipe it clean with a rag dabbed with glycerin, which is a natural solvent.

> To keep vegetable and meat bins clean, line them with a layer of wax paper. When it needs to be replaced, just wad it up and toss it in the trash—or if it's not stained with meat juices, you can add it to your compost pile.

> To keep fridge shelves clean, use plastic lids as coasters under food containers to catch any potential leaks. Drippy bottles and containers with leaks can create a big mess. If the lids get dirty, throw them in the dishwasher. Meanwhile, your fridge shelves will stay free of a sticky mess.

> To remove refrigerator odors, dab lemon juice on a cotton ball or sponge and leave it in the fridge for several hours. Remember to toss out any malodorous items that might be causing the bad smell.

Of course, you'll still want to put that box of baking soda inside your refrigerator to keep it smelling clean when you're done.

> If your kitchen stinker is your garbage disposer, freshen it up with salt. Just dump in 1/2 cup of salt, run the cold water, and start the disposer. The salt will dislodge stuck waste and neutralize odors.

Afterward, try sending a lemon rind down the disposer. It will waft a fresh citrus fragrance throughout the entire room. As a matter of fact, an easy way to deodorize your disposer is to save leftover lemon and orange peels and toss them down the drain once every month.

> **To mop up that flaky residue in a self-cleaning oven,** which is left over when it's done cleaning, don't waste an expensive roll of paper towels; wipe up that ashlike stuff up with a few sheets of moistened, crumpled newspaper.

> **To prevent splatters in your microwave,** use coffee filters to cover bowls or dishes when cooking food in your microwave oven. The filters, like all paper, are microwave safe.

> **Give your microwave a good cleaning** without scratching the surface with harsh cleansers or using a lot of elbow grease. Just mix 3 tablespoons of lemon juice into 1 1/2 cups of water in a microwave-safe bowl.

Microwave the mixture on High for 5 to 10 minutes, allowing the steam to condense on the inside walls and ceiling of the oven. Then just wipe away the softened food with a dishcloth.

First aid in the kitchen

In the kitchen, cuts and burns are an ever-present possibility. To be on the safe side, keep a first-aid chart and emergency phone numbers taped to the inside of a cabinet door. If you, or a family member, are seriously hurt, seek medical help right away, but for everyday nicks and burns, there are safe and soothing treatments right in your cabinet.

> **If you get burned** by accidentally grabbing a hot pot or getting splattered with grease, grab the vanilla extract from the cabinet to gain quick pain relief. The evaporation of the alcohol in the vanilla extract cools the burn.

> **To keep a burn from forming a blister,** it helps to apply an ice cube to the burn. The cold will also reduce the pain and speed recovery.

> **Another burn treatment:** Pour some baking soda into a container of ice water, soak a cloth in it, and apply it to the burn. Keep applying it until the burn no longer feels hot.

> **To remove a stubborn splinter,** soak it in vegetable oil. The oil will soften up your skin, perhaps just enough to ease that splinter out with your tweezers.

> **To disinfect a small cut** and stop bleeding, pour a few drops of lemon juice directly on the cut or apply the juice with a cotton ball and hold firmly in place for a minute. It will sting, but as your mother used to say, that only proves it is working.

Alternatively, you can clean and disinfect a minor cut with some alcohol-based mouthwash from the bathroom. Remember that before it became mouthwash, it was used as an antiseptic to prevent surgical infection.

> **Another quick fix for a bleeding finger:** Alum, the old-fashioned pickling salt at the back of your spice cupboard, is an astringent. In a pinch, sprinkle some on a minor cut to stanch the flow of blood.

Safe ways to clean grimy hands

Got your hands messy with grease or paint? Don't use smelly solvents to get them clean. Try one of these safer solutions:

■ Spray your hands with nonstick cooking spray, work it in well, then rinse. Wash with soap and water.

■ Pour 1 teaspoon of olive oil and 1 teaspoon of salt or sugar into your palms. Vigorously rub them over your hands and between your fingers for several minutes, then wash with soap and water. Your hands will be clean and very soft.

Extraordinary!

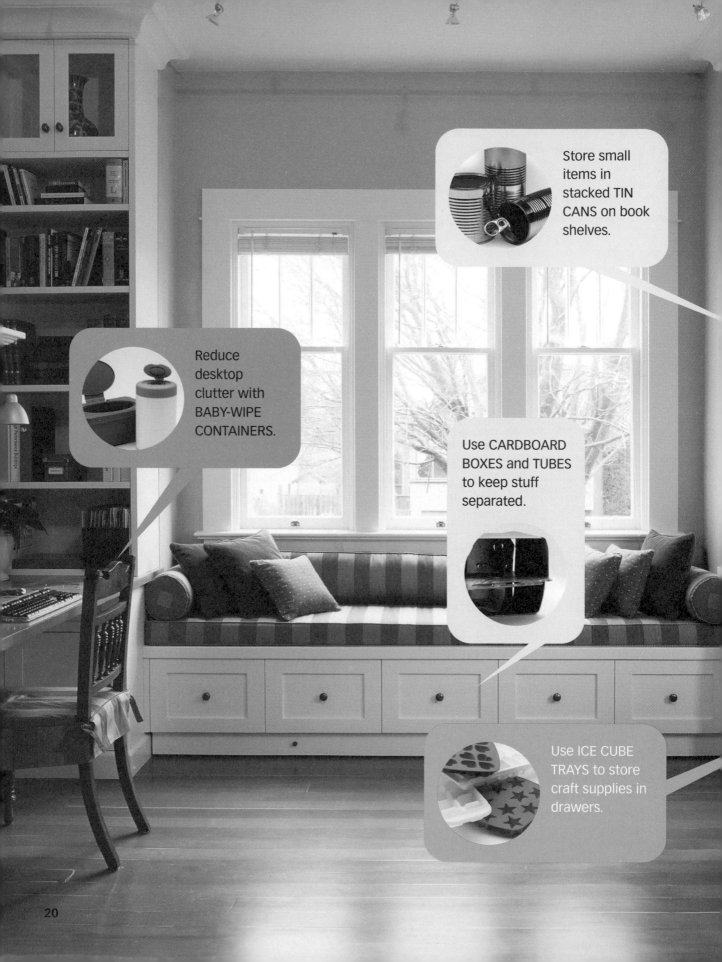

Store small items in stacked TIN CANS on book shelves.

Reduce desktop clutter with BABY-WIPE CONTAINERS.

Use CARDBOARD BOXES and TUBES to keep stuff separated.

Use ICE CUBE TRAYS to store craft supplies in drawers.

Ingenious
Storage
Solutions

Building new closets or more cabinets or installing storage systems costs a fortune! Here are free (or nearly free) ways to tame clutter, get organized, and find space for everything using everyday items.

Have you ever heard someone say, "Oh my, I have so much storage space I just don't know how to fill it all?" We haven't either. If you have an older home, you probably struggle constantly to find enough storage space. And even if you are fortunate enough have a new MacMansion—with a master bedroom walk-in larger than a New York apartment—storage space gets filled to overflowing in no time. Adding cabinets or new closets or one of those fancy storage systems with "a place for everything" can clean out your wallet faster than the extra storage can clean out your rooms.

There is an quick and easy solution to your storage problems, however, and it's right under your nose: creative use of everyday items—items that you already have in your house or have been recycling or throwing out, oblivious to their extraordinary capacity to tame your clutter.

Save that baby-wipe box!

If you have a baby in the house, there's an excellent chance you are also tossing out a lot of plastic boxes left from baby wipes; if not, you may be discarding a lot of those boxes from premoistened floor wipes. Quit throwing them out. These sturdy easily stacked plastic boxes can be used for storage in just about every room in the house. Wash and dry each box thoroughly, and it's ready to simplify your life and organize your home.

> **In the kitchen,** one of these boxes can make a dandy recipe-card file, while others can store seldom-used utensils like lobster crackers, cookie cutters, and serving pieces. Keep another box on the kitchen counter to store and organize coupons. Set one aside for cake decorating supplies, or use one to keep small snacks like boxes of raisins or fruit roll-ups handy.

> **In a child's room,** these boxes are terrific for storing small toys such as miniature cars, smaller blocks, and those "pocket" dolls and all their stuff. And be sure to set one aside as a "toy box to go" and fill it with small toys, sticker books, and other distractions for car trips, waiting in doctors' office, or restaurants, and visits to non-child-friendly places.

> **In the office,** use these boxes to store envelopes, notecards, pens and pencils, old floppy disks, or CDs. In the shop, store rags and paper towels in a plastic box to keep them clean and your workspace orderly. Turn one box into an easy-to-access first-aid kit with cleansing wipes, bandages, scissors, antibiotic cream or spray.

You can also fit about 40 to 50 plastic shopping bags, folded and the air squeezed out, in one of these boxes. Keep it next to Fido's leash for a ready supply of bags for picking up after him or put it where it's handy to line small trash cans. Pop-up, cylindrical wipe dispensers can also be put to good use—dispense kitchen twine, office string, or crafting yarn by tucking the ball into the cylinder and threading the end up through the opening in the lid.

Cardboard to the rescue!

Take the humble cardboard box. Most people just stuff things in cardboard boxes and stick them up in the attic, down in the basement, or out in the garage. But these simple items are whizzes at creating storage solutions for little or no cost—especially those superlatively strong boxes with dividers in which wine or liquor is shipped. (You don't have to drink to acquire these; just ask at any store that sells alcoholic beverages.)

An instant drying rack

An old umbrella with a curved handle can make a quick and portable drying rack. Remove the fabric, turn the umbrella upside down, and hang it wherever you need it. This is especially handy for camping or when on a trip and you need to wash some things out at a hotel.

Extraordinary!

> **For fragile items,** such as your fine glassware, candlestick holders, or vases, individually wrap the items in newspaper and store them in the sections. Carefully wrap and store all your Christmas ornaments to keep them safe until next year.

> **In your art area,** set a divided box to hold rolled paper, canvases, drawings, and so on.

> **In your workshop,** one of these divided boxes can hold measuring sticks, dowels, moldings, metal rods, or even folded extension cords.

> **In your gardening shed,** stack three divided boxes on top of each other (removing the bottoms from the top two), carefully matching the dividers, and use duct tape to secure the boxes together. Voilà! A perfect place to store brooms, hoes, rakes, and any other long-handled tools.

> **In your children's rooms,** cover a divided box with brightly colored self-adhesive paper and use it to hold lacrosse sticks, baseball bats, play swords, fishing poles, twirling batons, and more.

Put it in a tube

While we're on the subject of cardboard, have you ever thought of all the ways you can use cardboard tubes? From the short tubes found in the center of toilet paper rolls to the mega-tubes you can get from carpet or upholstery fabric stores, cardboard tubes are potential space savers you should never throw away.

> **Use smaller tubes** to keep electrical cords (appliance, computer, hair blower, curling iron) fanfolded and tidy. Or use one to keep strings from getting tangled. Cut a notch into each end of a smaller tube. Secure one end of a string in one notch, then wind the remaining string around the tube and secure the other end in the other notch.

Improbable uses for pantyhose

Even those old runny pantyhose can provide unexpected storage solutions.

1 Want to keep your rolls of **wrapping paper** neatly rolled and tear-free? Tuck them into tubes made from cutting the legs off a pair of pantyhose.

2 When you're bundling up your **blankets** for storage during the summer months, wrap them securely in the band cut from the waist of the pantyhose.

3 Get the maximum shelf life from your **onions** by tucking them in the cut-off leg of a clean pair of pantyhose, tying a knot between each onion. The air can circulate freely, keeping the onions fresh, and you can hang the onion string in a cool, dry area of your kitchen or pantry. When you need an onion, simply cut off the bottom one, leaving the knot above intact.

4 You can use the same technique to store **flower bulbs** over the winter.

> **Use longer tubes** (from paper-towel rolls, waxpaper or plastic wrap or aluminum foil) to store rolled fabric scraps, important documents, strings of decorative holiday lights, fluorescent lightbulbs, knitting needles, and more. If you have a lot of tubes with the same thing stored in them, stack them in a box for a cubbyhole effect.

Shoe bags aren't just for footwear

Sometimes you just have to look at something a different way to realize how useful it can be. A shoe bag, whether it's a traditional flat type with pockets or a more modern type with compartments, as shown at left, makes an outstanding organizer—and not just for shoes.

> In your mudroom or front closet, hang a shoe bag to keep gloves and mittens handy and together—and scarves, earmuffs, and knitted hats ready to go. In your office, hang one near your desk for scissors; staples and staplers; pens, pencils and markers; hole punches; envelopes both large and small; or even bills in date order.

> In a utility closet or room, tuck sponges, scrub brushes, old toothbrushes for cleaning tight corners, spray bottles, and cleaning clothes separated by use.

> In the bathroom, a bag on the door is invaluable (particularly for teenagers) to hold brushes, hair-grooming products, curling irons, hair dryers, sunscreen, lotions, shaving cream, and even makeup.

> In your own closet, add an extra bag to keep all your accessories like scarves, belts, small purses, ties, socks or stockings, even lingerie neatly stored and easy to find.

> In a child's room, display small beanbag animals, fashion dolls, plastic dinosaurs, or any other smaller collection of toys in a clear plastic shoe bag.

> For a long car trip with children, either find a small shoe bag or cut down a larger one and hang it on the back of the front car seats to give your kids in the backseat easy access to toys, games, audio equipment and disks, art supplies, and maybe even a water bottle and snacks.

3 Great uses for socks

Stop tossing orphan hosiery into the trash. Believe it or not, those unaccountable loners have lots of uses in the storage game. Here are three that you may not have thought of:

1 When **STORING DELICATE HOLIDAY ORNAMENTS** or decorations in those divine divided boxes, instead of enclosing them in newspaper or bubble wrap, simply slip them into a clean sock to prevent chips or breakage.

2 **GOING ON A TRIP?** Slip shoes into old, clean socks before packing them to keep everything else in your suitcase spotless. You can also use this trick in your closet to keep your best—and probably most expensive—shoes dust-free and protected between wearings.

3 **SHOP GOGGLES** are too big and bulky to fit in a regular eyeglass case, so slide them into a sock tacked to your workbench or tool wall, or attach it to your tool belt for a clean, convenient caddy.

Up a ladder

Consider the simple wooden ladder. Yes, it is invaluable for reaching high places, but have you ever thought about converting an old one to store or display things? Here are some interesting ways to do that.

> Make a freestanding display rack from a wooden ladder for plants or collectibles. It's relatively simple:

- Remove the folding metal spreaders.
- Using wood screws, securely attach small strips of wood to the inside of the back legs at exactly the height of the rungs on the front of the ladder. These wood strips will hold shelves, so be certain to get them level with the rungs.
- Cut shelves out of plywood or melamine that fit inside the ladder's legs and span from a rung to its corresponding wood strips. You can either place the shelves freely on the rung and wood strips or, for safety, attach them with screws or wood glue.
- Sand any rough edges and then paint the shelves and ladder any color you like.

> Display quilts and more. For that homespun feel, a ladder is a great way to display lacework, crochet, quilts and throws. To prevent rough surfaces from damaging delicate fabrics, smooth wooden ladder rungs with sandpaper or metal rungs with steel wool as necessary.

> Make a pot rack for your kitchen. Fancy metal racks cost hundreds of dollars—why not use an old wooden straight ladder instead? Saw off a section, smooth the rough spots with a little sandpaper, and hang it in your kitchen. Suspend it by chains from large metal screw hooks going into the ceiling joists and into the ladder. Put additional screw hooks on the ladder to hold your pots or create S-hooks from clothes-hanger wire.

Garden uses for ladders

Create a rustic trellis for your vines and trailing plants—either indoors or out! Just attach vinyl-covered hooks to the wall and hang a straight ladder from it so that the bottoms of its legs are just above the ground.

Lay an old straight ladder down flat in the garden to make small, contained beds for herbs, salad greens, or flowers.

If you have three straight wooden ladders, they can be turned into a wonderful archway for a garden path. Cut two of the ladders to the same height and position them on opposite sides of a path. Cut the third ladder to fit across the top and tie it to the upright ladders using supple grapevine, young willow twigs, or heavy jute twine.

Extraordinary!

Can we talk cans?

How many cans—and jars—do you open and toss into recycling each week? Are you aware of their enormous storage capability.

> **To organize your tool belt,** tuck a few clean, empty frozen-juice cans into it and transform those enormous nail-pocket pouches into an extremely efficient tote for your wrenches, pliers, and screwdrivers. Or keep your various nails and screws easily accessible yet separate.

> **For organizing your family,** coffee cans are incredibly useful. Designate one can for each member of your family, paint and label them, then set them up in the mudroom or hall so that everyone has a place to put keys, change, pagers, cell phones, and all those other small items that collect in our pockets throughout the day but that we need almost every day. Do the same in the laundry room for divvying up the stuff left in pockets before wash day.

> **To store your belts,** a coffee can with a see-through lid makes an ideal container—just the right size to keep belts from creasing, and the clear top lets you find the belt you need easily.

> **For your workshop,** drill a hole near the top edge of a few cans—coffee or any other type—and hang them from the pegboard or nails in the wall to keep nails, screws, small tools, bits of wood, glue bottles, and more off your work space.

> **Another snazzy shop trick** that will get small items off your bench is to hang jars on the bottom of a storage shelf. Screw the jar lids to the underside of a wooden shelf (be sure the screws don't poke through the top). Then sort your hardware into the jars and screw each jar into its own lid. Use this idea to make a hanging herb-and-spice holder or to tidy up your potting shed or gardening bench.

The cure for a messy desk

Want a great yet cheap organizer for your pens, pencils, rulers, paper clips, scissors, and such? Here is an organizer that is also terrific for kitchen utensils, art supplies, in the workshop, on a dresser for accessories, or anywhere else you have clutter to clear.

1 Assemble several clean, dry cans with labels removed in various sizes and heights.

2 Using a high-gloss enamel spray-paint the interior and exterior of the cans and let them dry (or cover them with felt or self-adhesive shelf paper).

3 Figure out the most useful arrangement for your needs—taller cans in back for pens and pencils, for example, and shallow tuna cans up front for paper clips and rubber bands.

4 Glue the cans together. Be sure to use glue that specifically works well with metal, such as PVC (polyvinyl chloride) liquid solder, or epoxy; hot glue will work only if the joints won't be subjected to any stress.

5 Finally, to protect a wooden desk or other surface, cover the bottom of the can arrangement with felt.

Big bonus: Adapt this idea to make your own set of pigeonholes. Just arrange the cans with the largest forming a base row and working up to the smallest cans. You can either set these on a table or desktop or, to keep surfaces clutter-free, hang your homemade pigeonholes on a handy wall.

Useful little compartments

Old egg cartons and ice-cube trays can be used to store many of the same tiny items—egg cartons provide a lid, which may sway your choice.

> **On your dresser,** both are excellent for storing earrings, rings, small brooches and other jewelry, sorting coins, or separating all the bits and pieces for a particular project.

> **In your sewing or crafting area,** egg cartons or ice-cube trays can be used to sort buttons, sequins, beads, snap fasteners, hooks and eyes, and other easy-to-lose objects.

> **In the workshop,** nails, screws, washers, nuts, and small bolts can be kept under control, in sequence if you are taking something apart.

> **For storing small Christmas ornaments,** egg cartons are ideal because of the lid, and because they stack readily in a larger cardboard box.

> **For the golfer** in the family, an egg carton is the ideal size for storing golf balls, keeping them clean and ready for teeing off.

> **In your junk drawer,** an ice-cube tray can bring order to all those bits and pieces—rolls of stamps, extra keys, tiny batteries, paper clips, rubber bands.

> **Another handy use:** organizing medications or vitamins for the day.

Storage potential all around you

As you can see, using everyday items in extraordinary ways can create solutions to storage shortages that you never imagined. Here are some more examples:

> **Tape can help you** store tubes of caulking, without taking up valuable shelf space. Cut a strip of adhesive or duct tape several inches long and fold it over the bottom edge of each tube, leaving a flap at the end. Punch a hole in the flap with a paper hole punch and hang the tube on a nail or hook. Another plus is you'll be able to find the tube you need quickly.

> **Small plastic baskets** can be summoned into use to keep all your medication bottles together in one place, to hold your sponges and soap pads at the kitchen sink (and let them dry thoroughly so they'll last longer, too), or attached one on top of the other to make a cagelike dispenser for kitchen twine, string, or yarn.

> **Plastic bottles** (1- or 2-liter soda type or milk or water jugs) can be transformed into boot trees (fill two 1-liter bottles with sand and upend your boots over them to dry completely), turned into a bag or string dispenser (just cut off the bottom and mount upside down), used to store leftover house paints, or trimmed down to store for those tiny items that always seem to slip through the cracks on your workbench.

> **Set a large flower pot or planter** next to your fireplace to hold kindling or small logs; set a smaller matching pot next to it to hold fireplace matches.

> **And one of our favorites:** Take an old (or new) tennis ball and carefully cut a 2-inch (5-cm) slit along one seam—you now have an ingenious place to hide you small valuables at the gym, in a locker, in your car . . . anywhere!

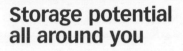

Clever
Home
Fixes

Why spend a fortune on home maintenance gear? Many common home-care and upkeep tasks can be handled perfectly well with simple everyday items.

Oh, how tempting it is, when something breaks or malfunctions around the house, just to rush out to the nearest home center and spend a small fortune. It is almost impossible to go into one of those warehouse stores for just the things you need to make a repair. All those endless aisles of stuff! It not only takes forever to chase down the thing you need, but if you're at all a home do-it-yourself type, you also have to make a supreme effort to rein in yourself; otherwise, you'll end up buying a lot of things that you don't need.

When you need to fix something, yes, you will often need to purchase something at a store—but that is not always the case and it certainly shouldn't be your first response. Before you run off to the giant home center or even your local hardware store, take a good look around you. You may find that there is some ordinary item lying around the house—a plastic bag, candle wax, or even beer—that you can use take care of the problem quite well.

And it will do the job at a fraction of the cost.

Making fixes to walls and windows

Let's start with the parts of the house that we look at most of the time—the walls and the windows in them. For the most part, they are trouble-free. And with a little quick attention to the problems that do happen, they should stay that way for a long time. Here are some fixes you can make using everyday household items:

> **Marks on walls** are a very noticeable problem—and a common one if you have children who are bursting with creativity that sometimes appears on your walls. Don't lose your cool; grab some white bread. Believe it or not, bread (with the crusts removed, naturally) miraculously scrubs away most marks on wallpaper (even the nonwashable kind) or walls.

> **For cleaning walls,** baking soda on a damp rag works well, too. Get rid of grease stains on wallpaper with a paste of 1 tablespoon of baking soda and 1 teaspoon of water. Rub it on the stain, let it set for 5 to 10 minutes, then rub off with a damp sponge. If your wall-paper needs brightening, wipe it with a rag or sponge moistened in a solution

of 2 tablespoons of baking soda dissolved in 4 cups of water.

> **To take down old wallpaper,** saturate it with a solution of 1 capful of fabric softener in 4 cups of water. Let the solution soak in for 20 minutes, then scrape the paper from the wall. If the wallpaper has a water-resistant coating, score it with a wire-bristle brush before treating it with the fabric-softener solution.

> **Loose windowpane?** A chunk of worn-out caulk has just fallen out, leaving you worried that the pane of glass will soon follow. Grab the gum—chewing gum, that is. Use a couple of freshly chewed wads as a temporary stopgap to hold the glass in place while you get to re-caulking.

> **To stabilize a broken windowpane** that threatens to fall and shatter, put on heavy leather gloves. Then carefully crisscross the glass with strips of adhesive or duct tape to hold the glass in place so that you can safely remove it.

> **To quickly clean up broken glass** on the floor, carefully pick up the larger pieces and put them in an old cardboard box. Then to gather smaller shards and tiny slivers, cover the affected area with a few sheets of wet newspaper, carefully

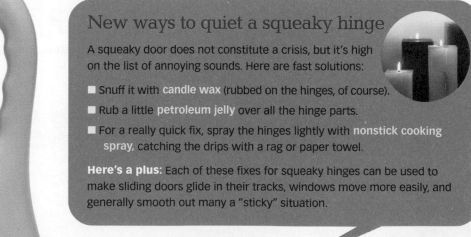

New ways to quiet a squeaky hinge

A squeaky door does not constitute a crisis, but it's high on the list of annoying sounds. Here are fast solutions:

- Snuff it with candle wax (rubbed on the hinges, of course).
- Rub a little petroleum jelly over all the hinge parts.
- For a really quick fix, spray the hinges lightly with nonstick cooking spray, catching the drips with a rag or paper towel.

Here's a plus: Each of these fixes for squeaky hinges can be used to make sliding doors glide in their tracks, windows move more easily, and generally smooth out many a "sticky" situation.

Extraordinary!

gather the paper up, and add it to the box. Make sure the box is marked "Broken Glass" so that your trash collector doesn't get cut.

> **To fix tiny holes** in your window screens, just dab some clear nail polish over the holes. It will stop those tiny (and often biting) insects in their tracks.

> **For a bigger hole** in a window screen, make a temporary patch by coating a piece of pantyhose with rubber cement, then placing the patch over the hole, pressing around the edges to be sure they're secured.

> **Dirty windows?** While dingy windows never actually hurt anyone, they are unattractive, any way you look at them. Fortunately, there's a couple of homemade solutions that work just as well if not better than those pricey store brands. Mix 1 cup of clear ammonia in 3 cups of water or dissolve 2 tablespoons of borax in 3 cups of water. Apply either with a soft cloth, then dry with a lint-free cloth, or even better, use crumpled sheets of newspaper.

> **Or make this window-cleaning spray:** Combine 2 tablespoons of cornstarch with 1/2 cup of ammonia and 1/2 cup of white vinegar in 3 quarts (3 liters) of warm water. Pour the milky solution into a spray bottle, spray the windows, wipe with a warm-water rinse, and dry with crumpled newspaper.

> **One final window-washing trick**: 1/2 cup of rubbing alcohol in 4 cups of water will cut grease, leave your windows shiny, and help prevent frost to boot.

Smooth-running baths and kitchens

Bathrooms and kitchens present one of the widest array of home repair and upkeep problems. Fortunately, the arsenal of ready-made solutions in your pantry is just as impressive.

> **Dreaded clogged drain?** Drop a couple of Alka-Seltzer tablets down the opening, then pour in a cup of vinegar. Wait a few minutes and then run hot water at full force to clear the clog.

Alternatively, drop a couple of denture cleaning tablets down the drain and run hot water. If the clog is stubborn, drop 3 dental tablets followed by 1 cup of white vinegar and wait a few minutes. Run hot water until the clog is gone.

> **Another easy clogged-drain fix:** Pour 1 cup of baking soda down the drain followed by 1 cup of hot vinegar (zap it in the microwave for 1 minute). Give it several minutes to work and enjoy

6 ways to make your toilet bowl gleam

Commercial toilet bowl cleaners are often expensive and environmentally questionable—forget them. For a shining and sanitized bowl, try one of these alternatives:

1 Sprinkle several tablespoons of **baking soda** directly into your toilet bowl and scrub it on any stains. Wait a few minutes, then flush.

2 Pour a mixture of 1/2 cup of **borax** in 1 gallon (3.8 liters) of water into your toilet bowl, scrub with a brush, then flush.

3 For a different approach, drop a **denture-cleaning tablet** into the bowl, wait for about 20 minutes, and then flush.

4 Pour 1/4 cup of **alcohol-based mouthwash** into the toilet bowl. Let it stand for a half hour, then swish with a toilet brush and flush.

5 For a really novel approach, spray **WD-40** into the bowl, then swish with a nylon toilet brush.

6 Pour half a box of **baking soda** directly into your toilet tank once a month. Let it stand overnight, then flush the toilet a few times the next morning. This actually cleans both the tank and the bowl.

the volcanic action, then add 4 cups of boiling water. Repeat if necessary.

> If the clog is mainly grease, use 1/2 cup each of baking soda and salt, followed by 1 cup of boiling water. Let the mixture work overnight, then rinse with hot tap water in the morning.

Or use a funnel and pour 1/2 cup of borax into the drain, then slowly pour in 2 cups of boiling water. Let the mixture set for 15 minutes, then flush with hot water. Repeat for stubborn clogs.

> For a gentle kitchen and bathroom cleanser, use plain baking soda. By now, you've noticed all the things you can do with and places you can use baking soda. The bathroom and kitchen are no exception. You can use baking soda to clean all of the surfaces—porcelain, ceramic, plastic laminate, vinyl, butcher block, what have you—without worrying about it doing any damage.

> For a particularly tough gunky patch, combine 2 parts baking soda with 1 part hydrogen peroxide. Rub the paste into the discolored area, let set for about 30 minutes, then scrub and rinse well. The paste will sweeten your drain on the way down, too.

For tough tile or porcelain stains, another good cleanser can be made from 1 cup of borax and 1/4 cup of lemon juice. Put some of the paste on a cloth or sponge and rub it into the stain, then rinse with running warm water. The stain should wash away with the paste.

For a stubborn bathtub stain, make a thick paste from cream of tartar and hydrogen peroxide. Apply the paste to the stain and let it dry. When you remove the paste, the stain will be gone.

> Keep bathroom tiles sparkling— and kill any mildew on them—by sponging them with 1/4 cup of ammonia in 1 gallon (3.8 liter) of water.

> To prevent grime and mildew altogether, first clean the soap-and-water residue off your tiles or shower stall. Then rub on a layer of car paste wax and buff with a clean, dry cloth. You'll need to do this only about once a year to keep it sparkling. (Note: Don't wax a bathtub—it will become dangerously slippery.)

> To keep your mirrors fog-free, apply a small amount of car paste wax to the mirror. Let it dry and then buff with a soft cloth. If you do this on bathroom fixtures, you'll prevent water spots, too.

> Weak shower spray? If the water in your area is hard, eventually your showerheads will suffer from mineral deposits. Combine 1/4 cup of baking soda with 1 cup of white vinegar in a self-sealing plastic bag. Place the bag over the showerhead, with the head completely covered with the solution. Loosely seal the bag (some of the gas needs to escape), and secure it with adhesive tape.

Let the solution work for about an hour. Then remove the bag and turn on your shower to wash off any remaining debris. Not only will the deposits disappear, but the showerhead will be back to its old shining self.

> To polish chrome to a fare-thee-well, rub a lemon rind over the chrome, rinse well, and dry with a soft cloth. Or try rubbing alcohol on a soft, absorbent cloth—no need to rinse, since rubbing alcohol evaporates quickly.

Caring for floors and carpets

We trudge around on them all day, subjecting them to all kinds of undeserved punishment, sometimes by dragging things across them. So it should come as no surprise that our floors, and the carpets and flooring that cover them, occasionally need a repair. And once again the items you need to solve the problem are often already at hand.

> If a vinyl floor tile comes loose, there's no reason to become unglued. Simply reposition the tile on the floor, cover it with aluminum foil and run a hot clothes iron over the area until you can feel the glue melting underneath.

Pile books or bricks on top of the tile to weight it down while the glue resets. The same technique also works well to smooth out bulges and straighten curled seams in sheet vinyl flooring.

> For a small gouge or hole in resilient flooring, grab the crayons. Select a crayon whose color most closely matches your floor, put it on a piece of wax paper, and microwave it, one minute at a time, until it is pliable.

Using a plastic or putty knife, fill the hole, then quickly smooth over the patch with a rolling pin or other flat object; the crayon should cool very quickly.

Finally, wax the floor to provide a clear protective coating.

> If wax buildup is yellowing your resilient flooring, on the other hand, it's time to remove the wax. Saturate the floor with 1 cup of ammonia stirred into 8 cups of water.

8 quick fixes for carpet stains

Carpet stains can really drive you crazy. No worries. Depending on the type of stain, one of these unexpectedly handy products may supply an instant solution. With any of the techniques listed, repeat as needed till the stain is gone.

Ammonia	Sponge the stain with a mixture of 1/2 cup of clear ammonia in 4 cups of warm water. Let dry thoroughly, and repeat if needed.
Baby wipes	For a fresh spill of almost any kind, grab a baby wipe and start blotting; this also works for stains on upholstery or clothing.
Baking soda	To get rid of grease or wine stains, blot up as much of the stain as possible with a paper towel, then sprinkle a liberal amount of baking soda over the spot. Give the baking soda at least an hour to absorb the stain, then vacuum up the remaining powder.
Beer	Pour a little beer on top of the carpet stain, rub it lightly into the material, and the stain should disappear.
Borax	Another great carpet stain remover is borax. Thoroughly wet the stained area, then rub in some borax. Let the area dry, then vacuum or blot it with a solution of equal parts vinegar and soapy water, and let dry again.
Cornstarch and milk	If you're attacking an ink stain on your carpet, mix a little milk with some cornstarch to make a paste. Apply the paste to the ink stain and let it dry for a few hours. Then brush the mixture to loosen it and just vacuum it up.
Shaving cream	If Junior spills something, don't fret: Blot up what you can, pat with a wet sponge, then squirt shaving cream on the spot. Wipe clean with a damp sponge. Works on clothes, too!
White wine and salt	Remove red wine stains by pouring a little white wine on top, then sponging with cold water. Now sprinkle the area with salt and wait about 10 minutes before vacuuming.

Let the solution sit for three to five minutes, then scrub with a nylon or plastic scouring pad to remove the old wax. Wipe away leftover residue with a clean cloth or sponge, then give the floor a thorough rinsing.

> **If a carpet needs freshening,** sprinkle baking soda or cornstarch lightly over the rug, let it settle in for 15 to 30 minutes or so, then vacuum it up. (Tuck a cotton ball soaked in vanilla extract or your favorite perfume in your vacuum clean bag for an even better scent.)

Keeping your furniture in tip-top condition

Good-quality furniture is an investment, so caring for it only makes sense—and it can be done for only cents, using things you already have around the house.

Give your sagging cane seat a lift

Saggy cane furniture? It's inevitable for cane to stretch and sag after a few years of use. But there is an easy solution:

Soak two cloths in a solution of **1/2 cup of baking soda** and **4 cups of hot water**. Saturate the top surface of the caning with one cloth while pushing the second up against the bottom of the caning to saturate the underside. Use a clean, dry cloth to soak up the excess moisture, then if the weather is nice, set the piece in the sun to dry.

> **Make a superb polish** for wood by combining 2 parts olive oil with 1 part lemon juice or white vinegar in a clean spray bottle. Shake vigorously, then spritz on your furniture. Let sit for a minute or two, then wipe off with a clean cloth.

> **Another wood polish:** In a pinch, flat beer actually makes a pretty good furniture polish, too.

> **Small scratches on wood?** Crayons are the answer! Choose a crayon in a color closest to the wood, soften the crayon slightly, then color over the scratches. Buff the repair with a clean rag to restore luster. It's a temporary repair that actually will last you for years, especially on a vertical surface. Just don't do this on a surface that you write on.

> **White rings from sweating glasses?** Make a paste of 1 tablespoon of baking soda and 1 teaspoon of water. Gently rub the spot in a circular motion over the white mark until it disappear. Remember not to use too much water.

> **Also get rid of white rings** by rubbing a dab of car paste wax lightly over the area with your finger. Let the wax dry and then buff.

Or rub a dab of petroleum jelly on the ring, leave it overnight, then wipe it off. The gentle friction of non-gel toothpaste will also work.

> **If your dresser drawers are sticking,** pull them out completely and rub the runners with a candle stub to coat them with wax. Slip the drawers back into place—quite a difference!

> **Yellowed piano keys** really detract from the beauty of the instrument. Remove age stains on your ivories (or plastic keys) by mixing a solution of 1/4 cup of baking soda in 4 cups of warm water. Apply to each key with a dampened cloth (you can place a thin piece of cardboard between the keys to avoid seepage). Wipe again with a cloth

Extraordinary!

dampened with plain water, then buff dry with a clean cloth.

> Other fixes for discolored piano keys include combining lemon juice and salt and proceeding as above. Or rub some mayonnaise over the keys, let it sit, then wipe with a damp cloth. Or just rub with a little non-gel toothpaste.

> For cleaning leather furniture, one of the best choices is WD-40. Spray it over the furniture and buff with a soft cloth. The combination of ingredients in WD-40 will clean, penetrate, lubricate, and protect the leather.

> Cleaning marble is trickier than it seems. Marble may look solid, but it is actually petrified calcium and quite porous. Here's the solution: Stir 3 tablespoons of baking soda into 4 cups of warm water. Dip a soft cloth into the solution and gently wipe over the marble surface. Let it stand for 15 to 30 minutes, then rinse with plain water and wipe dry.

> To remove mildew from wicker, wash the piece using a solution of 2 tablespoons of ammonia in 1 gallon (3.8 liters) of water. Use an old toothbrush to get into hard-to-reach places. Rinse well and let air-dry.

For efficient, comfortable heating and cooling

Even the heating, cooling, and humidifying units that control your home's climate sometimes have problems that you can solve with ordinary things you have around the house.

> For heating and cooling at peak efficiency—a smart idea given the cost of energy these days—you need to change the filters for your air conditioner and furnace frequently. If your units permit, buy washable filters instead of disposable ones, and clean them once a month.

Extraordinary !

Homemade dehumidifiers

Too much humidity is just as bad as too little. Overly damp basements, attics, or closets can ruin your possessions (and possibly impact your health). Try these simple tricks to keep a small enclosed space drier:

Take a **coffee can**, punch holes in the lid, and place a few charcoal briquettes inside. Then place the instant dehumidifier anywhere it's needed. Remember to replace the charcoal every few months.

In a slightly dampish closet, tie a few **sticks of chalk** together and hang them from the clothes bar. The chalk will absorb moisture and help prevent mildew.

To clean a filter and give it a clean smell, first vacuum off as much dust and dirt as possible, then wash it in a solution of 1 tablespoon of baking soda in 4 cups of water. Let the filter dry thoroughly before replacing it.

> If the air from your air conditioner smells musty, chances are one of the unit's drain holes is clogged. First, unscrew the front of the unit and locate the drain hole. (It's usually located under the barrier between the evaporator and compressor, or underneath the evaporator.)

Use a bent wire (from a spare coat hanger) to clear away any obstacles in the hole, then use an old turkey baster to flush it clean. You may also need to use the baster to remove any water pooling up at the bottom of the unit to gain access to the drain.

> Musty-smelling humidifier? For many, a humidifier is a must to combat the dry air from heating systems, but one can develop a stale moldy odor from time to time. Add 2 tablespoons of baking soda or 3 to 4 tablespoons of lemon juice to the water each time you change it to eliminate odors. (Note: Check the owner's manual or consult the unit's manufacturer before trying this.) The juice will not only remove the off odor but will replace it with a lemon-fresh fragrance. Repeat every couple of weeks.

> To increase the efficiency of cast-iron radiators, tape heavy-duty aluminum foil to cardboard with the shiny side of the foil facing out and place one reflector behind each radiator. The radiant heat waves will bounce off the foil into the room instead of being absorbed by the wall behind the radiator. If your radiators have covers, attach a piece of foil under the cover's top, too.

> Tired of fireplace cleanup? One of life's great pleasures is a fire on a chilly evening. But cleaning up the ashes is hardly enjoyable. Next time, line the bottom of the fireplace with a double layer of heavy-duty aluminum foil. Next day, when the ashes are completely cooled, just fold up the foil with the ashes inside and toss it.

> To clean grimy fireplace doors, you can just use ashes from the fire. Either mix some ashes with a bit of water and apply them with a damp cloth or sponge, or simply dip a wet sponge directly into the ashes. Rub the mixture over the doors' surfaces.

Rinse with a wet clean sponge, then dry with a clean cloth. The results will amaze you, but remember—wood ash was a key ingredient in old-fashioned lye soap.

> Another unexpected fireplace cleaner can be made by combining 1 tablespoon of ammonia, 2 tablespoons of vinegar, and 4 cups of warm water in a spray bottle. Spray on some of the solution; let it sit for several seconds, then wipe off with an absorbent cloth. Repeat if necessary—it's worth the extra effort.

Making fixes outside

The exterior of your house protects all the rest of your considerable home investment, and a leak in the roof or through the siding can be the start of a real disaster. But don't worry, there are quick fixes you can make with things just laying around the house. Some ordinary household items can also help you cope with winter's woes.

> A missing shingle on the roof is one of the things that can quickly throw most homeowners into a tizzy. Take a deep breath. There's an easy solution. Just cut a piece of corrugated cardboard the same size as a shingle, slip it into a self-sealing plastic bag, and slide it under the adjoining shingles.

Or cut a piece of 1/4-inch (6-mm) plywood to the size of a shingle and wrap strips of duct tape across the plywood. Wedge the makeshift shingle in place. Either quick fix will close the gap and repel water until you can effect a permanent repair.

> A hole in your vinyl siding— whether caused by flying debris or an accidental poke—also demands immediate attention. Again, duct tape to the rescue! Be sure the area around the tear is completely dry, then cover it in strips of duct tape (you can probably find tape close to the color of your siding).

Smooth the repair with your hand or a rolling pin, especially around the edges. This patch should last for a season or two.

Easier snow shoveling

Thoroughly coat your snow shovel's blade with nonstick cooking spray, vegetable shortening, WD-40, or car paste wax. The snow won't stick to your shovel anymore, so you won't work as hard.

Extraordinary!

> **Clearing icy walkways** is a common winter chore in the Snow Belt, but salt and commercial ice-melt formulations can stain or even eat away the concrete around your house. Try sprinkling steps and walkways with generous amounts of baking soda, then add some sand for improved traction.

> **To clean mildew off unfinished wooden patio furniture** (and all painted outdoor surfaces), use 1 cup of ammonia, 1/2 cup of vinegar, 1/4 cup of baking soda, and 1 gallon (3.8 liters) of water. Rinse thoroughly, then use old towels to dry completely.

Caring for your car

Our cars have become extensions of our homes in these fast-paced days, so keeping them working well and looking good is essential. Though most serious car repairs must be done by a mechanic, here are a few tricks to know:

> **To eliminate the corrosive buildup** on battery terminals, scrub them with a mixture of 3 tablespoons of baking soda and 1 tablespoon of warm water (use an old toothbrush). Wipe the terminals off with a wet towel and dry completely with another towel. Once they're dry, apply petroleum jelly around each terminal to deter future corrosive buildup.

> **For a sparkling windshield,** clean the glass with club soda. It will remove bird droppings and greasy stains from the surface, and the carbonation speeds the cleaning process.

> **If you have a small crack or nick in your windshield,** stop it from spreading by filling it in with clear nail polish on both sides of the glass. Do the repair in the shade, but move the car into the sun to let the polish dry.

> **What's the cure for a bug-covered grille?** Prevention! After washing, spray your clean grille with nonstick cooking spray or WD-40 and next time the bug guts will just wipe away.

> **Hiding small scratches on dashboard gauges** is easy. Just rub the plastic with a bit of baby oil.

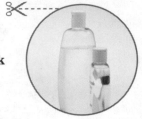

> **Give worn vinyl upholstery a quick pick-me-up** by rubbing it with a small amount of bath oil on a soft cloth. You can also wipe the dashboard, armrests, and other plastic surfaces. Polish with a clean cloth to remove any excess oil.

> **To get rid of road tar stains,** make a soft paste from 3 parts baking soda to 1 part water and apply the paste to the tar spots with a damp cloth. Let it dry for 5 minutes, then rinse clean.

> **To vanquish either tar or pine sap,** slather mayonnaise over the affected areas, let sit for several minutes, then wipe it all away with a clean, soft rag.

> **Small dents** getting you down? Grab your plumber's plunger, wet the edges, and just pull those dents out.

> **Broken taillight?** Patch it temporarily with red or yellow duct tape.

Stake delicate young saplings with PANTY-HOSE strips.

Foil slugs and snails with a BEER trap.

Control compost odor with wet shredded NEWSPAPER.

Mend a bent plant stem with TRANSPARENT TAPE.

Surprising Garden Secrets

Healthy plants, fewer bugs, brighter blooms—the answers are all in your pantry!

Grandpa really did know best when it came to gardening. In his time, all gardening was organic, and all gardeners were frugal and wise. They recycled household items in the garden, from their favorite old hat and shabby shoes to used egg and milk cartons, which they used for starting seeds. Those earlier generations were wonderful gardeners who grew glowing, healthy plants by heeding advice handed down from their grandparents—and so can you.

Whether you call it organic gardening or natural gardening, a chemical-free, earth-friendly approach to growing and caring for plants is great for both you and your garden. And it is a creative, money-saving style of gardening that makes regular use of a lot of everyday household items, including many things that you might otherwise toss out.

The natural approach to gardening also makes the most of laborsaving tricks for seeding, weeding, mulching, and creating slow-release fertilizers. Indeed, it is sometimes called "lazy gardening." And it saves not only time but money to boot!

But best of all, this approach helps you produce a balanced ecosystem where pesky bugs and diseases are kept at bay. And if occasional disease outbreaks or insect infestations do occur—or if drought threatens—you'll be prepared to nip the problem in the bud every time.

Start with soil

Good soil is like a balanced meal for plants. Plants growing in fertile, crumbly soil with sufficient moisture glow with health. They bloom longer, produce more fruits and vegetables, and have natural resistance to pests and diseases.

While few lawns and gardens are blessed from the outset with perfect soil, you can improve yours naturally by using mulch, compost, and organic fertilizers gleaned from your kitchen scraps, lawn clippings, and raked leaves.

Mulch is especially important because it slows erosion and evaporation, smothers weeds, and protects plant roots. The mulch you choose can be an organic material such as straw, bark chips, compost, or old newspapers (which, after all, is made from wood pulp). Or the mulch can be an inorganic material such as gravel, plastic sheeting, or even carpet scraps.

> One of the best and cheapest mulches is something that you throw out everyday—newspaper. Newspaper is excellent at retaining moisture and does an equally fine job of fighting off and suffocating weeds.

Just lay down several sheets of black-and-white newspaper. Then cover the paper with a 3-inch (8-cm) -thick layer of bark mulch so that it doesn't blow away. It's best to avoid using colored newspaper because the dyes in some color inks may be harmful to plants (and dangerous to you in vegetables). Renew your newspaper mulch each growing season.

> If you have an old carpet around, you have the making of a great mulch that will last you a couple of years or more. Just cut the carpet up and place the scraps upside down on your flowerbeds, with the natural jute backing facing up. Disguise it with a covering of bark mulch or straw.

> Don't throw out old coffee grounds. They're chock full o' nutrients that your acidic-loving plants crave. Save them to fertilize rosebushes, azaleas, rhododendrons, evergreens, and camellias. It's better to use grounds from a drip coffeemaker than the boiled grounds from a percolator. The drip grounds are richer in nitrogen.

Diaper your patio plants

Container gardens are great for sprucing up doorways, patios, and balconies, but they do dry out quickly. To keep your outdoor potted plants watered longer, place a clean, disposable diaper in the bottom of each flowerpot—absorbent side up—before adding soil and plants. It will absorb water that would otherwise drain out the bottom, and it will slowly release the water to the soil as the soil dries out.

Extraordinary!

> **Sprinkle used tea leaves** (loose or in tea bags) around your rosebushes and cover with mulch to give them a mid-summer boost. When you water the plants, the nutrients from the tea will be released into the soil, spurring growth. Roses love the tannic acid that occurs naturally in tea.

> **Save those banana peels, too.** Roses and other established plants also benefit from potassium-rich banana-peel mulch. Dry out banana peels on screens during the winter months. In spring, grind them up in a food processor or blender and use as a mulch to give new plants and seedlings a healthy start.

Enrich your compost pile

Compost is often called black gold, and with good reason. This nutrient-rich soil conditioner, which is endowed with disease-inhibiting qualities, can be worked into new or existing garden beds or used as mulch. Best of all, you can make it from yard clippings, dried leaves, and kitchen vegetable scraps. Even some unexpected nonfood throw-aways are fodder for your compost heap.

> **To collect food scraps for your compost** heap, keep an old milk carton near the kitchen sink so that you can throw the scraps into it instead of the garbage disposal.

> **Calcium-rich eggshells** are especially good toss-outs to add to your compost, because calcium is a nutrient that helps plants to thrive. Crushing them before you put them in your heap helps them break down faster.

> **Overripe whole bananas** as well as peels are also a welcome addition to any compost pile because of their high content of potassium and phosphorus—and they don't have to be dried as they do when you use them for mulch. The fruit breaks down especially fast in hot temperatures.

The 1-to-3 recipe for compost

Whatever you put in your compost pile, always keep this basic formula in mind:

■ Mix **one part moist ingredients,** such as vegetable scraps and coffee grounds, with **three parts dry ones,** such as straw, dried grass, leaves, or paper.

■ Put them in a pile or compost bin, and in about three months, you'll have fluffy, black, sweet-smelling compost ready to enrich your garden.

Don't forget to remove any glued-on tags from the peels, and be sure to bury bananas deep within your pile—otherwise, they may simply turn out to be a meal for a four-legged visitor.

> **Brown paper bags** make an unlikely but great contribution to any garden compost heap. Not only do they contain less ink and pigment than newsprint, but they will also attract more earthworms to your pile. (In fact, the only thing earthworms like better than paper bags is cardboard.) Shred the bags and wet them well before adding to your pile to help them break down faster.

> **A good way to reduce odor** from your compost heap, however, is to add wet, shredded newsprint—in moderate amounts and printed in black ink only. It also gives earthworms a tasty treat.

> **To speed up the decomposition** process and enrich your compost, here's another tip: Pour a few cups of strongly brewed tea into the heap. The liquid tea will hasten decomposition and draw acid-producing bacteria, creating desirable acid-rich compost.

Be warned, however, composting is addictive—when you start, you'll want to make more and better compost.

Seeds and seedlings

As winter starts to loosen its grip on the earth, the gardener's mind naturally turns to buying and starting seeds for the upcoming growing season. Here are some tips about unexpected ways to use things around the house to make the process of starting seedlings indoors and planting seeds outdoors easier.

> **For biodegradable starting pots** for seedlings, don't waste your hard-earned money buying ones at the garden supply store. Just save and use the cardboard tubes from paper towels and toilet paper.

Cut each toilet paper tube into two open-ended "pots," or each paper towel tube into four. Fill a tray with the cut cylinders packed tightly against each other so that they won't tip when you water the seedlings.

Now fill each bottomless pot with seed-starting mix, gently pack it down, and sow your seeds. When you plant the seedlings, break down the side of the roll and completely bury the cardboard.

> **Other good starting pots for seeds** include paper egg cartons, milk cartons, and eggshells.

> **Making straight rows with light-weight seeds**—particularly ones for vegetables—is often harder than it looks. But all you need for perfect rows is some string. String can help you plant dozens of seeds in a snap.

Just cut the string to the length of a row and wet it thoroughly. Then sprinkle the seeds directly on it. The moisture will make the seeds stick long enough for you to lay the string in a prepared furrow. Just cover the seed-studded string with soil and you're done!

> **When planting large seeds,** such as beans, string can also help you. But the best approach is to just put sticks in the ground at each end of a row and run a piece of string between them to guide you as you plant.

> **Another way to plant seeds** spaced evenly in straight rows is to use a scrap board with some old wine corks that you saved attached to it.

Determine the spacing you want between plants and mark the board at that interval. Drive a drywall screw through the board at each mark, letting the end of the screw protrude about 3/4 inch (9 mm) from the board. Now twist a wine cork onto each screw.

Just press the board, corks-side down, into your garden bed and, voilà! Instant seed holes.

Sowing seeds with coffee

Did you know that mixing coffee with your seeds can increase your carrot harvest? Just mix the seeds with fresh-ground coffee before sowing. Not only does the extra bulk make the tiny seeds easier to sow, but the coffee aroma may help repel root maggots and other pests. And as an added bonus, the grounds will help add nutrients to the soil as they decompose around the plants.

Extraordinary!

Getting rid of pesky critters

Creepy crawly creatures of all types are wily garden opponents, but don't despair or run out and buy the latest chemical solution. You can outsmart these unwelcome critters with secret weapons liberated from your pantry and trash bin.

> Make a trap for slugs and snails with beer. Like some people, some pest—especially slugs and snails—find the golden beverage irresistible. If you're having problems with these slimy invaders in your garden, set a shallow container in the area where you've seen the pests, pour in about half a can of warm leftover beer, and leave it overnight.

The next morning, you're likely to find a horde of pests, drunk and drowned.

> Another way to get rid of slugs and snails is just to take a container of salt into the garden and douse the offenders. They won't survive long.

> To foil ravenous cutworms, which thrive in late spring when tender seedlings are especially vulnerable, all you need are some old aluminum cans. Remove both ends of each can, set it over a seedling, and push it into the earth. This will keep the cutworms from severing the seedling stems.

> Keeping melons free of pests and disease is trickier, especially because they grow big, juicy, and unwieldy. But you can keep melons off the ground by making protective sleeves for them from old pantyhose.

Cut the legs off the pantyhose. As your young melons start to develop, slide each one into a foot section and tie the leg to a stake to suspend the melon above the ground. The nylon holders will stretch as the fruits mature, keeping them from touching the damp soil, where they would be susceptible to rot or hungry insects.

> If mosquitoes have made a meal of you, stop the itching instantly by applying a drop or two of ammonia directly to the bites. But don't use ammonia on a bite you've already scratched open, though; the itch will be replaced by a nasty sting.

> Stung by a bee? Then grab an onion slice from the picnic table and place it over the area where you got stung. It will ease the soreness. (Of course, if you are badly allergic to bee or other insect stings, seek medical attention at once.)

An effective
homemade
insecticide

You can quickly whip this up using ordinary ingredients from your kitchen. It will deter most soft-bodied pests but won't harm your plants— or you, your kids, or your pets.

MIX	
	several crushed **garlic cloves**
	1/4 cup **canola oil**
	3 tablespoons **hot pepper sauce**
	1/2 teaspoon mild **liquid soap**
	1 gallon (3.8 liters) **water**

POUR	
	some into your spray bottle, and shake well before spraying it on vulnerable plants.

Larger pests— birds and animals

In the spring, birds are a real delight to have as garden residents; they are courting, nesting, singing—and eating insect pests. But by midsummer, they are beginning to size up your fruit and berry plants for snacks. And in sheer size as well as in the damage they can do, deer are in a league of their own when it comes to garden pests—and squirrels aren't much better.

> To throw deer off the scent, savvy gardeners have been hanging out bits of soap for some time but you might be interested to know that tallow-based soap works especially well to stop deer from making lunch out of your shrubbery. Hang the soap in its wrapper or a cloth bag to keep it from dissolving too fast. Hang it from a stake, not a branch.

> To deter pesky birds—and maybe some hungry squirrels as well—dangle strips of aluminum foil or old deflated metallic balloons from the branches of your vulnerable trees. Use monofilament fishing line to attach them.

> Another way to scare birds is to hang some foil-wrapped seashells, which will add a bit of noise to startle the fine-feathered thieves. Or just hang up old aluminum pie pans in pairs that will bang together.

> Put a damper on squirrels that snack on your bulbs by planting each bulb in one of those small plastic baskets that berries come in. Just place the basket at the correct depth, then insert the bulb and cover with soil.

> For guarding young plants, berry baskets are also the answer. Just place the inverted berry baskets over the plants. The baskets will let water, sunlight, and air in but keep raccoons and squirrels out. Make sure the basket is buried below ground level and tightly secured (placing a few good-sized stones around it may suffice).

> To protect young trees in winter when small varmints like to feed on their bark, you'll find a cheap and effective deterrent in your kitchen drawer. Simply wrap the tree trunks with a double layer of heavy-duty aluminum foil in late fall and remove it in spring.

Killing weeds

Some weeds, such as bull and Russian thistle, are tough customers. Many will give up the ghost after a dose of vinegar (see "A Nontoxic Weed Killer" on page 83). If they don't, head for the garage for good old WD-40—after a spritz, they'll soon wither and die.

When using herbicides to kill weeds in your garden, you have to be careful not to also spray and kill surrounding plants. To isolate the weed you want to kill . . .

STEP ONE	Cut a 2-liter soda bottle in half.
STEP TWO	Place the top half over the weed you want to spray.
STEP THREE	Direct your pump's spraying wand through the regular opening in the top of the bottle and blast away.

After the spray settles down, pick up the bottle and move on to your next target. Always wear goggles and gloves when spraying chemicals in the garden.

Keeping your landscape lush

Planting costly permanent landscaping plants such as trees, shrubs, and perennials is a major investment that you want to pay off in the future. And here, too, you can use a lot of everyday things from your kitchen and recycling bin to make sure that these expensive plants thrive.

> To reseed bare spots on your lawn in spring, don't shell out big bucks for a spreader. It wastes seed by throwing it everywhere, and only a small fraction will land on target. For precision seeding, fashion a spot seeder from an empty coffee can and a pair of plastic lids.

Drill small holes into one lid to let grass seed pass. Snap this lid in place when reseeding and keep the other, nonpierced lid snapped over the can's bottom end. When you're done reseeding, simply reverse the lids to seal in unused seed.

> To secure a young tree, use a short length of old garden hose to tie it to its stake. Young trees often need a little help to stand up straight, but you must take care not to damage the tender bark when you stake them. A length of hose is perfect because it is flexible enough to stretch when the tree moves in the wind, and it won't damage the bark.

> To stake young delicate plants or saplings, use strips of pantyhose to attach the stems to the stakes. The nylon will stretch as plants fill out and mature, and it is nearly invisible.

> Making an instant trellis for climbers from an old umbrella is a great way to add a distinctive feature to your garden. Remove the fabric from the umbrella and bury the handle into the ground and use it to support vines such as morning glories. The umbrella's shape covered with flowers will look terrific.

> Creating support for flowering plants—especially top-heavy ones such as peonies—is another good use for an old umbrella. The ribs from an umbrella make excellent stakes that are strong but not very noticeable. As a matter of fact, if the wind destroys your umbrella, be sure to remove the umbrella's ribs before tossing it because you may need them. On such a stormy day, your flowers are also likely to have taken a beating and need staking.

Impromptu frost guard

If the weather report predicts a killing frost, don't worry—sacrifice an old umbrella to save the seedlings. Open the umbrella and cut off the handle. Then place the umbrella over the seedlings to keep the frost from settling on them. The next morning, close the umbrella and stash it in your garden shed for the next unexpected spring frost.

> If a plant stem gets bent by blustery winds, wrap the damaged area of the stem with transparent tape and leave the tape on until it mends.

> When raking up autumn leaves, there's no reason to strain your back by constantly lifting piles of leaves into a wheelbarrow or bag when an old sheet can solve the problem. Just lay the sheet on the ground and rake the leaves onto it. Then gather the four corners and drag the sheet to the curb or leaf pile.

> To protect delicate shrubs from the cold, look for scraps from sheets of Styrofoam insulation tossed away at construction sites. They're waterproof and block wind and road salt. (You can use plastic-foam packing material, but it won't last as long as the foam insulation.)

Extraordinary!

To give moderate protection to a plant, cut some of the foam insulation into two same-size sheets. Poke holes in one end of each sheet and lash them together to form a pup tent over the plant. To hold the pieces in place, drive a bamboo garden stake through the bottom of each piece and into the ground.

> For more substantial protection against the elements, fit pieces of the foam insulation together to form a box around a plant on four sides. Put a stake inside each corner and join the pieces with duct or packing tape.

Tools and garden helpers

Your gardening tools are meant to last a lot longer than your perennials, so you'll want to keep them clean and protected from the elements. And you want to keep your garden watered during droughts. You can do both by recycling some old containers.

> For your garden hand tools, such as pruners and trowels, just fill an old coffee can with sand and a little motor oil and use it the same way to clean and oil them.

> To make a great shovel cleaner, you need an old 5-gallon (19-liter) plastic bucket—the kind that bulk paint and plaster come in and that you can find tossed out at any building site. Pickles and prepared foods also come in these buckets, so you can find them in deli and supermarket waste bins, too.

Fill the bucket with builder's sand (available at masonry supply and home centers) and pour in about 1 quart (1 liter) of clean motor oil.

Then, to clean and lubricate a shovel—or other large garden tool—just plunge the blade into the sand a few times. You can even leave the tool blades in the bucket of sand for storage to prevent rust.

> To water your plants during dry spells, it's a good idea to place several drip irrigators around your garden that will get water down to the roots of your plants. Again the solution is in your recycling bin. Make your drip irrigators from 1-gallon (3.8-liter) plastic juice or detergent jugs.

Cut a large hole in the bottom of a clean jug, and then drill two to five tiny—about 1/16-inch (1.6-mm)—holes in or around the cap. Keep the holes small so that the water seeps out slowly.

Bury the capped jugs upside down about three-quarters submerged beneath the soil near the plants you need to water. Fill them with water through the hole on top as often as needed.

Indoor gardening tips

For garden lovers, paradise is having lots of fertile outdoor space and a warm, moist climate year-round. For the rest of us, there are houseplants. Here are clever ways to keep our indoor plant friends clean and healthy.

> Block plant overspray with an umbrella. Houseplants love to be misted with water, but your walls don't love to get soaked with overspray. Stick an open umbrella between the plants and the wall and give your plants a house-friendly shower.

> Protect surfaces with mouse pads. Most potted plant containers have hard ceramic bottoms. To protect your hardwood floors or shelves from scratches, place the pots on one or more computer mouse pads. Another choice that works equally well is carpet remnants.

> To prevent soil erosion in houseplants, put a piece of pantyhose at the bottom of a pot before filling it with soil and plants. The pantyhose will act as a line that allows the excess water to flow out without draining the soil along with it.

> **To rid an indoor plant of bugs,** put the plant in a clear plastic bag, such as a cleaning bag, add a few mothballs, and seal for a week. When you take the plant out of the bag, your plant will be bug-free. It'll also keep moths away for a while!

> **Use basters to water your indoor plants.** Kitchen basters—the type used to keep turkeys moist while cooking—are perfect for getting underneath dense leaves and getting water right to the soil. You can also use a baster to water a Christmas tree and to add small, precise amounts of water to cups containing seedlings. Basters are also great at removing old water from flower arrangements. Just suction out the old water and add fresh.

> **If your potted houseplants dry out** too quickly after watering, when you repot them, try this simple trick: Tuck a damp sponge in the bottom of the pot before filling it with soil. It'll act as a water reservoir. And it will also help prevent a gusher if you accidentally overwater your houseplant.

Keep on recycling

Savvy recycling ideas for gardeners didn't stop in Grandpa's day. You should always be on the lookout for new things around the house that you can use in the garden, and maybe you can even start a frugal gardening tradition of your own. Here are a couple of ideas to get you started:

> **To create cushions for your knees** when you're working in the garden, just recycle tired computer mouse pads. You can kneel on them or attach them directly to the legs of your old gardening pants with duct tape.

> **To make sidewalk or driveway reflectors,** use discarded CDs (especially those that come in the mail). They are a lot more attractive than those ugly orange reflectors. Drill small holes in each CD and screw it to your mailbox post or onto a wooden stake and push it into the ground. Install several of them to light a nighttime path to your front door or through your garden.

Isn't technology wonderful? It gives us not only amazing inventions but also new products to recycle.

4 ways to clean a leaf

Houseplants often get dusty and dirty, and misting them with water merely moves the dirt around and leaves spots. Here are smarter ways to keep plant leaves clean and healthy:

1 Wipe down each leaf with the inside of a **banana peel**. It'll remove the gunk on the surface and replace it with a lustrous shine.

2 Put a bit of **hair conditioner** on a soft cloth and rub the plant leaves to remove dust and provide a shine.

3 Professional florists use this trick frequently: Rub a little **mayonnaise** on the leaves with a paper towel, and the leaves will stay bright and shiny for weeks and even months.

4 Add a few drops of **shampoo** to a pot of water, dunk in a cloth, wring it out, and wipe dusty leaves clean.

Make
MOTHBALLS
dance in water.

Launch
your own
ALKA-SELTZER
rocket.

Make a LEMON-
powered
battery.

Float a
PAPER CLIP
on water.

Rainy Day Kids' Projects

16 surprising science experiments, for children and grown-ups alike, that require only the most ordinary of stuff.

You'll be pleasantly surprised at how easy it is to explore the mystery and wonder of science with the kids in your life. And, just as important, you'll be rewarded yourself when you take time from the crazy, fast-paced lives we all live to see what makes our universe tick. So, slow down and see for yourselves that there's something to be discovered everywhere you look.

These science projects use ordinary items that you're sure to have around the house—a lemon, a few pieces of construction paper, some coins, a few Alka-Seltzer tablets—to create a little magic. Depending on the age of the children you're working with, you may be able to have them to do the experiments while you read the instructions. In a few cases, you'll have to do the bulk of the work while they lend a hand. Either way, you're sure to enjoy working together on these simple and surprising projects. So, gather up your ingredients, and read directions carefully. Then go on and amaze your kids—and yourself.

Launch a mini rocket ship

Turn "plop, plop, fizz, fizz" into "whoosh, whoosh, gee whiz" with this Alka-Seltzer rocket.

Bring the space program into your own backyard with this test of rocket propulsion. This science project gives a lot of bang for very little effort. The rocket gets its thrust from the gas created when you drop a couple of Alka-Seltzer tablets into some water inside a film canister.

WHAT YOU'LL NEED

Using just the right components is important. Use only a plastic Film canister from a roll of Fuji 35-mm film. This is the only type of film canister that has a lid that fits inside the lip of the canister. Canisters with lids that fit around the outside of the lip won't work. If you don't have the right kind of canister on hand, drop into your local camera shop and ask for an empty one to do this experiment.

You'll also need a couple of pieces of construction paper, transparent tape, scissors, and, of course, Alka-Seltzer tablets and refrigerated water—cold water is vital to a successful liftoff.

HOW TO PROCEED

1. Form the body of the rocket by wrapping a piece of construction paper around the canister with the canister's open end facing out the bottom end of the tube. Tape the paper in place.

2. Form a quarter-sheet of construction paper into a nose cone. Then trim it on the bottom and tape it onto the top of the rocket body.

3. To launch the rocket, fill the canister about halfway with refrigerated water. Plop in two Alka-Seltzer tablets. Quickly pop on the lid and set the rocket on the ground. Stand back.

4. The gas will quickly build up pressure in the canister, causing the canister's lid to pop off and the rocket to launch several feet into the air. The effect is surprising and a lot of fun!

Try this!

For even greater effect, try launching it from a stack of books or off the railing of the back porch.

Blow up a balloon

Harness the amazing power of a simple chemical reaction.

Nearly every kid has seen or created a baking-soda-and-vinegar volcano, but this project harnesses that powerful combination to work for you. It uses the gas produced by mixing baking soda and vinegar to blow up a balloon.

WHAT YOU'LL NEED

All you need are white vinegar, baking soda, a funnel, an average-size balloon, and a narrow-neck bottle (such as an empty water bottle). Use a clear glass or plastic vessel so you can witness the chemical reaction.

HOW TO PROCEED

1. Pour 1/2 cup of vinegar into the bottom of the bottle.

2. Insert a funnel into the mouth of the balloon and pour 5 tablespoons of baking soda through the funnel into the balloon.

3. Carefully stretch the mouth of the balloon over the opening of the bottle.

4. Gently lift up the balloon so that the baking soda empties into the vinegar at the bottom of the bottle.

5. The vinegar solution will start foaming vigorously—and the gas will soon inflate the balloon!

What's happening?

The fizzing and foaming you see are actually the result of a chemical reaction between the baking soda and the vinegar. All this bubbling is caused by the carbon-dioxide gas that the reaction creates.

Trick your brain

Sometimes you can't believe what you think you see.

You were able to see what happened when you inflated the balloon. Now here is a simple experiment where your eyes play a trick on you. Scientists use optical illusions to show how the brain can be tricked.

WHAT YOU'LL NEED

Assemble a small piece of stiff paper, some colored pencils for drawing, transparent tape, and a pencil.

HOW TO PROCEED

1. Trim the paper to about 2 inches (5 cm) square.

2. Turn the square so that it's a diamond. Then use the colored pencils to draw an animal or a person on one side.

3. On the other side of the diamond, draw a setting for the animal or a hat and hair for the person. For example, if you drew a cheetah on one side, draw grasslands on the other. If you drew a little boy on one side, draw a baseball cap on the other side.

4. Tape the bottom point of the diamond onto the point of a pencil.

5. Hold the pencil so the picture is upright and twirl the pencil rapidly between your hands.

What do you see?

You should see both images at the same time. The cheetah should appear in his habitat; the boy should be wearing the hat! The images blend because of the after-image.

Project
4

Make mothballs dance

Discover the magic that can happen when mothballs meet a few everyday ingredients.

You'll think your eyes are playing tricks on you in this experiment, but they're not. You can make mothballs dance and get a basic science lesson, too.

WHAT YOU'LL NEED

All that's required is a glass jar, water, vinegar, baking soda, and some mothballs.

HOW TO PROCEED

1. Fill the jar about two-thirds full with water.

2. Add about 1/4 to 1/3 cup of vinegar and 2 teaspoons of baking soda. Stir gently and toss in a few mothballs.

3. In no time, they'll start bouncing up and down. You've got to admit, it's funny and strange to watch.

What's happening?

The vinegar and baking soda create carbon dioxide just as they did for our rocket. The carbon-dioxide bubbles cling to the irregular surfaces of the mothballs. And when enough bubbles accumulate to lift the weight of a mothball, it rises to the surface of the water.

Once a mothball is on the surface, some of the bubbles escape into the air and the mothball sinks to the bottom of the jar to start the cycle again.

The dance will last longer if the container is sealed.

Make indoor lightning

Project 5

Witness a dazzling display of static electricity in action.

If you still have those balloons handy, here's a little experiment that helps children see the phenomenon of static electricity up close but not too personal.

You experience a discharge of static electricity when you touch a doorknob after shuffling across a carpet. But, with the exception of a lightning storm, you rarely see this phenomenon. This experiment offers a dazzling display of static electricity in action.

WHAT YOU'LL NEED

Assemble a package of nonflavored gelatin powder, a piece of paper, a balloon, and a woolen sweater. This is the kind of experiment that kids will want to see over and over again, so be sure to have a few extra packets of gelatin around.

HOW TO PROCEED

1. Empty the package of gelatin powder onto the paper.

2. Blow up the balloon, rub it on the sweater, and then hold it about an inch over the powder.

3. The gelatin particles will arch up toward the balloon.

What's happening?

The slightly negatively charged electrons—the built-up static electricity on the balloon—are attracting the positively charged protons in the gelatin powder. Voilà—instant lighting!

Project
6 Follow the sun

This simple sundial experiment is a great way to show how the sun's path changes.

One of the most essential lessons an adult can give a child is an understanding of the natural world. When we know how things work, we can feel a sense of security that leads to further inquiry and greater knowledge. A simple sundial experiment is a great way for kids to observe how the sun's path changes every day.

WHAT YOU'LL NEED

All you need is some cardboard, a stick, a screw or nail, a small board, and a pencil or pen.

HOW TO PROCEED

1. Just take a 10-inch (25-cm) square piece of cardboard and poke a stick through the middle. If necessary, attach a small board with a screw or nail to the bottom of the stick to hold it upright. This is your sundial.

2. Place the sundial in a sunny spot. At each hour, have the kids mark where the stick's shadow falls on the cardboard.

3. Check again the next day, and sure enough, the sundial seems pretty accurate.

4. Check a week later, though, and you'll find that the shadows don't align with the marks at the right times.

What's going on?

Here's your chance to discuss the natural world with your kids. You can start by suggesting they search the Internet for a reason why the mark's don't match from week to week. Give them this hint: The earth is tilted on its axis. And now you can have a world of interesting discussion.

Create a world in a jar

Build a biosphere and watch your kids learn about ecology—in miniature!

Now that you've looked at the sun in the sky, turn your gaze earthward. Discuss with your kids what the sun does for us here on earth and how everything is interconnected.

Children take these things for granted, so it's a real surprise when they realize just what an important part the sun plays in keeping us all alive and healthy. And you can demonstrate this by making a miniature biosphere.

WHAT YOU'LL NEED

Start with a large, wide-mouthed jar with a lid that you've cleaned thoroughly. You'll also need some pebbles, charcoal chips, potting soil, small plants, water, and some decorative items such as seashells and driftwood. It's important to use sterilized soil to avoid introducing unwanted organisms.

HOW TO PROCEED

1. Place a handful of pebbles and charcoal chips in the bottom of the jar.

2. Add several inches of slightly damp, sterilized potting soil.

3. Select a few plants that like similar conditions (such as ferns and mosses, which both like moderate light and moisture). Add a few colorful stones, seashells, or a piece of driftwood.

4. Add water to make the terrarium humid—but not drenching wet.

5. Tighten the lid and place the jar in a dimly lit location for two days. Then display it in bright light but not direct sunlight. When should I add more water? You shouldn't need to add water—it cycles from the plants to the soil and back again. The charcoal chips filter the water as it recycles.

Project
8

Let's get buggy

Help your bug-loving budding entomologist observe and preserve insects.

Some kids love to study insects, and just like the pros, your budding entomologist can preserve bugs—using nail polish remover.

WHAT YOU'LL NEED

Use a nail polish remover that contains the solvent acetone. (Check the label or sniff it for a banana-like odor.)

You'll also need a clean, wide-mouth jar, like a peanut butter jar, some cotton balls, a few facial tissues, straight pins, and corkboard or some corrugated cardboard. You may need a second jar to collect the insects.

HOW TO PROCEED

1. Collect a few live insects.

2. Soak some cotton balls with the nail polish remover and place them in the jar.

3. Add several tissues and your live insects. The tissues prevent the insects from damaging their wings.

4. Seal the jar tightly with a lid, and the specimens will quickly dehydrate.

5. Open the lid, turn the jar on its side, and carefully remove the insects.

6. Use a straight pin stuck through the insect's body to mount it on a corkboard or corrugated cardboard.

What kind of bugs do you have?

Consult the Internet or your local library to see what kinds of insects you've collected and to learn their characteristics. In what ways are those you collected alike? In what ways are they different from one another?

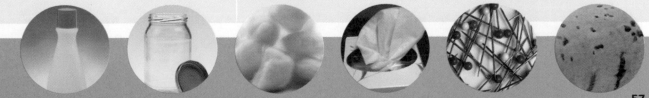

Learn Newton's law with a funny hat

*Hands-on experience is the best way to learn anything—
especially science!*

Physics is a complex science, but we are constantly surrounded by its truths. Here's a fun way to demonstrate Newton's first law of physics.

WHAT YOU'LL NEED

Get some modeling clay, a wire coat hanger, and a pair of pliers that you'll use to cut and shape the hanger.

HOW TO PROCEED

1. Make two medium-size balls from modeling clay.

2. Cut the coat hanger and bend a length of wire from it to form a large loopy **M** with hooks on each end.

3. Holding the wire in the middle, attach one clay ball to each of the hooks.

4. Place the low center point of the **M** on top of your head.

5. Slowly turn your head to the left or right. The inertia of the balls will be enough to keep them in place.

What's happening?

You're demonstrating Newton's law that "objects at rest tend to stay at rest."

With practice, you can actually turn all the way around and the balls will remain still.

Gravity lesson

Help your kids get a grip on gravity—using a tennis ball and a Ping-Pong ball!

Most kids are fascinated by gravity, especially the idea of a gravity-free environment, where they might be able to float! In this gravity experiment, you'll have fun as your kids learn that gravity exerts equal force on all objects, regardless of an object's weight.

Start out by asking your kids to guess which ball will fall faster—the tennis ball or the Ping-Pong ball? They'll become instantly involved as they discover the answer.

WHAT YOU'LL NEED

All that is required is two tennis balls, a Ping-Pong ball, and a chair you can stand on.

HOW TO PROCEED

1. Stand on the chair, holding the two tennis balls, one in each hand. Extend your arms so they're at the same distance from the floor.

2. Ask the kids to watch closely as you release both balls at once. Did the balls hit the floor at the same time?

3. Replace one of the tennis balls with a much lighter weight Ping-Pong ball. Before releasing the balls, ask the kids which ball they think will land first. Most will guess the heavier one, the tennis ball.

4. Release the balls, and the kids will discover that both balls will land at about the same time.

Why do they land at the same time?

Because gravity exerts the same force on all objects, regardless of their weight.

If you try this with a ball and a feather, the kids will also learn that less dense objects fall more slowly not because of their weight difference but because of air resistance.

Pierce a potato with air power

Demonstrate the power of air pressure—using nothing but a potato, a straw, and your finger!

When it's humid outside, you can get a clear sense of what air pressure is all about. But otherwise, children may have a hard time understanding it. Here's a way to demonstrate the power of air pressure.

WHAT YOU'LL NEED

You'll need only a potato and a couple of plastic straws.

HOW TO PROCEED

1. Grasp a straw in the middle and try to plunge it into a potato. It crumples and bends, unable to penetrate the potato.

2. Grasp another straw in the middle, but this time, put your finger over the top. The straw will plunge right into the tuber.

 Why did it work?

When the air is trapped inside the straw, it presses against the straw's sides, stiffening the straw enough to plunge into the potato. In fact, the deeper the straw plunges, the less space there is for the air and the stiffer the straw gets.

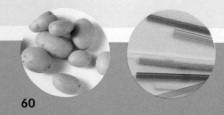

Make a battery with a lemon

Help your young scientist learn about electricity with just a penny and a lemon!

Children get a kick out of this simple experiment that involves a lemon, coins, and a human tongue. In it, you demonstrate how to turn a lemon into a battery. It won't start your car, but you will be able to feel the current with your tongue.

WHAT YOU'LL NEED

Assemble a lemon, a sharp knife to cut it, a clean copper penny, and a clean dime.

HOW TO PROCEED

1 Roll the lemon on a flat surface to activate its juices.

2 Cut two small slices in the lemon about 1/2 inch (13 mm) apart. Place a penny into one slot and a dime into the other.

3 Touch your tongue to the penny and the dime at the same time. You'll feel a slight electrical tingle.

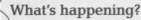

What's happening?

The acid in the lemon reacts with the two metals to produce an electrical charge on each. But it produces different charges with each type of metal. With the copper coin, it produces a positive electric charge, while with the silver one it produces a negative charge. When you put your tongue on both coins at once, your tongue conducts the charges, causing a small amount of electricity to flow.

For your young budding scientist, here's a chance to talk not only about how electrical current works but also the dangers of electricity.

Project 13

Coat a nail with copper

Use this experiment to demonstrate the power of electrical currents created between everyday objects.

Use regular copper pennies for this metal-plating experiment. Gather 25 pennies. Don't worry about how old or dirty they are.

WHAT YOU'LL NEED:

Besides the 25 pennies, you'll also need white vinegar, salt, a glass jar, a large iron nail, some baking soda, and a sponge.

HOW TO PROCEED

1 Mix 1/2 cup of vinegar with 1/4 teaspoon of salt in the glass jar. Gently drop in the pennies and let them sit for about 5 minutes in the solution.

2 Meanwhile, dampen the sponge and coat it with baking soda. Clean the nail with it and then rinse clean.

3 Place the cleaned nail into the jar with the pennies.

4 After about 15 minutes you should see a change. The pennies should shine like new and the nail will be coated with copper.

What happened?

The acetic acid in the vinegar combined with the copper on the pennies to create a new compound—copper acetate. This removed copper from the surface of the pennies and left them shiny.

At the same time, a mild electrical current was created between the two metals in the presence of the acidic solution, just as in the lemon and coins experiment on the previous page. As the current flowed from the copper pennies to the iron nail, it carried the newly produced copper acetate with it, depositing the copper on the nail.

Project
14

See the rainbow effect

Show how all colors are combinations of the primary colors—red, blue, and yellow.

In the previous project, you transferred copper from pennies to a nail, changing the look and colors of both. Now here's an experiment that separates color to its components.

WHAT YOU'LL NEED

You need only a paper towel, a batch of colorful markers, and a glass jar filled with water.

HOW TO PROCEED

1 Cut a paper towel into strips. Use felt-tip markers of different colors to draw a rectangle or large circle on one end of each strip. Use just one color per strip and include black on one strip.

2 Place the unmarked end of the strip into the glass jar filled with water. Leave the colored end dry and draped over the side of the jar. Be patient.

3 After about 20 minutes, the water from the jar will have traveled up the strip and down the outside into the color blot. As it does, it will separate the colors into their primary components.

What colors make up a rainbow?

Let your kids in on the secret of ROY-G-BIV. Each letter of this memory device stands for a different color of the rainbow. Red-Orange-Yellow-Green-Blue-Indigo-Violet.

It's like walking on water

Amaze your kids as you both discover how to make a paper clip float!

Try this experiment as a challenge. Ask your children if they can make a paper clip float on water. Of course it will sink when they put it in the water. But you can make it float with a little help.

WHAT YOU'LL NEED

All that you need is a bowl of water, a paper towel, and a paper clip.

HOW TO PROCEED

1. Take a piece of paper towel larger than the paper clip and place it on top of the water.

2. Put the paper clip on top of the paper towel.

3. After a few seconds the paper towel will sink into the water—leaving the clip floating!

What's happening?

It's not magic. The surface tension of the water allows the clip to float. As the paper towel sinks, it lowers the paper clip onto the water without breaking the surface tension. If the tension had been broken, the clip would have sunk.

What's a bag's bursting strength?

*Use this experiment to help the environment—
one plastic bag at a time!*

Have you ever wondered how much weight a strong flexible material like plastic can hold before it breaks? The next time you go grocery shopping with the kids, see if they can guess how much a plastic grocery bag will hold. Most are meant to carry about 20 pounds (9 kg) of groceries before you need to double-bag.

How much do your kids think a bag can hold without its handles breaking?

WHAT YOU'LL NEED

For this experiment, you will need a kitchen scale, a plastic bag, and a bunch of rocks.

HOW TO PROCEED

1. Place the bag on the scale. Fill it with rocks until the scale reads 10 pounds (4.5 kg). Lift the bag. Does it hold?

2. Have your kids add more rocks in 2-pound (1 kg) increments, testing the bag's strength after each addition.

3. When the handles start to tear, they'll know the bag's actual strength.

4. Continue the learning (and keep your child busy while you shop) by asking him or her to add up the weight of what you're buying and guessing how many bags you'll need to carry your groceries home.

Which bag should I choose?

The eternal struggle—paper vs. plastic. If you're trying to be environmentally conscious—and hoping to pass that value on to your children—the simple answer is as follows: Whichever you choose, reuse.

Each time you reuse a bag or don't use an extra one for double-bagging, you save it from being added to a landfill. Plus, you keep a new one from being made.

Amazingly versatile vinegar— for kitchen and bath, laundry and garden, housecleaning and car cleaning, even pet care and personal care

The Miracle of
Vinegar

Cleaning, healing, fixing, improving—there's no end to what you can do with nature's most practical liquid. Here are 188 ideas to get you started!

Easier Housecleaning

CLEAN YOUR WINDOW BLINDS

Give your mini-blinds or vene-tians "the white glove treatment." Just put on a white cotton glove and moisten the fingers in a solution of equal parts white vinegar and hot tap water. Now simply slide your fingers across both sides of each slat to quickly clean them. Periodically rinse the glove in a container of clean water.

GET RID OF SMOKE ODOR

Remove the lingering odor of burned food or cigarettes by setting out shallow bowls about three-quarters full of white or cider vinegar. The odor should be gone in less than a day. To quickly dispense of the smell of fresh cigarette smoke, moisten a cloth with vinegar and wave it around a bit.

ERASE BALLPOINT-PEN MARKS

Has a budding young artist just decorated a painted wall with a ballpoint original?
Dab on some full-strength white vinegar, using a sponge. Repeat until the marks are gone.

RESTORE YOUR RUGS

Does your rug or carpet look worn and dingy? Bring it back to life by brushing it with a clean push broom dipped in a solution of 1 cup white vinegar in 1 gallon (3.8 liters) water. Your faded threads will perk up, and you don't even need to rinse off the solution.

KEEP RUGS FROM MILDEWING

To prevent mildew from forming on the bottoms of carpets and rugs, mist the backs with full-strength white vinegar from a spray bottle.

REVITALIZE WOOD PANELING

To liven up dull wood paneling, mix 2 cups warm water, 4 table-spoons white or cider vinegar, and 2 tablespoons olive oil in a container, give it a couple of shakes, and apply with a clean cloth. Let it soak in for several minutes, then polish with a dry cloth.

BRIGHTEN UP BRICKWORK

To clean brick floors without breaking out the polish, just go over them with a damp mop dipped in 1 cup white vinegar mixed with 1 gallon (3.8 liters) warm water. Brighten fireplace bricks the same way.

WIPE AWAY MILDEW

To remove mildew stains, reach for white vinegar. It can be safely used without additional ventilation and can be applied to almost any surface—bathroom fixtures and tile, clothing, furniture, painted surfaces, plastic curtains, and more. For heavy mildew accumulations, use it full strength. For light stains, dilute it with an equal amount of water.

UNGLUE STICKERS, DECALS, AND PRICE TAGS

To remove a sticker or decal on painted furniture or a painted wall, saturate the corners and sides of the sticker with full-strength white vinegar and carefully scrape it off, using an expired credit or phone card. Remove any residue by pouring on a bit more vinegar. Let it sit for a minute or two, then wipe with a clean cloth. This is equally effective for removing price tags and other stickers from glass, plastic, and other glossy surfaces.

CLEAN YOUR PIANO KEYS

To get grimy fingerprints and stains off piano keys, dip a soft cloth into a solution of 1/2 cup white vinegar mixed with 2 cups water, squeeze it out thoroughly, then gently wipe each key. Use a second cloth to dry each key as you move along. Let the keyboard dry uncovered for 24 hours.

FRESHEN A MUSTY CLOSET

Got a closet that doesn't smell fresh? Empty it, then wash the walls, ceiling, and floor with a cloth dampened in a solution of 1 cup vinegar, 1 cup ammonia, and 1/4 cup baking soda in 1 gallon (3.8 liters) water. Let the interior dry with the door open before refilling it.

REMOVE CARPET STAINS

You can lift out many stains from your carpet with vinegar.

■ Rub **light carpet stains** with a mixture of 2 tablespoons salt dissolved in 1/2 cup white vinegar. Let dry, then vacuum.

■ For **larger or darker stains**, add 2 tablespoons borax to the mixture and use in the same way.

■ For **tough, ground-in dirt** and other stains, make a paste of 1 tablespoon vinegar with 1 tablespoon cornstarch, and rub on with a dry cloth. Let it set for two days, then vacuum.

Floor Cleaning

Damp-mopping with a mild vinegar solution is widely recommended as a way to clean wood and no-wax vinyl or laminate flooring. But, if possible, check with your flooring manufacturer first. Even when diluted, vinegar's acidity can ruin some floor finishes, and too much water will damage most wooden floors. If you want to try vinegar on your floors, use 1/2 cup white vinegar mixed in 1 gallon (3.8 liters) warm water. Start with a trial application in an inconspicuous area. Before applying the solution, squeeze out the mop thoroughly (or just use a spray bottle to moisten the mop head).

TO MAKE Spray-on spot and stain remover

You will need: two spray bottles, water, vinegar, and ammonia

1	Fill one spray bottle with
	   5 parts water
	   1 part vinegar

2	Fill a second spray bottle with
	   5 parts water
	   1 part nonsudsy ammonia

3	Saturate the stain with the vinegar solution. Let it settle for a few minutes, then blot thoroughly with a clean, dry cloth.
4	Then spray on the ammonia solution and blot again.
5	Repeat until the stain is gone.

Cleaning Your Stuff

CLEAN YOUR EYEGLASSES

To remove dirt, sweat, and fingerprints from glass lenses, apply a few drops of white vinegar and wipe with a soft cloth; it will leave them spotless. But don't use vinegar on plastic lenses.

SHINE YOUR SILVER

Make your silverware—as well as your pure silver jewelry—shine like new by soaking it in a mixture of 1/2 cup white vinegar and 2 tablespoons baking soda for two to three hours. Rinse under cold water and then dry with a soft cloth.

POLISH BRASS AND COPPER ITEMS

Put the shimmer back in brass, bronze, and copper objects by making a paste of equal parts white vinegar and salt, or vinegar and baking soda (wait for the fizzing to stop before using). Use a clean, soft cloth to rub the paste into the item until the tarnish is gone. Rinse with cool water and polish with a soft towel until dry.

➕ **TAKE CARE** Don't apply vinegar to jewelry containing pearls or gemstones, because it can damage their finish or, in the case of pearls, actually disintegrate them. Don't attempt to remove tarnish from antiques, because removing the tarnish could diminish their value.

CLEAR DIRT OFF PCS AND PERIPHERALS

To keep your computer, printer, and other home office gear clean and dust-free, dampen a clean cloth in equal parts white vinegar and water, squeeze it out well, and start wiping. Before you start, make sure that your equipment is shut off, and never use a spray bottle; you don't want to get liquid on the circuits inside. Have a few cotton swabs on hand for getting into tight spaces (like between the keys of your keyboard).

CLEAN YOUR COMPUTER MOUSE

If you have a mouse with a removable tracking ball, use a 50-50 vinegar-water solution to clean it. First, remove the ball from underneath the mouse by twisting off its cover. Use a cloth, dampened with the solution and wrung out, to wipe the ball and the mouse itself. Then use a moistened cotton swab to clean out the ball chamber. (Let it dry a couple of hours before reinserting the ball.)

BURNISH YOUR SCISSORS

When your scissor blades get sticky or grimy, don't wash them in water, which might cause rust. Instead, wipe them with a cloth dipped in full-strength white vinegar, then dry.

GET THE SALT OFF YOUR SHOES

Winter ice, slush, and snow are rough enough on your shoes and boots, but all the rock salt used to melt them is worse. Besides leaving unsightly white stains, it can cause your footwear to crack and even disintegrate. To remove it and prevent long-term damage, wipe fresh stains with a cloth dipped in undiluted white vinegar.

DEODORIZE LUNCH BOXES AND FOOTLOCKERS

Does your old footlocker smell musty? Or does your child's lunch box stink of week-old tuna? Soak a slice of white bread in white vinegar and leave it in the space overnight. The smell should be gone by morning.

Furniture Care

REMOVE CANDLE WAX

To remove candle wax on fine wood furniture, soften it with a blow-dryer on its hottest setting and blot up as much as you can with paper towels. Then remove what's left by rubbing with a cloth soaked in a solution of equal parts white vinegar and water. Wipe clean with a soft cloth.

CONCEAL SCRATCHES IN WOOD FURNITURE

To make a scratch on a wooden tabletop much less noticeable, mix some distilled or cider vinegar and iodine in a small jar and paint over the scratch with a small artist's brush. Use more iodine for darker woods; more vinegar for lighter shades.

GET RID OF WATER RINGS ON FURNITURE

To remove white rings left by wet glasses on wood furniture, mix equal parts vinegar and olive oil and apply it with a soft cloth while moving with the wood grain. Use another clean, soft cloth to shine it. To get white water rings off leather furniture, dab them with a sponge soaked in full-strength white vinegar.

WIPE OFF WAX OR POLISH BUILDUP

To get built-up polish off wood furniture, dip a cloth in equal parts white vinegar and water and squeeze it out well. Then, moving with the grain, clean away the polish. Wipe dry with a soft cloth. Most leather tabletops will come clean simply by wiping them down with a soft cloth dipped in 1/4 cup vinegar and 1/2 cup water. Dry with a clean towel.

REVITALIZE LEATHER FURNITURE

Has your leather sofa lost its luster? Restore it by mixing equal parts white vinegar and boiled linseed oil in a spray bottle. Shake the mixture well and spray it on. Spread it evenly over the leather using a soft cloth, wait a couple of minutes, then rub it off with a clean cloth.

➕ **TAKE CARE** Don't use vinegar on tabletops, countertops, or floors made of marble. Its acidity can dull or even pit the protective coating—and possibly damage the stone itself. Also, avoid using vinegar on travertine and limestone; the acid eats through the calcium in the stonework.

It Lasts Almost Forever

You just came across an old, unopened bottle of vinegar, and you wonder: Is it still any good? The answer is an unqualified yes. In fact, vinegar has a practically limitless shelf life. Its acid content makes it self-preserving and even negates the need for refrigeration (although many people mistakenly believe in refrigerating their open bottles). You won't see any changes in white vinegar over time, but some other types may change slightly in color or develop a hazy appearance or a bit of sediment. However, these are strictly cosmetic changes; the vinegar itself will be virtually unchanged.

A Spotless Kitchen

CLEAN CHROME AND STAINLESS STEEL

To clean chrome and stainless-steel fixtures, lightly mist them with undiluted white vinegar from a spray bottle. Buff with a soft cloth to brighten.

STEAM-CLEAN YOUR MICROWAVE

To clean your microwave, place a glass bowl filled with 1/4 cup vinegar in 1 cup water inside, and zap the mixture for five minutes on the highest setting. Once the liquid cools, dip a cloth into it and wipe off stains and splatters.

BRUSH-CLEAN CAN OPENER BLADES

To clean and sanitize that dirty wheel blade on your electric can opener, dip an old toothbrush in white vinegar and position the bristles around the wheel. Turn on the appliance, and let the blade scrub itself clean.

SANITIZE JARS, CONTAINERS, AND VASES

Want to clean out a peanut butter jar? Or get the slimy residue out of a vase? Just fill it with equal parts vinegar and warm, soapy water and let it stand for 10 to 15 minutes. Close a bottle or jar and give it a few good shakes; otherwise, use a bottle brush to scrape off the remains before thoroughly rinsing.

CLEAN YOUR TEAKETTLE

To eliminate lime and mineral deposits in a teakettle, bring 3 cups full-strength white vinegar to a full boil for five minutes and leave it overnight. Rinse with cold water the next day.

CLEAR THE AIR IN YOUR KITCHEN

If the smell of yesterday's boiled cabbage or fish stew is still hanging around, boil 1/2 cup white vinegar in 1 cup water until the liquid is almost gone.

WASH OUT YOUR DISHWASHER

To remove built-up soap film in your dishwasher, pour 1 cup undiluted white vinegar into the bottom of the unit—or in a bowl on the top rack. Then run the machine through a full cycle without any dishes or detergent. Do this once a month, especially if you have hard water. *Note:* If there's no mention of vinegar in your dishwasher owner's manual, check with the manufacturer first.

REFRESH YOUR ICE TRAYS

If your plastic ice trays are covered with hard-water stains—or if it's been a while since you've cleaned them, soak them in undiluted vinegar for four to five hours, then rinse well under cold water and let dry.

DISINFECT CUTTING BOARDS

Water and dishwashing detergent can weaken surface fibers on wood cutting boards and butcher-block countertops. Instead, wipe them with full-strength white vinegar after each use. The acetic acid in the vinegar is a good disinfectant, effective against many harmful bugs. When your wood cutting surface needs deodorizing as well, spread some baking soda over it and then spray on undiluted white vinegar. Let it foam and bubble for five to ten minutes, then rinse with a cloth dipped in clean cold water.

PURGE BUGS FROM YOUR PANTRY

Are there moths or other insects in your cupboard? Fill a small bowl with 1 1/2 cups cider vinegar and a couple of drops of liquid dish detergent. Leave it in there for a week; it will attract the bugs, which will fall into the bowl and drown. To prevent their return, empty the area, give it a thorough washing, and toss all pasta, flour, and other wheat products.

DEODORIZE YOUR GARBAGE DISPOSAL

To keep your garbage disposal unit sanitized and smelling clean, mix equal parts water and vinegar in a bowl, pour the solution into an ice cube tray, and freeze it. Then simply drop a couple of "vinegar cubes" down your disposal every week or so, followed by a cold-water rinse.

MAKE A SCRUB FOR POTS AND PANS

Want an effective, safe scouring mix for metal cookware that costs pennies? Simply combine equal parts salt and flour and add just enough vinegar to make a paste. Work the paste over the utensil inside and out, then rinse and dry.

CLEAN YOUR COFFEEMAKER

If your coffee is bitter, odds are, your coffeemaker needs cleaning. Fill the decanter with 2 cups white vinegar and 1 cup water. Place a filter in the machine, and pour the solution into the water chamber. Run the coffeemaker through a brew cycle. Replace the filter with a fresh one and run clean water through the machine for two cycles, replacing the filter again for the second brew. If you have soft water, clean your coffeemaker after 80 brew cycles—after 40 cycles if you have hard water.

QUICK CLEANING
Glass and China

Here's how to put the sparkle back in your glassware and china with vinegar.

■ To keep everyday **glassware** gleaming, add 1/4 cup vinegar to your dishwasher's rinse cycle.

■ To rid **drinking glasses** of cloudiness or spots caused by hard water, heat a pot of equal parts white vinegar and water (use full-strength vinegar if your glasses are very cloudy), and let them soak in it for 15 to 30 minutes. Scrub well with a bottle brush and rinse.

■ When cleaning good **crystal glasses,** add 2 tablespoons vinegar to your dishwater. Rinse in a solution of 3 parts warm water to 1 part vinegar and air-dry.

■ To wash delicate crystal and **fine china,** add 1 cup vinegar to a basin of warm water. Gently dunk the glasses in the solution and let dry.

■ To get coffee stains and other discolorations off **china teacups,** scrub them with equal parts vinegar and salt, and rinse under warm water.

Speed Cleaning in Your Kitchen

Distilled white vinegar is one of the best grease eliminators around. Here's how to put it to good use.

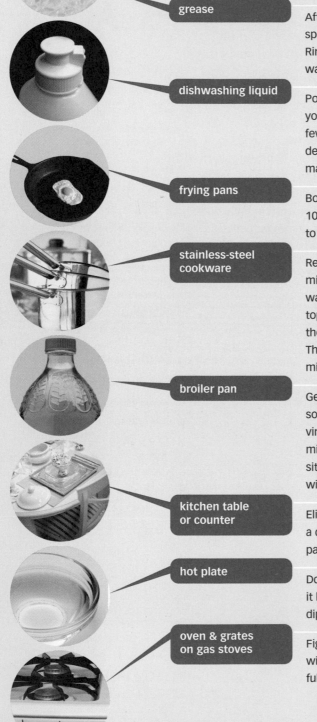

grease

After frying, wash off grease splatters with a sponge dipped in undiluted white vinegar. Rinse with another sponge soaked in cold water, then dry with a soft cloth.

dishwashing liquid

Pour 3 to 4 tablespoons white vinegar into your dishwashing liquid bottle and give it a few shakes. The vinegar will increase the detergent's grease-fighting capabilities and make it last longer.

frying pans

Boiling 2 cups vinegar in your pans for 10 minutes will help keep food from sticking to it for several months at a time.

stainless-steel cookware

Remove burned-on grease and food by mixing 1 cup distilled vinegar in enough water to cover the material (if it's near the top of a large pot, you may need to increase the amount of vinegar). Boil for five minutes. The material should come off with some mild scrubbing.

broiler pan

Get blackened, cooked-on grease off by softening it up with a solution of 1 cup cider vinegar and 2 tablespoons sugar. Apply the mixture while the pan is still hot, and let it sit for an hour or so. The grime will slide off with a light scrubbing.

kitchen table or counter

Eliminate grease stains by wiping them with a cloth dampened in a solution of equal parts white vinegar and water.

hot plate

Does it look more like a grease pan? To get it back in shape, wash it with a sponge dipped in full-strength white vinegar.

oven & grates on gas stoves

Fight grease buildups in your oven by wiping the inside with a sponge soaked in full-strength white vinegar once a week.

UNCLOG AND DEODORIZE DRAINS

Vinegar used in combination with baking soda or salt is gentler on your pipes (and wallet) than commercial drain cleaners.

▪ To clear clogs in sink and tub drains, pour in 1/2 cup baking soda followed by 1 cup vinegar. When the foaming subsides, flush with hot tap water. Wait five minutes and then flush again with cold water. This also washes away odor-causing bacteria.

▪ To speed up a slow drain, pour in 1/2 cup salt followed by 2 cups boiling vinegar, then flush with hot and cold tap water.

MULTIPURPOSE CLEANER #1

For cleaning glass, stainless steel, and plastic laminate surfaces, fill a spray bottle with 2 parts water, 1 part distilled white vinegar, and a couple of drops of dishwashing liquid.

MULTIPURPOSE CLEANER #2

For walls and other painted surfaces, mix 1/2 cup white vinegar, 1 cup ammonia, and 1/4 cup baking soda in 1 gallon (3.8 liters) water and pour some into a spray bottle. Spritz it on spots and stains and wipe with a clean towel.

CLEAN A DIRTY THERMOS

To clean a thermos bottle, fill it with warm water and 1/4 cup white vinegar. If you see any residue, add some uncooked rice to help scrape it off. Close and shake well. Rinse and air-dry.

REFRESH YOUR REFRIGERATOR

Vinegar is an effective, safe cleanser for your fridge. To prevent mildew, wash the interior walls and the vegetable and fruit bin interiors with full-strength white vinegar. Also use undiluted vinegar to wipe away accumulated dust and grime on top of the fridge. Use vinegar diluted half and half with water to wash everything else, including the door gasket. When you're done, put a box of baking soda inside to maintain the clean smell.

TRAP FRUIT FLIES

Did you bring home fruit flies from the market? Make a trap for them by filling an old jar halfway with apple cider. Punch a few holes in the lid and screw it back on.

QUICK CLEANING
Cooking Stains

Nothing will do a better job of removing stubborn cooking stains on your pots, pans, and ovenware than vinegar.

▪ To remove discolorations from **stainless-steel pots and pans,** soak them in 2 cups white vinegar for 30 minutes. Rinse with hot, soapy water, then with cold water.

▪ For those dark stains on your **aluminum cookware** (caused by cooking acidic foods), add 1 teaspoon white vinegar for every cup of water needed to cover the stains. Let it boil for a couple of minutes, then rinse with cold water.

▪ To get cooked-on food stains off **glass ovenware,** fill them with 1 part vinegar and 4 parts water and let it boil at a low level for five minutes. After the mixture cools, mild scrubbing should remove the stains.

▪ For mineral stains on **nonstick cookware,** rub with a cloth dipped in undiluted distilled vinegar. To loosen up stubborn stains, mix 2 tablespoons baking soda, 1/2 cup vinegar, and 1 cup water and boil for 10 minutes.

A Sparkling Bathroom

SHINE CERAMIC TILES

Brighten soap-dulled ceramic tiles by scrubbing them with 1/2 cup white vinegar, 1/2 cup ammonia, and 1/4 cup borax mixed in 1 gallon (3.8 liters) warm water. Rinse well.

WHITEN STAINED TILE GROUT

Use an old toothbrush dipped in undiluted white vinegar to scrub dinginess from the grout lines between tiles and restore their original shade of white.

CLEAN SINKS AND BATHTUBS

To put the shine back in a porcelain sink or tub, scrub it with full-strength white vinegar and rinse with cold water.

RID YOUR TUB OF HARD-WATER STAINS

Pour in 3 cups white vinegar as you fill the tub with running hot water that covers the hard-water stains. Let it soak for four hours, then drain. The stains should scrub off easily.

SHINE YOUR SHOWER DOORS

To leave glass shower doors sparkling clean—and to remove annoying water spots—wipe them with a cloth dipped in a solution of 1/2 cup white vinegar, 1 cup ammonia, and 1/4 cup baking soda mixed in 1 gallon (3.8 liters) warm water.

WIPE DOWN FIXTURES

Pour a bit of undiluted white vinegar onto a soft cloth and use it to wipe chrome faucets, towel racks, bathroom mirrors, doorknobs, and other such surfaces. It'll leave them gleaming.

CLEAN OUT SHOWER DOOR TRACKS

Get rid of accumulated grime in shower door tracks. Fill them with full-strength white vinegar and let it sit for three to five hours. (If the tracks are really dirty, microwave the vinegar in a glass container for 30 seconds first.) Then pour hot water over the track to flush away the gunk. Use a small scrub brush for tough stains.

REMOVE MINERAL DEPOSITS FROM SHOWERHEADS

Clear blockages and mineral deposits from your showerheads with vinegar.

■ If you have a **removable** metal showerhead, place it in 1 quart (1 liter) boiling water with 1/2 cup distilled vinegar for 10 minutes. (Use hot, not boiling, liquid if you are cleaning a plastic showerhead.)

■ If you have a **nonremovable** showerhead, fill a small plastic bag half full with vinegar and tape it over the showerhead. Let it sit for about one hour, then remove the bag and wipe off the showerhead.

FIGHT BATHROOM MOLD AND MILDEW

To remove and inhibit bathroom mold and mildew, mix 3 tablespoons white vinegar, 1 teaspoon borax, and 2 cups hot water in a spray bottle. Spray the mixture on painted surfaces, tiles, windows, or wherever you see mold or mildew spots. Work the solution into the stains with a soft scrub brush or just let it soak in.

DISINFECT TOILET BOWLS

Keep your toilet looking and smelling clean. Pour 2 cups white vinegar into the bowl and let it soak overnight. Doing this weekly will also help keep the bowl from developing an ugly water ring.

WASH YOUR RINSE CUP

If several family members use the same rinse cup after brushing, clean it weekly: Fill it with equal parts water and white vinegar and let it sit overnight. Rinse thoroughly.

CLEAN YOUR TOOTHBRUSH HOLDER

Get the grime, bacteria, and caked-on toothpaste drippings out of the openings of a toothbrush holder by cleaning them with a cotton swab moistened with white vinegar.

➕ **TAKE CARE** Combining vinegar with bleach—or any other product containing chlorine, such as chlorinated lime (sold as bleaching powder)—may produce chlorine gas. In low concentrations, this toxic, acrid-smelling gas can cause damage to your eyes, skin, or respiratory system. High concentrations are often fatal.

Laundry Magic

STOP REDS FROM RUNNING

Prevent red—or other brightly dyed—washable clothes from ruining your wash loads. Soak new garments in a few cups of undiluted white vinegar for 10 to 15 minutes before their first washing.

MAKE NEW CLOTHES READY TO WEAR

Get the chemicals, dust, odor, and whatever else out of your brand-new or secondhand clothes by pouring 1 cup white vinegar into the wash cycle the first time you wash them.

WHITEN DINGY CREW SOCKS

Are your white crew socks an unwelcome gray? Add 1 cup vinegar to 6 cups water in a large pot and bring to a boil. Pour into a bucket and soak your socks overnight. The next day, wash them normally.

GET THE YELLOW OUT OF CLOTHING

To restore yellowed clothing, soak the garments overnight in a solution of 1 cup vinegar to 3 quarts (3 liters) warm water. Wash them the next morning.

CLEAN YOUR WASHING MACHINE

To remove soap scum and disinfect your washer, pour in 2 cups vinegar, then run it through a full cycle without any clothes or detergent. If your washer is particularly dirty, fill it with very hot water, add 2 gallons (7.5 liters) vinegar, and let the agitator run for 8 to 10 minutes. Turn off the washer and let the solution stand overnight. In the morning, empty the washer and run it through a complete cycle.

SHARPEN YOUR CREASES

For neater creases, lightly spray your clothes with equal parts water and vinegar before ironing. For truly sharp creases, dampen the garment using a cloth moistened in a solution of 1 part white vinegar and 2 parts water. Then place a brown paper bag over the crease and start ironing.

DULL THE SHINE IN YOUR SEAT

To get rid of that shiny seat on your dark pants or skirt, just brush the area lightly with an old soft toothbrush dipped in equal parts white vinegar and water. Pat dry with a soft towel.

➕ **TAKE CARE** Keep cider vinegar out of the laundry. Using it to pretreat clothes or adding it to wash or rinse water may actually create stains rather than remove them. Use only distilled white vinegar for laundering.

QUICK CLEANING
Laundry Loads

Just adding 1 cup of white vinegar to your washer's rinse cycle yields many benefits. It will:

▪ Kill off any bacteria in your wash load, especially if it includes cloth diapers and the like.

▪ Make your clothes come out of the wash soft and smelling fresh—eliminating the need for fabric-softening liquids or sheets.

▪ Brighten small loads of white clothes.

▪ Keep your clothes lint- and static-free if added to the last rinse.

▪ Set the color of newly dyed fabrics if added to the last rinse.

Speed Cleaning in Your Laundry Room

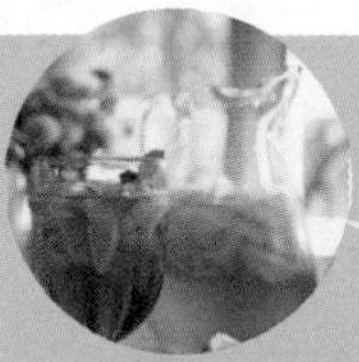

FOOD STAINS

Water-soluble stains include beer, fruit juices, black coffee and tea, and vomit. Pat the spot with a cloth moistened with undiluted white vinegar just before washing. For large stains, soak the garment overnight in a solution of 3 parts vinegar to 1 part cold water before washing.

DYE STAINS

Dye stains, which include cola, hair dye, ketchup, and wine, are more difficult to remove. Sponge the spot with undiluted vinegar within 24 hours and launder immediately. For severe stains, add 1 or 2 cups vinegar to the wash cycle as well.

UNDERARM STAINS

For perspiration and deodorant stains on shirts and other garments, pour a little undiluted vinegar on the stain and gently rub it into the fabric before laundering.

RING AROUND THE COLLAR

Scrub rings on collars and cuffs of shirts and dresses with a paste made from 2 parts white vinegar and 3 parts baking soda. Let the paste set for at least half an hour before washing.

LIGHT MILDEW STAINS

Apply a vinegar-baking soda paste as described above for ring around the collar to eliminate mildew stains.

PEN AND INK

Wet the stain with white vinegar, then rub in a paste of 2 parts vinegar to 3 parts cornstarch. Let the paste dry thoroughly before washing.

BLOODSTAINS

Pour full-strength white vinegar on the stain before it sets. Let it soak in for 5 to 10 minutes, then blot well with a cloth. Repeat if necessary, then wash immediately. Bloodstains are relatively easy to remove before they set but can be nearly impossible to wash out after 24 hours.

RUST

Moisten the spot with full-strength vinegar and then rub in a little salt. Let it dry in the sunlight (in winter, a sunny window will do), then toss it in the wash.

CRAYON STAINS

Rub crayon stains on clothing with an old toothbrush soaked in undiluted vinegar before washing.

REMOVE CIGARETTE SMELL FROM SUITS

If you have the lingering smell of cigarette smoke on your good suit or dress, add 1 cup vinegar to a bathtub filled with the hottest water your tap can muster. Close the door and hang your garments above the steam. The smell should be gone within hours.

SPRAY AWAY WRINKLES

You can often get wrinkles out of a garment after drying by misting it thoroughly with a solution of 1 part vinegar to 3 parts water. Hang it up and let it air-dry. You may find this works better for some clothes than ironing.

FLUSH YOUR IRON'S INTERIOR

To eliminate mineral deposits and prevent corrosion on your steam iron, clean it occasionally by filling the reservoir with undiluted white vinegar. Place the iron in an upright position, switch on the steam setting, and let the vinegar steam through it for 5 to 10 minutes. Then refill the chamber with clean water and repeat. Finally, give the water chamber a good rinsing with cold, clean water.

MAKE OLD HEMLINES DISAPPEAR

Want to make those needle marks from an old hemline disappear? Just moisten the area with a cloth dipped in equal parts vinegar and water, then place it under the garment before ironing.

RESHAPE YOUR WOOLENS

Shrunken woolen sweaters can usually be stretched back to their former size or shape after boiling them in a solution of 1 part vinegar to 2 parts water for 25 minutes. Let the garment air-dry after stretching it.

SOFTEN YOUR BLANKETS

To remove soap residue from a cotton or wool blanket, add 2 cups white vinegar to your washer's rinse water. It will feel fresh and soft as new.

SPIFF UP YOUR SUEDE

You can generally tone up suede items by lightly wiping them with a sponge dipped in vinegar.

REMOVE GREASE ON SUEDE

To get rid of a greasy spot on a suede garment, gently brush the stain with a soft toothbrush dipped in white vinegar. Let the garment air-dry, then brush with a suede brush. Repeat if necessary.

ERASE SCORCH MARKS

You can often eliminate slight scorch marks by rubbing the spot with a cloth dampened with white vinegar, then blotting it with a clean towel. Repeat if necessary.

CLEAN YOUR IRON'S SOLEPLATE

To remove scorch marks from the soleplate of your iron, scrub it with a paste made by heating up equal parts vinegar and salt in a small pan. Use a rag dipped in clean water to wipe away the remaining residue.

Buying Vinegar

Vinegar comes in a surprising number of varieties—including herbal organic blends, Champagne, rice, and wine. For household chores, however, plain distilled white vinegar is the best and by far the least expensive choice. You can buy it by the gallon (3.8 liters) to save even more money. Apple cider vinegar runs a close second in usefulness—especially for cooking and home remedies. All other types of vinegar are strictly for ingestion and can be pretty pricey as well.

Better Cooking

KEEP CORNED BEEF FROM SHRINKING

Stop your corned beef from shrinking by adding a couple of tablespoons of cider vinegar to the water when boiling it.

REMOVE ODORS FROM YOUR HANDS

Strong onion, garlic, or fish odors are a lot easier to wash off your hands if you rub some distilled vinegar on them before and after you slice vegetables or clean fish.

WASH STORE-BOUGHT PRODUCE

Before serving fruits and vegetables, eliminate hidden dirt, pesticides, and even insects by rinsing them in 4 tablespoons cider vinegar dissolved in 1 gallon (3.8 liters) cold water.

GET RID OF BERRY STAINS

Use undiluted white vinegar to remove stains from berries and other fruits on your hands.

TENDERIZE AND PURIFY MEATS AND SEAFOOD

Soak a lean or inexpensive cut of red meat in a couple of cups of full-strength vinegar overnight to break down tough fibers and kill any potentially harmful bacteria. You can tenderize seafood steaks the same way. Experiment with different vinegar varieties for added flavor, or use cider or white vinegar if you intend to rinse it off before cooking.

MAKE BETTER HARD-BOILED EGGS

Add 2 tablespoons distilled vinegar for every quart (liter) of water to keep hard-boiled eggs from cracking. It also makes them easier to shell.

MAKE BETTER POACHED EGGS

Add a couple of tablespoons of vinegar to the water to keep your poached eggs in tight shape. It keeps the egg whites from spreading.

A vinegar with pedigree

The world's most highly prized—and priced—vinegar is that delectable version from Italy, balsamic vinegar. Authentic balsamic vinegar comes solely from Trebbiano grapes, a particularly sweet white variety grown in the hills surrounding the town of Modena. Italian law mandates the vinegar be aged in wooden barrels made of chestnut, juniper, mulberry, or oak. There are only two grades of true balsamic vinegar: *tradizionale vecchio*, vinegar that is at least 12 years old; and *tradizionale extra vecchio*, vinegar that is aged for at least 25 years. Some balsamic vinegars have aged successfully for more than 100 years. A top-quality, authentic balsamic vinegar can sell for more than $50 an ounce. But its flavor is so intense, you might need only a single drop to provide its full flavor to a dish. Then again, true aficionados drink a one-ounce shot glass of balsamic vinegar each day "for their health."

Health and Beauty

GIVE DANDRUFF THE BRUSH-OFF

Rinse your hair after each shampoo with 2 cups cider vinegar mixed in 2 cups cold water. Or, massage 3 tablespoons vinegar into your hair and scalp before shampooing. Wait a few minutes, then rinse and wash as usual.

PUT LIFE BACK INTO LIMP OR DAMAGED HAIR

Combine 1 teaspoon cider vinegar with 2 tablespoons olive oil and 3 egg whites. Rub the mixture into your hair and cover it for 30 minutes with a shower cap. Then shampoo and rinse as usual.

MAKE A POULTICE FOR CORNS AND CALLUSES

To treat corns and calluses, soak a piece of white bread in 1/4 cup white vinegar for 30 minutes. Break off a piece big enough to completely cover the corn and secure it with adhesive tape overnight. It will dissolve the hard, callused skin, making the corn easy to remove. Older, thicker calluses may require several treatments.

PAMPER YOUR SKIN

After washing your face, mix 1 tablespoon cider vinegar with 2 cups water and use it as a finishing rinse to cleanse and tighten your skin. You can also make your own facial treatment by mixing 1/4 cup cider vinegar with 1/4 cup water. Gently apply the solution to your face and let it dry.

APPLY AS ANTIPERSPIRANT

To keep your underarms smelling fresh, splash a little white vinegar under each arm in the morning, and let it dry. And you avoid deodorant stains on garments.

SOAK ACHING MUSCLES

Adding 2 cups cider vinegar to your bathwater is a great way to soothe aches and pains or to take the edge off a stressful day.

FRESHEN YOUR BREATH

To sweeten your garlic or onion breath, dissolve 2 tablespoons cider vinegar and 1 teaspoon salt in a glass of warm water and rinse your mouth.

EASE SUNBURN

To cool a bad sunburn, gently dab the skin with a cotton ball saturated with white or cider vinegar, preferably before the burn starts to sting.

CALM BUG-BITE ITCHING

Applying a cotton ball dipped in vinegar also helps stop the itch of mosquito and other insect bites, as well as poison ivy or poison oak rashes.

BANISH BRUISES

You can speed healing and prevent black-and-blue marks by putting a piece of cotton gauze soaked in white or cider vinegar on the injured area for an hour.

A Cancer Dectector?

Some researchers believe vinegar will ultimately be used to diagnose cervical cancer in women—especially those living in impoverished nations. In tests conducted over a two-year period, midwives in Zimbabwe used a vinegar solution to detect more than 75 percent of potential cancers in 10,000 women (the solution turns tissue containing precancerous cells white). Although the test is not as accurate as a Pap smear, doctors believe it will soon be an important screening tool in developing countries, where only 5 percent of women are currently tested for this often fatal disease.

TREAT AN ACTIVE COLD SORE

You can usually dry up a cold sore in short order by dabbing it with a cotton ball saturated in white vinegar three times a day. The vinegar will quickly soothe the pain and swelling.

SAY GOOD-BYE TO AGE OR SUN SPOTS

To remove brown spots on your skin caused by overexposure to the sun or hormonal changes, pour full-strength cider vinegar onto a cotton ball and apply it to the spots for 10 minutes at least twice a day. The spots should fade or disappear within a few weeks.

PROTECT BLOND HAIR FROM CHLORINE

To keep your golden locks from turning green in a chlorinated pool, rub 1/4 cup cider vinegar into your hair and let it set for 15 minutes before diving in.

GET THE JUMP ON ATHLETE'S FOOT

You can often quell the infection and ease the itching of athlete's foot by rinsing your feet three or four times a day for a few days with undiluted cider vinegar. Also soak your socks or stockings in a mixture of 1 part vinegar and 4 parts water for 30 minutes before laundering.

SOFTEN YOUR CUTICLES

Before manicuring your nails, soak your fingers (or toes) in a bowl of undiluted white vinegar for five minutes to soften the cuticles.

MAKE NAIL POLISH LAST LONGER

Your nail polish will stay on longer if you dampen your nails with vinegar on a cotton ball and let it dry before applying polish.

TREAT A JELLYFISH OR BEE STING

A jellyfish can pack a nasty sting. If you have an encounter with one, pouring some undiluted vinegar on the sting will take away the pain in no time and let you scrape out the stinger with a plastic credit card. The same treatment can also be used to treat bee stings. But using vinegar on stings inflicted by the jellyfish's cousin, the Portuguese man-of-war, is now discouraged because vinegar may actually increase the amount of toxin released under the skin. *Warning*: If you have difficulty breathing or the sting area becomes inflamed and swollen, get medical attention at once; you could be having an allergic reaction.

Relief for Colds and Sore Throats

Here are some ways to ease those dreary cold symptoms.

Congestion caused by a cold or sinus infection	Add 1/4 cup white vinegar to the water in your hot-steam vaporizer. (Don't add vinegar to a cool-mist vaporizer without first checking with the manufacturer.)
Raw throat from a bad cough	Get fast relief by dissolving 1 tablespoon cider vinegar and 1 teaspoon salt in a glass of warm water and gargling several times a day.
Sore throat from a cold or flu	Combine 1/4 cup cider vinegar and 1/4 cup honey and take 1 tablespoon every four hours.
Cough and an irritated throat	Mix 1/2 cup vinegar, 1/2 cup water, 4 teaspoons honey, and 1 teaspoon hot sauce. Swallow 1 tablespoon four or five times daily, including before bed.

WARNING: Never give honey to children under one year old.

Garden Tricks

TEST SOIL ACIDITY OR ALKALINITY

To do a quick test for excess alkalinity in your soil, place a handful of earth in a container and then pour in 1/2 cup white vinegar. If the soil fizzes or bubbles, it's definitely alkaline. Similarly, to see if your soil has a high acidity, mix the earth with 1/2 cup water and 1/2 cup baking soda. This time, fizzing would indicate acid in the soil. To find the exact pH level of your soil, have it tested or pick up a simple, do-it-yourself kit or meter.

TREAT RUST AND OTHER PLANT DISEASES

Vinegar can treat a host of plant diseases, including rust, black spot, and powdery mildew. Mix 1 tablespoon cider vinegar in 4 cups water, and pour some into a recycled spray bottle. Spray the affected plants in the morning or early evening (when temperatures are cooler and there's no direct light on the plant) until the condition is cured.

CLEAN A HUMMINGBIRD FEEDER

Hummingbirds won't flock around a dirty, sticky, crusted-over sugar-water feeder. Regularly wash your feeders in equal parts cider vinegar and hot water. Rinse well with cold water, and air-dry in full sunlight before refilling.

A Nontoxic Weed Killer?

Looking for a nontoxic alternative to commercial weed killers? Vinegar is the way to go. In field and greenhouse studies, researchers at the Agricultural Research Service in Beltsville, Maryland, proved vinegar effective at killing five common weeds—including the all-too-common Canada thistle—within their first two weeks aboveground. The vinegar was hand-sprayed in concentrations varying between 5 and 10 percent. But that's old news to seasoned gardeners who've been using undiluted apple cider vinegar for ages to kill everything from poison ivy to crabgrass (and, regrettably, the occasional ornamental plant that grew too close to the target).

SPEED GERMINATION OF FLOWER SEEDS

Get woody seeds, such as moon-flower, passionflower, morning glory, and gourds, off to a healthier start by scarifying them—that is, lightly rubbing them between a couple of sheets of fine sandpaper—and soaking them overnight in a solution of 1/2 cup cider vinegar and 2 cups warm water. Next morning, remove the seeds, rinse them off, and plant them. You can also use the solution (minus the sand-paper treatment) to start many herb and vegetable seeds.

KEEP CUT FLOWERS FRESH

To keep cut flowers around as long as pos-sible, mix 2 tablespoons cider vinegar and 2 tablespoons sugar with the vase water before adding the flowers. Be sure to change the solution every few days to enhance your flowers' longevity.

ELIMINATE INSECTS AROUND THE GARDEN

If bugs are feasting on fruits and vegetables in your garden, try this simple, nontoxic trap. Fill a 2-liter soda bottle with 1 cup cider vinegar and 1 cup sugar. Slice a banana peel into small pieces, put them in the bottle, add 1 cup cold water, and shake. Tie a piece of string around the neck of the bottle and hang it from a low tree branch, or place it on the ground. Replace the traps as needed.

WIPE AWAY MEALYBUGS

Nip a mealybug invasion in the bud by dabbing the insects with cotton swabs dipped in full-strength white vinegar. You may need to use a handful of swabs, but the vinegar will kill the fluffy monsters and any eggs left behind. Be vigilant for missed targets, and break out more vinegar-soaked swabs if you spot bugs.

CLEAN YOUR LAWN MOWER BLADES

Before you park your mower back in the garage, wipe down the blades with a cloth dampened with undiluted white vinegar. It will clean off leftover grass on the blades, as well as any pests that may have been planning to hang out awhile.

ENCOURAGE BLOOMS ON AZALEAS AND GARDENIAS

A little bit of acid goes a long way toward bringing out the blooms on your azalea and gar-denia bushes—especially if you have hard water. Both bushes do best in acidic soils (with pH levels between 4 and 5.5). To keep them healthy and to pro-duce more flowers, water them every week or so with 3 table-spoons white vinegar mixed in 1 gallon (3.8 liters) water. Don't apply the solution while the bush is in bloom, however; it may shorten the life of the flowers or harm the plant.

STOP YELLOW LEAVES ON PLANTS

The sudden appearance of yellow leaves on plants accustomed to acidic soils—such as azaleas, hydrangeas, and gardenias—could signal a drop in the plant's iron intake or a shift in the ground's pH above a comfortable 5.0 level. Either problem can be resolved by watering the soil around the plants once a week for three weeks with 1 cup of a solution made by mixing 2 table-spoons cider vinegar in 1 quart (1 liter) water.

KEEP OUT FOUR-LEGGED CREATURES

Some animals—including cats, deer, rabbits, and raccoons—can't stand the scent of vinegar even after it has dried. To keep these unauthorized visitors out of your garden, soak several rags in white vinegar and place them on stakes around your veggies. Resoak the rags about every 7 to 10 days.

EXTERMINATE DANDELIONS AND UNWANTED GRASS

Got dandelions sprouting in the cracks of your driveway or along the fringes of your patio? Make them disappear by spraying them with full-strength white or cider vinegar. Early in the season, give each plant a single spritz of vinegar in its midsection or in the middle of the flower before the plants go to seed. Aim another shot near the stem at ground level so the vinegar can soak down to the roots. Keep an eye on the weather, though; if it rains, you'll need to give the weeds another spraying.

Great Outdoors

CLEAN OUTDOOR FURNITURE AND DECKS

Before resorting to bleach to remove mildew on your deck or your patio furniture, try these milder vinegar-based solutions.

■ Keep full-strength white vinegar in a spray bottle and use it wherever you see mildew. The stain will wipe right off most surfaces, and the vinegar will keep it from coming back for a while.

■ Remove mildew from wood decks and wood patio furniture by sponging them off with a solution of 1 cup ammonia, 1/2 cup white vinegar, and 1/4 cup baking soda in 1 gallon (3.8 liters) water. Use an old toothbrush to work the solution into tight spaces.

■ To deodorize and inhibit mildew growth on outdoor plastic mesh furniture and patio umbrellas, mix 2 cups white vinegar and 2 tablespoons dishwashing liquid in a bucket of hot water. Use a soft brush to work it into the grooves of the plastic and for scrubbing seat pads and umbrella fabric. Rinse with cold water; then dry in the sun.

GIVE ANTS THE BOOT

Pour equal parts white vinegar and water into a spray bottle and spray it on anthills and around areas where you see ants. Ants hate vinegar, and it won't take long for them to move on. Also spray picnic and children's play areas to keep ants away. If you have lots of anthills, pour full-strength vinegar over them.

ANOTHER WAY TO REPEL BUGS

To keep gnats and mosquitoes at bay, moisten a cotton ball with white vinegar and rub it over your exposed skin.

USE AS INSECT REPELLENT

Going camping or fishing? Here's an old army trick to keep away ticks and mosquitoes: About three days before you leave, start taking 1 tablespoon cider vinegar three times a day. Continue throughout your outing, and you just might return home without a bite.

A Storied Liquid

Taken literally, vinegar is nothing more than wine that's gone bad; the word derives from the French *vin* (wine) and *aigre* (sour). But, in fact, anything used to make alcohol can be turned into vinegar, including apples, honey, malted barley, molasses, sugarcane, rice, and even coconuts. Vinegar's acidic, solvent properties were well known even in ancient times. According to one popular legend, Cleopatra is said to have wagered she could dispose of a fortune in the course of a single meal. She won the bet by dissolving a handful of pearls in a cup of vinegar...and then consuming it.

Vinegar and Eau de Skunk

If Fido has an encounter with a skunk, here are some ways to get rid of the smell:

■ Bathe your pet in a mixture of 1/2 cup white vinegar, 1/4 cup baking soda, and 1 teaspoon liquid soap in 4 cups of 3 percent hydrogen peroxide. Work the solution deep into his coat, give it a few minutes to soak in, then rinse him thoroughly.

■ Bathe your pet in equal parts water and vinegar (preferably outdoors in a large washtub). Then repeat using 1 part vinegar to 2 parts water, followed by a good rinsing.

■ If you have an unscheduled meeting with skunk yourself, soak your clothes in undiluted vinegar overnight to get the smell out.

MAINTAIN FRESH WATER WHEN HIKING

Keep your water fresh and clean tasting when camping by adding a few drops of cider vinegar to your water bottle. Also clean your water container at the end of each trip with a half-vinegar, half-water rinse to kill bacteria and remove residue.

MAKE A TRAP FOR FLYING INSECTS

Keep gnats, flies, mosquitoes, or other six-legged pests away from your backyard cookout. Place a bowl filled with cider vinegar near some food, but away from you and guests. By the evening's end, most of your uninvited guests will be floating inside the bowl.

CLEAN OFF BIRD DROPPINGS

Make those messy droppings disappear in no time by spraying them with full-strength cider vinegar. Or pour the vinegar onto a rag and wipe them off.

REMOVE RUST STAINS ON CONCRETE

Did a left-out tool or a piece of metal furniture leave an ugly rust stain on your concrete patio or driveway? To get rid of the stain, just pour undiluted white vinegar on it and let it soak in for several minutes before wiping it up. Repeat if the stain is stubborn.

DEODORIZE YOUR PICNIC COOLER

If your picnic cooler smells a little musty when you first pull it out for the summer, you don't want your food to pick up the odor. First, wash out the cooler well using dishwashing liquid and warm water and let it dry. Then fill a small bowl with vinegar and put it in the cooler. Close the lid and leave it overnight. The next day, the odor will be gone and the cooler will smell fresh as a daisy.

KEEP YOUR WICKS BURNING LONGER

If you use a propane lantern when you go camping, you can make your wicks last longer and burn brighter with this trick. After you buy new wicks, soak them in undiluted white vinegar for several hours, then let them dry completely. When you use them, you'll find that the wickers not only don't burn out as fast but also give off more light.

Pet Care

KEEP THE KITTIES AWAY

If you want to keep Snowball and Fluffy out of the kids' playroom, or discourage them from using your favorite easy chair as a scratching post, sprinkle some full-strength distilled white vinegar around the area or onto the object itself. Cats don't like the smell of vinegar and will avoid it.

ADD TO A DOG'S DRINKING WATER

Adding a teaspoon of cider vinegar to your dog's drinking water provides needed nutrients to its diet, gives it a shinier, healthier-looking coat, and acts as a natural deterrent to fleas and ticks.

PROTECT AGAINST FLEAS AND TICKS

To give your dog effective flea and tick protection, fill a spray bottle with equal parts water and vinegar and apply it directly to the dog's coat and rub it in well.

CLEAN YOUR PET'S EARS

If Rover has been scratching around his ears a lot more than usual, a bit of vinegar could bring him some big relief. Swabbing your pet's ears with a cotton ball or soft cloth dabbed in a solution of 2 parts vinegar and 1 part water keeps them clean and helps deter ear mites and bacteria. It also soothes minor itches from mosquito bites and such.

Warning: Do not apply vinegar to open cuts. If you see a cut in your pet's ears, seek veterinary treatment.

UNMARK YOUR PET'S SPOTS

When housebreaking a puppy or kitten, it'll often wet previously soiled spots. After cleaning up, it's essential to remove the scent. And nothing does that better than vinegar.

▪ On a **floor**, blot up as much of the stain as possible. Then mop with equal parts white vinegar and warm water. (On a wood or vinyl floor, test a few drops of vinegar in an inconspicuous area to make sure it won't harm the finish.) Dry with a cloth or paper towel.

▪ For **carpets, rugs, and upholstery**, thoroughly blot the area with a towel or some rags. Then pour a bit of undiluted white vinegar over the spot. Blot it up with a towel, then reapply the vinegar and let air-dry.

The World's Only Vinegar Museum

The International Vinegar Museum, located in Roslyn, South Dakota, is housed in a building that was the former town hall. It is operated by Dr. Lawrence J. Diggs, an international vinegar consultant also known as the Vinegar Man. (You can visit him online at www.vinegarman.com.) The museum showcases vinegars from around the world, has displays on the various methods used to make vinegar, and lets visitors sample different types of vinegars. It's among the world's least expensive museums: Admission for adults is $2; for those under 18, $1; and "instant scholarships for those too poor to pay."

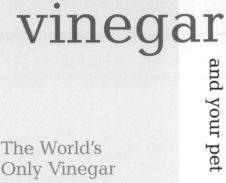

A Cleaner Car

Here are four easy ways to use vinegar to keep your car clean:

Remove bumper stickers

To take off a tattered old bumper sticker, saturate the top and sides with undiluted white vinegar and wait 10 to 15 minutes for the vinegar to soak through. Then use an expired credit card to scrape it off. Use more full-strength vinegar to get rid of any residue. Remove decals on the back windshield the same way.

Clean windshield wiper blades

If your windshield actually gets blurrier after you turn on the wipers, your wiper blades are probably dirty. To clean them, dampen a cloth or rag with full-strength white vinegar and run it down the length of each blade once or twice.

Care for your car's carpets

After vacuuming up the sand and other debris from your car's carpeting, get rid of stains or ground-in dirt by sponging a solution of equal parts water and white vinegar into the carpet. Wait a couple of minutes; then blot with a paper towel. This will also eliminate salt residues left on car carpets in winter.

Keep car windows frost-free

To keep frost from forming on your car's windows when you park outside in winter, spray the outsides of the windows with a solution of 3 parts white vinegar to 1 part water. Each coating may last up to several weeks—although it won't ward off a heavy snowfall.

Do-It-Yourself Projects

WASH CONCRETE OFF YOUR SKIN

Even though you wear rubber gloves when working with concrete, some of the stuff inevitably splashes on your skin. Prolonged contact with wet concrete can cause your skin to crack and may even lead to eczema. Use undiluted white vinegar to wash dried concrete or mortar off your skin, then wash with warm, soapy water.

DEGREASE GRATES, FANS, AND AIR-CONDITIONER GRILLES

Air-conditioner grilles, heating grates, and fan blades eventually develop a layer of dust and grease. To clean them, wipe them with full-strength white vinegar. Use an old toothbrush to work the vinegar into tight spaces.

DISINFECT AIR-CONDITIONER AND HUMIDIFIER FILTERS

An air-conditioner or humidifier filter can become inundated with dust, soot, pet dander, and even harmful bacteria. Every 10 days or so, clean your filter in equal parts white vinegar and warm water. Soak the filter in the solution for an hour, then squeeze it dry before using. Soak filters that are particularly dirty overnight.

GET RID OF RUST

To clean rusted old tools, soak them in full-strength white vinegar for several days. Vinegar is equally effective at removing the rust from corroded nuts and bolts. And you can pour it on rusted hinges and screws to loosen them for removal.

PEEL OFF WALLPAPER

Get old wallpaper to peel off easily. Spray equal parts white vinegar and water on it until it is saturated and wait a few minutes. Then zip the stuff off with a wallpaper scraper. If it is stubborn, try carefully scoring the wallpaper with the scraper before you spritz.

SLOW HARDENING OF PLASTER

Want to keep plaster pliable a bit longer to get it all smoothed out? Just add a couple of tablespoons of white vinegar to your plaster mix. It will slow down the hardening process to give you the extra time you need.

Vinegar, the Painter's Friend

■ To remove **dried-on paint** from a synthetic-bristle paintbrush, soak it in full-strength white vinegar until the paint dissolves and the bristles are soft and pliable, then wash in hot, soapy water.

■ Is your **paintbrush hardened** beyond hope? Before you toss it, try boiling it in 1 to 2 cups vinegar for 10 minutes, then thoroughly wash in soapy water.

■ Paint on **cement floors** and galvanized metal has a tendency to peel. To keep the paint stuck longer, coat the surface with white vinegar and let it dry before painting.

■ To dispel the **strong odor** in a freshly painted room, set out a couple of shallow dishes filled with undiluted white vinegar.

Clothespins, cardboard tubing, a length of string—seemingly worthless objects like these can be extraordinarily useful all around your **home** and **yard**.

Extraordinary Uses

for 60 Objects

Our team of investigators set out to find the most clever, most extraordinary uses for some of the most common household items. And here is what they found—hundreds of tips guaranteed to simplify your day and save you a fortune!

Adhesive Tape

Remove a splinter

Is a splinter too tiny or too deep to remove with tweezers? Avoid the agony of digging it out with a needle. Instead, cover the splinter with adhesive tape. After about three days, pull the tape off and the splinter should come out with it.

Stop ants in their tracks

Is an army of ants marching toward the cookie jar on your countertop or some sweet prize in your pantry? Create a "moat" around the object by surrounding it with adhesive tape placed sticky side up.

Make a lint-lifter

To lift lint and pet hair off clothing and upholstery, you don't need a special lint remover. Just wrap your hand with adhesive tape, sticky side out.

Hang glue and caulk tubes

Got an ungainly heap of glue and caulk tubes on your workbench? Cut a strip of adhesive or duct tape several inches long and fold it over the bottom of each tube, leaving a flap at the end. Punch a hole in the flap with a paper hole punch and hang the tube on a nail or hook. You'll free up counter space, and you'll be able to find the right tube fast.

Reduce your hat size

Got a hat that's a bit too big for your head? Wrap adhesive tape around the sweatband—it might take two or three layers depending on the size discrepancy. As a bonus, the adhesive tape will absorb brow sweat on hot days.

Clean a comb

To remove the gunk that builds up between the teeth of your comb, press a strip of adhesive tape along the comb's length and lift it off. Then dip the comb in a solution of alcohol and water, or ammonia and water, to sanitize it. Let dry.

Cover casters

Prevent your furniture from leaving marks on your wood or vinyl floor by wrapping the furniture's caster wheels with adhesive tape.

Safely remove broken window glass

Removing a window sash to fix a broken pane of glass can be dangerous; there's always the possibility that a sharp shard will fall out and cut you. To prevent this, crisscross both sides of the broken pane with adhesive tape before removing the sash. And don't forget to wear heavy leather gloves when you pull the glass shards out of the frame.

How Band-Aids Were Invented

In the 1920s, **Josephine Dickson,** an **accident-prone** New Jersey housewife, inspired the invention of the Band-Aid bandage. Her husband, **Earle,** who tended her various burns and wounds, hit upon the idea of sticking small squares of sterile gauze onto adhesive tape, covering it with a layer of **crinoline,** then rolling it back up so that Josephine could cut off and apply the ready-made bandages herself.

Earle's employer, **Johnson & Johnson,** soon began producing the first Band-Aids. By the time Earle died in 1961—by then a member of the company's board of directors—Band-Aid sales exceeded $30 million a year.

GET A GRIP ON TOOLS

Adhesive tape has just the right texture for wrapping tool handles. It gives you a positive, comfortable grip, and it's highly absorbent so that tools won't become slippery if your hand sweats. When you wrap tool handles, overlap each wrap by about half a tape width and use as many layers as needed to get the best grip. Here are some useful applications:

■ **Screwdriver handles** are sometimes too narrow and slippery to grip well when you drive or remove stubborn screws. Wrap layers of adhesive tape around the handle until the tool feels comfortable in your hand—this is especially useful if you have arthritis in your fingers.

■ Take a tip from carpenters who wrap **wooden hammer handles** that can get slippery with sweat. Wrap the whole gripping area of the tool. A few wraps just under the head will also protect the handle from damage caused by misdirected blows.

■ Plumbers also keep adhesive tape in their tool kits: When they want to cut a pipe in a spot that's too tight for their hacksaw frame, they make a mini-hacksaw by removing the **hacksaw blade** and wrapping one end of the blade to form a handle.

Alka-Seltzer

Clean your coffeemaker

Fill your percolator or the water chamber of your drip coffeemaker with water and plop in four Alka-Seltzer tablets. When the Alka-Seltzer has dissolved, put the coffeemaker through a brew cycle to clean the tubes. Rinse the chamber out two or three times, then run a brew cycle with plain water before making coffee.

Clean a vase

That stuck-on residue at the bottom of narrow-neck vases may seem impossible to scrub out, but you can easily bubble it away. Fill the vase halfway with water and drop in two Alka-Seltzer tablets. Wait until the fizzing stops, then rinse the vase clean. The same trick works for cleaning glass thermoses.

Clean glass cookware

Say so long to scouring those stubborn stains off your ovenproof glass cook-ware. Just fill the container with water, add up to six Alka-Seltzer tablets, and let it soak for an hour. The stains should easily scrub away.

Clean your toilet

The citric acid in Alka-Seltzer com-bined with its fizzing action is an effective toilet bowl cleaner. Simply drop a couple of tablets into the bowl and find something else to do for 20 minutes or so. When you return, a few swipes with a toilet brush will leave your bowl gleaming.

Clean jewelry

Drop your dull-looking jewelry in a glass of fizzing Alka-Seltzer for a couple of minutes. It will sparkle and shine when you pull it out.

Unclog a drain

Drain clogged again? Get almost instant relief: Drop a couple of Alka-Seltzer tablets down the opening, then pour in a cup of vinegar. Wait a few minutes and then run the hot water at full force to clear the clog. This is also a good way to eliminate kitchen drain odors.

Soothe insect bites

Mosquito or other insect bite driving you nuts? To ease the itch, drop two Alka-Seltzer tablets in half a glass of water. Dip a cotton ball in the glass and apply it to the bite. *Caution:* Don't do this if you are allergic to aspirin, which is a key ingredient in Alka-Seltzer.

Attract fish

All avid anglers know fish are attracted to bubbles. If you are using a hollow plastic tube jig on your line, just break off a piece of Alka-Seltzer and slip it into the tube. The jig will pro-duce an enticing stream of bubbles as it sinks.

Baby Powder

Give sand the brush-off

How many times have you had a family member return from a day at the beach only to discover that a good portion of the beach has been brought back into your living room? Minimize the mess by sprinkling some baby powder over sweaty, sand-covered kids (and adults) before they enter the house. In addition to soaking up excess moisture, the powder makes sand incredibly easy to brush off.

Cool sheets in summer

Are those sticky, hot bed sheets giving you the summertime blues when you should be deep in dreamland? Cool things down by sprinkling a bit of baby powder between your sheets before hopping into the sack on warm summer nights.

Dry-shampoo your pet

Is the pooch's coat in need of a pick-me-up? Vigorously rub a handful or two of baby powder into your pet's fur. Let it settle in for a couple of minutes, and follow up with a thorough brushing. Your dog will both look and smell great! You can even occasionally "dry shampoo" your own, or someone else's, hair by following the same technique.

Absorb grease stains on clothing

Frying foods can be dangerous business—especially for your clothes. If you get a grease splatter on your clothing, try dabbing the stain with some baby powder on a powder puff. Make sure you rub it in well, and then brush off any excess powder. Repeat until the mark is gone.

Clean your playing cards

Here's a simple way to keep your playing cards from sticking together and getting grimy: Loosely place the cards in a plastic bag along with a bit of baby powder. Seal the bag and give it a few good shakes. When you remove your cards, they should feel fresh and smooth to the touch.

Slip on your rubber gloves

Don't try jamming and squeezing your fingers into your rubber gloves when the powder layer inside the gloves wears out. Instead, give your fingers a light dusting with baby powder. Your rubber gloves should slide on good as new.

Remove mold from books

If some of your books have been stored in a less than ideal environment and have gotten a bit moldy or mildewed, try this: First, let them thoroughly air-dry. Then, sprinkle some baby powder between the pages and stand the books upright for several hours. Afterward, gently brush out the remaining powder from each book. They may not be as good as new, but they should be in a lot better shape than they were.

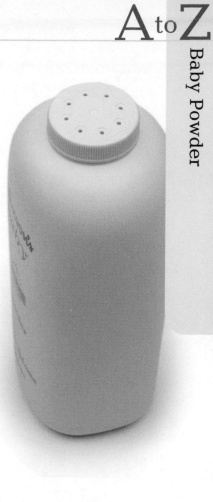

Dust off your flower bulbs

Many savvy gardeners use medicated baby powder to dust flower bulbs before planting them. Simply place 5 or 6 bulbs and about 3 tablespoons of baby powder in a sealed plastic bag and give it a few gentle shakes. The medicated-powder coating helps both reduce the chance of rot and keep away moles, voles, grubs, and other bulb-munching pests.

Baby Wipes

Use for quick, on-the-move cleanups

Baby wipes can be used for more than just cleaning babies' bottoms. They're great for wiping your hands after pumping gas, mopping up small spills in the car, and cooling your sweaty brow after a run. In fact, they make ideal travel companions. So, next time you set off on the road, pack a small stack of wipes in a tightly closed self-sealing sandwich bag and put it in the glove compartment of your car or in your purse or knapsack.

Shine your shoes

Most moms know that a baby wipe does a pretty good job of brightening Junior's white leather shoes. But did you ever think of using one to put the shine back in your leather pumps—especially with that 10 a.m. meeting fast approaching?

Recycle as dust cloths

Believe it or not, some brands of baby wipes—Huggies, for instance—can be laundered and reused as dust cloths and cleaning rags for when you straighten up. It probably goes without saying, but only "mildly" soiled wipes should be considered candidates for laundering.

Buff up your bathroom

Do you have company coming over and not much time to tidy up the house? Don't break out in a sweat. Try this double-handed trick: Take a baby wipe in one hand and start polishing your bathroom surfaces. Keep a dry wash-cloth in your other hand to shine things up as you make your rounds.

Clean your PC keyboard

Periodically shaking out your PC's keyboard is a good way to get rid of the dust and debris that gathers underneath and in between the keys. But that's just half the job. Use a baby wipe to remove the dirt, dried spills, and unspecified gunk that builds up on the keys themselves. Make sure to turn off the computer or unplug the keyboard before you wipe the keys.

Soothe your skin

Did you get a bit too much sun at the beach? You can temporarily cool a sunburn by gently patting the area with a baby wipe. Baby wipes can also be used to treat cuts and scrapes. Although most wipes don't have any antiseptic properties, there's nothing wrong with using one for an initial cleansing before applying the proper topical treatment.

Remove makeup

It's one of the fashion industry's worst-kept secrets: Many models consider a baby wipe to be their best friend when it comes time to remove that stubborn makeup from their faces, particularly black eyeliner. Try it and you can see for yourself.

Balloons

Protect a bandaged finger

Bandaging an injury on your finger is easy; keeping the bandage dry as you go about your day can be a different story. But here's the secret to skipping those wet-bandage changes: Just slip a small balloon over your finger when doing dishes, bathing, or even simply washing your hands.

Keep track of your child

Those inexpensive floating helium-filled balloons sold in most shopping malls can be more than just a treat for a youngster; they could be invaluable in locating a child who wanders off into a crowd. Even if you keep close tabs on your kids, you can buy a little peace of mind by simply tying (though not too tightly) a balloon to your child's wrist on those weekend shopping trips.

Transport cut flowers

Don't bother with awkward, water-filled plastic bags and such when traveling with freshly cut flowers. Simply fill up a balloon with about 1/2 cup of water and slip it over the cut ends of your flowers. Wrap a rubber band several times around the mouth of the balloon to keep it from slipping off.

Use as a hat mold

To keep the shape in your freshly washed knit cap or cloth hat, fit it over an inflated balloon while it dries. Use a piece of masking tape to keep the balloon from tilting over or falling onto the ground.

Mark your campsite

Bring along several helium-filled balloons on your next camping trip to attach to your tent or a post. They'll make it easier for the members of your party to locate your campsite when hiking or foraging in the woods.

Protect your rifle

A dirty rifle can jam up and just be downright dangerous to use. But you can keep dust and debris from accumulating in your rifle barrel by putting a sturdy latex balloon over the barrel's front end.

Make an ice pack

Looking for a flexible ice pack you can use for everything from icing a sore back to keeping food cold in your cooler? Fill a large, durable balloon with as much water as you need and put it in your freezer. You can even mold it to a certain extent into specific shapes—for example, put it under something flat like a box of pizza if you want a flat ice pack for your back. Use smaller latex balloons for making smaller ice packs for lunch boxes, etc.

Freeze for cooler punch

To keep your party punch bowl cold and well filled, pour juice in several balloons (use a funnel) and place them in your freezer. When it's party time, peel the latex off the ice, and periodically drop a couple into the punch bowl.

Repel unwanted garden visitors

Put those old deflated shiny metallic balloons—the ones lying around your house from past birthday parties—to work in your garden. Cut them into vertical strips and hang them from poles around your vegetables and on fruit trees to scare off invading birds, rabbits, and squirrels.

MAKE A PARTY INVITATION

How's this for an imaginative invitation? Inflate a balloon (for sanitary purposes, use an electric pump, if possible). Pinch off the end, but don't tie a knot in it. Write your **invitation details** on the balloon with a **bright permanent marker;** make sure the ink is dry before you deflate it. Place the balloon in an envelope, and mail one out to each guest. When your guests receive it, they'll have to blow it up to see what it says.

Bleach

Sterilize secondhand items

Remember Mom saying, "Put that down. You don't know where it's been"? She had a point—especially when it comes to toys or kitchen utensils picked up at thrift shops and yard sales. Just to be safe, soak your used, waterproof items for 5 to 10 minutes in a solution containing 3/4 cup of bleach, a few drops of antibacterial dish-washing liquid, and 1 gallon (3.8 liters) warm water. Rinse well, then air-dry, preferably in sunlight.

Brighten up glass dishware

Put the sparkle back in your glasses and dishes by adding a teaspoon of bleach to your soapy dishwater as you're washing your glassware. Be sure to rinse well, and dry with a soft towel.

Shine white porcelain

Want to get your white porcelain sink, candleholder, or pottery looking as good as new? In a well-ventilated area on a work surface protected by heavy plastic, place several paper towels over the item (or across the bottom of the

sink) and carefully saturate them with undiluted bleach. Let soak for 15 minutes to a half hour, then rinse and wipe dry with a clean towel. *Note:* Do not try this with antiques; you can diminish their value or cause damage. And never use bleach on colored porcelain, because the color will fade.

Clean butcher block cutting boards and countertops

Don't even think about using furniture polish or any other household cleaner to clean a butcher block cutting board or countertop. Rather, scrub the surface with a brush dipped in a solution of 1 teaspoon of bleach diluted in 2 quarts (2 liters) of water. Scrub in small circles, and be careful not to saturate the wood. Wipe with a slightly damp paper towel, then immediately buff dry with a clean cloth.

Disinfect trash cans

Even the best housekeepers must confront a gunked-up kitchen garbage pail every now and then. On such occasions, take the pail outside, and flush out any loose debris with a garden

hose. Then add 1/2 to 1 cup of bleach and several drops of dishwashing liquid to 1 gallon (3.8 liters) of warm water. Use a toilet brush or long-handled scrub brush to splash and scour the solution on the bottom and sides of the container. Empty, then rinse with the hose, empty it again, and let air-dry.

Increase cut flowers' longevity

Freshly cut flowers will stay fresh longer if you add 1/4 teaspoon of bleach per quart (1 liter) of vase water. Another popular recipe calls for 3 drops of bleach and 1 teaspoon of sugar in 1 quart (1 liter) of water. This will also keep the water from getting cloudy and inhibit the growth of bacteria.

➕ **TAKE CARE** Never mix bleach with ammonia, lye, rust removers, oven or toilet-bowl cleaners, or vinegar. Any combination can produce toxic chlorine gas fumes, which can be deadly. Some people are even sensitive to the fumes of undiluted bleach itself. Always make sure you have adequate ventilation in your work area before you start pouring.

CLEAN OFF MOLD AND MILDEW

Bleach and ammonia are both useful for removing mold and mildew inside and outside your home. However, the two should never be used together. Bleach is especially suited for the following chores:

- Wash mildew out of **washable fabrics.** Wet the mildewed area and rub in some powdered detergent. Then wash the garment in the hottest water setting permitted by the clothing manufacturer using 1/2 cup of chlorine bleach. If the garment can't be washed in hot water and bleach, soak it in a solution of 1/4 cup of oxygen bleach (labeled "all fabric" or "perborate") in 1 gallon (3.8 liters) of warm water for 30 minutes before washing.

- Remove mold and mildew from the **grout between your bathroom tiles.** Mix equal parts of chlorine bleach and water in a spray bottle, and spray it over grout. Let it sit for 15 minutes, then scrub with a stiff brush and rinse off. You can also do this just to make your grout look whiter.

- Get mold and mildew off your **shower curtains.** Wash them—along with a couple of bath towels (to prevent the plastic curtains from crinkling)—in warm water with 1/2 cup of chlorine bleach and 1/4 cup of laundry detergent. Let the washer run for a couple of minutes before loading. Put the shower curtain and towels in the dryer on the lowest temperature setting for 10 minutes, then immediately hang-dry.

- Rid your rubber **shower mat** of mildew. Soak in a solution of 1/8 cup of chlorine bleach in 1 gallon (3.8 liters) of water for 3 to 4 hours. Rinse well.

- Get mildew and other stains off **unpainted cement, patio stones, or stucco.** Mix a solution of 1 cup of chlorine bleach in 2 gallons (7.6 liters) of water. Scrub vigorously with a stiff or wire brush and rinse. If any stains remain, scrub again using 1/2 cup of washing soda (this is sodium carbonate, not baking soda) dissolved in 2 gallons of warm water.

- Remove mildew from **painted surfaces and siding.** Make a solution of 1/4 cup of chlorine bleach in 2 cups of water and apply with a brush to mildewed areas. Let the solution set for 15 minutes, then rinse. Repeat as necessary.

Make a household disinfectant spray

Looking for a good, all-purpose disinfectant to use around the house? Mix 1 tablespoon of bleach in 1 gallon (3.8 liters) of hot water. Then fill a clean, empty spray bottle and use it on a paper towel to clean countertops, tablecloths, lawn furniture—basically, wherever it's needed. Just be sure not to use it in the presence of ammonia or other household cleaners.

Kill weeds in walkways

Do weeds seem to thrive in the cracks and crevices of your walkways? Try pouring a bit of undiluted bleach over them. After a day or two, you can simply pull them out, and the bleach will keep them from coming back. Just be careful not to get bleach on the grass or plantings bordering the walkway.

Sanitize garden tools

You cut that diseased stalk off your rosebush with your branch clipper. Unless you want to spread the disease the next time you use the tool, sterilize it by washing it with 1/2 cup of bleach in 1 quart (1 liter) of water. Let the tool air-dry in the sun, then rub on a few drops of oil to prevent rust.

Clean plastic lawn furniture

Is your plastic-mesh lawn furniture looking dingy? Before you place it curbside, try washing it with some mild detergent mixed with 1/2 cup of bleach in 1 gallon (3.8 liters) of water. Rinse it clean, then air-dry.

Get rid of moss and algae

To remove slippery and unsightly moss and algae on your brick, concrete, or stone walkways, scrub them with a solution of 3/4 cup of bleach in 1 gallon (3.8 liters) of water. Be careful not to get bleach on your grass or ornamental plants.

➕ **TAKE CARE** Some folks skip the bleach when cleaning their toilets, fearing that lingering ammonia from urine—especially in households with young children—could result in toxic fumes. Unless you are sure there is no such problem, you may want to stick with ammonia for this job.

Borax

Clear a clogged drain

Before you reach for a caustic drain cleaner to unclog that kitchen or bathroom drain, try this much gentler approach: Use a funnel to insert 1/2 cup of borax into the drain, then slowly pour in 2 cups of boiling water. Let the mixture set for 15 minutes, then flush with hot water. Repeat for stubborn clogs.

Rub out heavy sink stains

Get rid of those stubborn stains—even rust—in your stainless steel or porcelain sink. Make a paste of 1 cup of borax and 1/4 cup of lemon juice. Put some of the paste on a cloth or sponge and rub it into the stain, then rinse with running warm water. The stain should wash away with the paste.

Remove mildew from fabric

To remove mildew from upholstery and other fabrics, soak a sponge in a solution of 1/2 cup of borax dissolved in 2 cups of hot water, and rub it into the affected areas. Let it soak in for several hours until the stain disappears, then rinse well. To remove mildew from clothing, soak it in a solution of 2 cups of borax in 2 quarts (2 liters) of water.

Clean your toilet

Want a way to disinfect your toilet bowl and leave it glistening without having to worry about dangerous or unpleasant fumes? Use a stiff brush to scrub it using a solution of 1/2 cup of borax in 1 gallon (3.8 liters) of water.

Sanitize your garbage disposal

A garbage disposal is a great convenience but can also be a great breeding ground for mold and bacteria. To maintain a more sanitary disposal, every couple of weeks pour 3 tablespoons of borax down the drain and let it sit for 1 hour. Then turn on the disposal and flush it with hot water from the tap.

Get out rug stains

Remove stubborn stains from rugs and carpets. Thoroughly dampen the area, then rub in some borax. Let the area dry, then vacuum or blot it with a solution of equal parts vinegar and soapy water and let dry. Repeat if necessary. Don't forget to first test the procedure on an inconspicuous corner of the rug or on a carpet scrap before applying it to the stain.

Make your own dried flowers

Give your homemade dried flowers the look of a professional job. Mix 1 cup of borax with 2 cups of cornmeal. Place a 3/4-inch (2-cm) coating of the mixture in the bottom of an airtight container, like a large flat plastic food storage container. Cut the stems off the flowers you want to dry, then lay them on top of the powder and lightly sprinkle more of the mixture on top of the flowers (be careful not to bend or crush the petals or other flower parts). Cover the container, and leave it alone for 7 to 10 days. Then remove the flowers and brush off any excess powder with a soft brush.

✚ **TAKE CARE** Borax, like its close relative, boric acid, has relatively low toxicity levels, and is considered safe for general household use, but the powder can be harmful if ingested in sufficient quantities by young children or pets. Store it safely out of their reach.

Borax is toxic to plants, however. In the yard, be very careful when applying borax onto or near soil. It doesn't take much to leach into the ground to kill off nearby plants and prevent future growth.

Clean windows and mirrors

Want to get windows and mirrors spotless and streakless? Wash them with a clean sponge dipped in 2 tablespoons of borax dissolved in 3 cups of water.

Keep away weeds and ants

Get the jump on those weeds that grow in the cracks of the concrete outside your house by sprinkling borax into all the crevices where you've seen weeds grow in the past. It will kill them off before they have a chance to take root. When applied around the foundation of your home, it will also keep ants and other six-legged intruders from entering your house.

But be very careful when applying borax—it is toxic to plants (see Take Care warning, page 101).

Control creeping Charlie

Is your garden being overrun by that invasive perennial weed known as creeping Charlie (*Glechoma hederacea,* also known as ground ivy, creeping Jenny and gill-over-the-ground)? You may be able to conquer Charlie with borax. First, dissolve 8 to 10 ounces (230 to 280 grams) of borax in 4 ounces (120 ml) of warm water. Then pour the solution into 2 1/2 gallons (9.5 liters) of warm water—this is enough to cover 1,000 square feet (93 square meters).

Apply this treatment only one time in each of two years. If you still have creeping Charlie problems, consider switching to a standard herbicide. (See Take Care warning about using borax in the garden, page 101.)

Eliminate urine odor on mattresses

Toilet training can be a rough experience for all the parties involved. If your child has an "accident" in bed, here's how to get rid of any lingering smell: Dampen the area, then rub in some borax. Let it dry, then vacuum up the powder.

MAKE SOME OOEY, GOOEY PLAY STUFF

Help your children brew up some **slime**—that gooey, stretchy stuff kids love to play with.

THE RECIPE

■ First, mix 1 cup **water,** 1 cup **white glue,** and 10 drops **food coloring** in a medium bowl.

■ Then, in a second, larger bowl, stir 4 teaspoons **borax** into 1 1/3 cups **water** until the powder is fully dissolved.

■ Slowly pour the contents of the first bowl into the second. Use a wooden mixing spoon to roll (don't mix) the glue-based solution around in the borax solution four or five times.

■ Lift out the globs of glue mixture, then knead it for 2 to 3 minutes. Store your homemade slime in an airtight container or a self-sealing plastic storage bag.

Bottles

Using bottles around the house

Make a foot warmer

Walking around on harsh winter days can leave you with cold and tired tootsies. But you don't need to shell out your hard-earned money on a heating pad or a hot-water bottle to ease your discomfort. Just fill up a 1- or 2-liter soda bottle with hot water, then sit down and roll it back and forth under your feet.

Recycle as a chew toy

If Lassie has been chewing on your slippers instead of fetching them, maybe she's in need of some chew toys. A no-cost way to amuse your dog is to let her chew on an empty plastic 1-liter soda bottle. Maybe it's the crunchy sound they make, but dogs love them! Just be sure to remove the label and bottle cap (as well as the loose plastic ring under it). And replace it before it gets too chewed up—broken pieces of plastic are choke hazards.

Make a bag or string dispenser

An empty 2-liter soda bottle makes the perfect container for storing and dispensing plastic grocery bags. Just cut off the bottom and top ends of the bottle, and mount it with screws upside down inside a kitchen cabinet or closet. Put washers under the screw heads to keep them from pulling

through the plastic. Fill it with your recycled bags (squeeze the air out of them first) and pull them out as needed. You can make a twine dispenser the same way, using a 1-liter bottle and letting the cord come out the bottom.

Place in toilet tank

Unless your house was built relatively recently, chances are you have an older toilet that uses a lot of water each flush. To save a bit of money on your water bills, fill an empty 1-liter soda bottle with water (remove any labels first) and put it in the toilet tank to cut the amount of water in each flush.

Cut out a toy carryall

If you're fed up with Lego or erector-set pieces underfoot, make a simple carryall to store them in by cutting a large hole in the side of a clean gallon jug with a handle. Cut the hole opposite the handle so you or your youngster can easily carry the container back to the playroom after putting the pieces away. For an easy way to store craft materials, crayons, or small toys, just cut the containers in half and use the bottom part to stash your stuff.

Store your sugar

The next time you bring home a 5-pound (2.2-kg) bag of sugar from the supermarket, try pouring it into a clean, dry 1-gallon (3.8-liter) jug with a handle. The sugar is less likely to

harden, and the handle makes it much easier to pour it out.

Fashion a funnel

To make a handy, durable funnel, cut a cleaned milk jug, bleach, or liquid detergent container with a handle in half across its midsection. Use the top portion (with the spout and handle) as a funnel for easy pouring of paints, rice, coins, and so on.

Using bottles away from home

Make a scoop or boat bailer

Cut a clean plastic half-gallon (2-liter) jug with a handle diagonally from the bottom so that you have the top three-quarters of the jug intact. You now have a handy scoop that can be used for everything from removing leaves and other debris from your gutters, to cleaning out the litter box and poop-scooping up after your dog. Use it to scoop dog food from the bag, spread sand or ice-melt on walkways in winter, or bail water out of your boat (you might want to keep the cap on for this last application).

Keep the cooler cold

Don't let your cooler lose its cool while you're on the road. Fill a few clean plastic jugs with water or juice and keep them in the freezer for use when transporting food in your cooler. This is not only good for keeping food cold; you can actually drink the water or juice as it melts. It's also not a bad idea to keep a few frozen jugs in your freezer if you have extra space; a full freezer actually uses less energy and can save money on your electric bill. When filling a jug, leave a little room at the top for the water to expand as it freezes.

Use for emergency road kit in winter

Don't get stuck in your car the next time a surprise winter storm hits. Keep a couple of clean gallon (3.8-liter) jugs with handles filled with sand or kitty litter in the trunk of your car. Then you'll be prepared to sprinkle the material on the road surface to add traction under your wheels when you need to get moving on a slippery road. The handle makes it easier to pour them.

Using bottles in the garden

Feed the birds

Why spend money on a plastic bird feeder when you probably have one in your recycling bin? Take a clean 1/2-gallon (2-liter) juice or milk jug and carve a large hole on its side to remove the handle. (You might even drill a small hole under the large one to insert a sturdy twig or dowel for a perch.) Then poke a hole in the middle of the cap and suspend it from a tree with a piece of strong string or monofilament fishing line. Fill it up to the opening with birdseed, and enjoy the show.

Make a watering can

No watering can? It's easy to make one from a clean 1-gallon (3.8-liter) juice, milk, or bleach jug with a handle. Drill about a dozen tiny (1/16-inch or 1.5-mm is good) holes just below the spout of the jug on the side opposite the handle. Or carefully punch the holes with an ice pick. Fill it with water, screw the cap on, and start sprinkling.

Mark your plants

Want an easy way to make ID badges for all the vegetables, herbs, and flowers in your garden? Cut vertical strips from a couple of clear 1-gallon (3.8-liter) water jugs. Make the strips the same width as your seed packets but double their length. Fold each strip

CUTTING PLASTIC CONTAINERS SAFELY

Cutting plastic containers can be a tricky, dangerous business—especially when you reach for your sharpest kitchen knife. But you can greatly minimize the risk by visiting your local fabric or crafts store and picking up a **rolling cutter knife** (this is not the same device used to slice pizza, by the way). The device usually sells for between $6 and $10. Be careful, though. These knives use blades that are razor sharp, but they make life much easier when it's time to cut into a hard plastic container.

USING BOTTLES FOR DO-IT-YOURSELF JOBS

- **Build a paint bucket** Tired of splattering paint all over as you work? Make a neater paint dispenser by cutting a large hole opposite the handle of a clean 1-gallon (3.8-liter) jug. Pour in the paint so that it's about an inch below the edge of the hole, and use the edge to remove any excess paint from your brush before you lift your brush. You can also cut jugs in half and use the bottom halves as disposable paint buckets when several people work on the same job.

- **Store your paints** Why keep leftover house paints in rusted or dented cans when you can keep them clean and fresh in plastic jugs? Use a funnel to pour the paint into a clean, dry milk or water jug, and add a few marbles (they help mix the paint when you shake the container before your next paint job). Label each container with a piece of masking tape, noting the paint manufacturer, color name, and the date.

- **Use as workshop organizers** Are you always searching for the right nail to use for a particular chore, or for a clothespin, picture hook, or small fastener? Bring some organization to your workshop with a few 1- or 1/2-gallon (3.8- or 2-liter) jugs. Cut out a section near the top of each jug on the side opposite the handle. Then use the containers to store and sort all the small items that seem to "slip through the cracks" of your workbench. The handle makes it easy to carry a jug to your worksite.

- **Use as a level substitute** How can you make sure that shelf you're about to put up is straight if you don't have a level on hand? Easy. Just fill a 1-liter soda bottle about three-quarters full with water. Replace the cap, then lay the bottle on its side. When the water is level, so is the shelf.

- **Make a weight for anchoring or lifting** Fill a clean, dry gallon (3.8-liter) jug with a handle with sand and cap it. You now have an anchor that is great for holding down a tarp covering your cut firewood, securing a shaky patio umbrella, or steadying a table for repair. The handle makes it easy to move or attach a rope. Or use a pair of sand-filled bottles as exercise weights, varying the amount of sand to meet your lifting capacity.

over an empty packet to protect it from the elements, and staple it to a strong stick or chopstick.

Secure garden netting

If you find yourself having to constantly re-stake the loose netting or plastic lining over your garden bed, place some water-filled large plastic jugs around the corners to keep the material in place.

Use as an attachable trash can or harvest basket

Here's a great tip for weekend gardeners and pros alike: Cut a large hole opposite the handle of a 1/2- or 1-gallon (2-or 3.8-liter) container, and loop the handle through a belt or rope on your waist. Use it to collect the debris—rocks, weeds, broken stems—you encounter as you mow the lawn or stroll through your garden. Use the same design to make an attachable basket for harvesting berries, cherries, and other small fruits or vegetables.

Build a bug trap

Do yellow jackets, wasps, or moths swarm around you every time you set foot in the yard? Use an empty 2-liter soda bottle to make an environment-friendly trap for them. First, dissolve 1/2 cup of sugar in 1/2 cup of water in the bottle. Then add 1 cup of apple cider vinegar and a banana peel (squish it up to fit it through). Screw on the cap and give the mixture a good shake before filling the bottle halfway with cold water. Cut or drill a 3/4-inch (2-cm) hole near the top of the bottle, and hang it from a tree branch where the bugs seem especially active. When the trap is full, toss it into the garbage and replace it with a new one.

Space seeds in garden

Want an easy way to perfectly space seeds in your garden? Use an empty soda bottle as your guide. Find the distance that the seed company recommends between seeds and then cut off the tapered top of the bottle so its diameter equals that distance. When you start planting, firmly press your bottle, cut edge down, into the soil and place a seed in the center of the circle it makes. Then line up the bottle so that its edge touches the curve of the first impression, and press down again. Plant a seed in the center, and repeat until you've filled your rows.

Set up a backyard sprayer

When temperatures soar outdoors, keep your kids cool with a homemade backyard sprayer. Just cut three 1-inch (2.5-cm) vertical slits in one side of a clean 2-liter soda bottle. Or make the slits at different angles so the water will squirt in different directions. Attach the nozzle of the hose to the bottle top with duct tape (make sure it's fastened on tight). Turn on the tap, and let the fun begin!

Bread

Remove scorched taste from rice

Did you leave the rice cooking too long and let it get burned? To get rid of the scorched taste, place a slice of white bread on top of the rice while it's still hot. Replace the pot lid and wait several minutes. When you remove the bread, the burned taste should be gone.

Soften up hard marshmallows

You reach for your bag of marshmallows only to discover that they've gone stale. Put a couple of slices of fresh bread in the bag and seal it shut (you may want to transfer the marshmallows to a self-sealing plastic bag). Leave it alone for a couple of days. When you reopen the bag, your marshmallows should taste as good as new.

Absorb vegetable odors

Love cabbage or broccoli, but hate the smell while it's cooking? Try putting a piece of white bread on top of the pot when cooking up a batch of "smelly" vegetables. It will absorb most of the odor.

Soak up grease and stop flare-ups

To paraphrase a famous bear: Only you can prevent grease fires. One of the best ways to prevent a grease flare-up when broiling meat is to place a couple of slices of white bread in your drip pan to absorb the grease. It will also cut down on the amount of smoke produced.

Pick up glass fragments

Picking up the large pieces of a broken glass or dish is usually easy enough, but getting up those tiny slivers can be a real pain (figuratively if not literally). The easiest way to make sure you don't miss any is to press a slice of bread over the area. Just be careful not to prick yourself when you toss the bread into the garbage.

Dust oil paintings

You wouldn't want to try this with an original Renoir, or with any museum-quality painting for that matter, but you can clean off everyday dust and grime that collects on an oil painting by gently rubbing the surface with a piece of white bread.

Bubble Pack

Prevent toilet-tank condensation

If your toilet tank sweats in warm, humid weather, bubble pack could be just the right antiperspirant. Lining the inside of the tank with bubble pack will keep the outside of the tank from getting cold and causing condensation when it comes in contact with warm, moist air. To line the tank, shut off the supply valve under the tank and flush to drain the tank. Then wipe the inside walls clean and dry. Use silicone sealant to glue appropriate-sized pieces of bubble pack to the major flat surfaces.

Protect patio plants

Keep your outdoor container plants warm and protected from winter frost damage. Wrap each container with bubble pack and use duct tape or string to hold the wrap in place. Make sure the wrap extends a couple of inches above the lip of the container. The added insulation will keep the soil warm all winter long.

Keep cola cold

Wrap soft-drink cans with bubble pack to keep beverages refreshingly cold on hot summer days. Do the same for packages of frozen or chilled picnic foods. Wrap ice cream just before you leave for the picnic to help keep it firm en route.

Protect produce in the fridge

Line your refrigerator's crisper drawer with bubble pack to prevent bruises to fruit and other produce. Cleanup will be easier, too—when the lining gets dirty, just throw it out and replace it with fresh bubble pack.

Protect tools

Reduce wear and tear on your good-quality tools and extend their lives. Line your toolbox with bubble pack. Use duct tape to hold it in place.

Add insulation

Cut window-size pieces of wide bubble pack and duct-tape them to inside windows for added warmth and savings on fuel bills in winter. Lower the blinds to make it less noticeable.

Cushion your work surface

When repairing delicate glass or china, cover the work surface with bubble pack to help prevent breakage.

Make a bedtime buffer

Keep cold air from creeping into your bed on a chilly night by placing a large sheet of bubble pack between your bedspread or quilt and your top sheet. You'll be surprised at how effective it is in keeping warm air in and cold air out.

Cushion bleachers and benches

Take some bubble pack out to the ballgame with you to soften those hard stadium seats or benches. Or stretch a length along a picnic bench for more comfy dining.

Bubble Wrap Wallpaper?

Yep, that's right. Wallpaper was what inventors **Alfred Fielding** and **Marc Chavannes** had in mind when they began developing the product in Saddle Brook, New Jersey, in the late 1950s. Perhaps they had the padded-cell market in mind. In any case, they soon realized their invention had far greater potential as packaging material. In 1960 they raised $85,000 and founded the **Sealed Air Corporation.**

Today Sealed Air is a Fortune 500 company with $3.5 billion in annual revenues. The company produces Bubble Wrap cushioning in a multitude of sizes, colors, and properties, along with other protective packaging materials such as **Jiffy padded mailers.**

Cans

Keep tables together

When you're having a large dinner party, lock card tables together by setting adjacent pairs of legs into empty cans. You won't have to clean up any spills caused by the tables moving this way and that.

Make light reflectors

It's simple to make reflectors for your campsite or backyard lights. Just remove the bottom of a large empty can with a can opener and take off any label. Then use tin snips to cut the can in half lengthwise. You've just made two reflectors.

Tuna can egg poacher

An empty 6-ounce (170-gram) tuna can is the perfect size to use as an egg poacher. Remove the bottom of the can as well as the top and remove any paper label. Then place the metal ring in a skillet of simmering water, and crack an egg into it.

Store jewelry in candy tins

You are late for the party but you can only find one earring from the pair that matched your dress so nicely. To prevent pairs of small earrings from going their separate ways, store them together in a little candy tin and you'll be right on time for the next party. You can also keep necklaces and chain bracelets separate and tangle-free in their own individual candy tins. And don't lose all the little pieces of that

broken jewelry you plan to have repaired someday. Keep the pieces together and safe in a small candy tin.

Make a birthday keepsake

Decorate the outside of a small candy tin, line it with felt or silk, and insert a penny or, if you can find one, a silver dollar from the birth year of your friend or loved one.

Organize your sewing with candy tins

Use a small candy tin to store snaps, sequins, buttons, and beads in your sewing box. Label the lids or glue on a sample for easy identification of the contents. A small candy tin is also just the right size for an emergency sewing kit. Use it to hold a handy selection of needles, thread, and buttons in your purse or briefcase for on-the-spot repairs.

Store workshop accessories

Candy tins are great for storing brads, glazing points, setscrews, lock washers, and other small items that might otherwise clutter up your workshop.

Make a miniature golf course

Arrange cans with both ends removed so the ball must go through them, go up a ramp into them, or ricochet off a board through them.

Quick floor patch

Nail can lids to a wooden floor to plug knotholes and keep rodents out. If you can get access to the hole from the basement, nail the lid in place from underneath so the patch won't be obvious.

Keep the laundry room neat

Have an empty coffee can nearby as you're going through the kids' pockets before putting up a load of wash. Use it to deposit gum and candy wrappers, paper scraps, and other assorted items that kids like to stuff into their pockets. Keep another can handy for coins and bills.

Make planters more portable

Don't strain your back moving a planter loaded with heavy soil. Reduce the amount of soil and lighten the load by first filling one-third to one-half of the bottom of the planter with empty, upside-down aluminum cans. Finish filling with soil and add your plants. In addition to making the planter lighter, the rustproof aluminum cans also help it to drain well.

Create a decorative snowman

Wrap an old soda can with white paper and tape with transparent tape. For a head use a styrene foam ball and tape it to the top of the can. Cover the body with cotton batting or cotton bandaging material and tape or glue it in place. Make a cone-shaped paper hat. Make eyes and a nose with buttons. To add arms, punch holes in the sides of the can and insert twigs. Use dots from a black marker pen to make buttons down the snowman's front. Make a scarf from a scrap of wooly fabric.

Feed the birds

A bird doesn't care if the feeder is plain or fancy as long as it is filled with suet. For a feeder that's about as basic as you can get, wedge a small can filled with suet between tree branches or posts.

The Invention of the Airtight Can

Tin cans are often described as **"hermetically sealed,"** but do you know the origin of the term? The word hermetic comes from Hermes Trismegistus, a legendary **alchemist** who is reputed to have lived sometime in the first three centuries A.D. and to have invented a magic seal that keeps a vessel airtight.

The hermetically sealed can was invented in 1810 by British merchant **Peter Durand.** His cans were so thick they had to be hammered open! Two years later, Englishman **Thomas Kensett** set up America's first cannery on the New York waterfront to can oysters, meats, fruits, and vegetables.

Cat Litter

Make a mud mask

Make a deep-cleansing mud mask. Mix two handfuls of fresh cat litter with enough warm water to make a thick paste. Smear the paste over your face, let it set for 20 minutes, and rinse clean with water. The clay from cat litter detoxifies your skin by absorbing dirt and oil from the pores. When your friends compliment you on your complexion and ask how you did it, just tell them it's your little secret.

Sneaker deodorizer

If your athletic shoes reek, fill a couple of old socks with scented cat litter, tie them shut, and place them in the sneakers overnight. Repeat if necessary until the sneakers are stink-free.

Add traction on ice

Keep a bag of cat litter in the trunk of your car. Use it to add traction when you're stuck in ice or snow.

Prevent grease fires

Don't let a grease fire spoil your next barbecue. Pour a layer of cat litter into the bottom of your grill for worry-free outdoor cooking.

Stop musty odors

Get rid of that musty smell when you open the closet door. Just place a shallow box filled with cat litter in each musty closet or room. Cat litter works great as a deodorant.

Preserve flowers

The fragrance and beauty of freshly cut flowers is such a fleeting thing. You can't save the smell, but you can preserve their beauty by drying your flowers on a bed of cat litter in an air-tight container for 7 to 10 days.

Remove foul stench

Just because your garbage cans hold garbage doesn't mean they have to smell disgusting. Sprinkle some cat litter into the bottom of garbage cans to keep them smelling fresh. Change the litter after a week or so or when it becomes damp. If you have a baby in the house, use cat litter the same way to freshen diaper pails.

Freshen old books

You can rejuvenate old books that smell musty by sealing them overnight in a can with clean cat litter.

Repel moles

Moles may hate the smell of soiled cat litter even more than you do. Pour some down their tunnels to send them scurrying to find new homes.

Keep tents must-free

Keep tents and sleeping bags fresh smelling and free of must when not in use. Pour cat litter into an old sock, tie the end, and store inside the bag or tent.

Make grease spots disappear

Get rid of ugly grease and oil spots in your driveway or on your garage floor. Simply cover them with cat litter. If the spots are fresh, the litter will soak up most of the oil right away. To remove old stains, pour some paint thinner on the stain before tossing on the cat litter. Wait 12 hours and then sweep clean.

The Origins of Kitty Litter

Ed Lowe might not have gotten the idea for cat litter if a neighbor hadn't asked him for some sand for her cat box one day in 1947. Ed, who worked for his father's company selling industrial absorbents, suggested clay instead because it was more absorbent and would not leave tracks around the house. When she returned for more, he knew he had a winner. Soon he was crisscrossing the country, selling bags of his new **Kitty Litter** from the back of his Chevy Coupe. By 1990 Edward Lowe Industries, Inc., was the nation's largest producer of cat box filler with retail sales of more than $210 million annually.

Chewing Gum

Use as makeshift window putty

Worried that a loose pane of glass may tumble and break before you get around to fixing it? Hold it in place temporarily with a wad or two of fresh-chewed gum.

Lure a crab

You'll be eating plenty of crab cakes if you try this trick: Briefly chew a stick of gum so that it is soft but still hasn't lost its flavor, then attach it to a crab line. Lower the line and wait for the crabs to go for the gum.

Fill cracks

Fill a crack in a clay flowerpot or a dog bowl with piece of well-chewed gum.

Retrieve valuables

Oops, you just lost an earring or other small valuable down the drain. Try retrieving it with a just-chewed piece of gum stuck to the bottom of a fishing weight. Dangle it from a string tied to the weight, let it take hold, and reel it in.

Treat flatulence and heartburn

Settle stomach gases and relieve heartburn by chewing a stick of spearmint gum. The oils in the spearmint act as an antiflatulent. Chewing stimulates the production of saliva, which neutralizes stomach acid and corrects the flow of digestive juices. Spearmint also acts as a digestive aid.

Repair glasses

When your glasses suddenly have a lens loose, put a small piece of chewed gum in the corner of the lens to hold it in place until you can get the glasses properly repaired.

A Brief History of Chewing Gum

Humans have been chewing gum a long time. Ancient Greeks chewed mastiche, a chewing gum made from the resin of the **mastic tree.** Ancient Mayans chewed **chicle,** the sap from the sapodilla tree. North American Indians chewed the sap from spruce trees, and passed the habit on to the **Pilgrims.** And other early American settlers made chewing gum from spruce sap and beeswax. **John B. Curtis** produced the first commercial chewing gum in 1848 and called it State of Maine Pure Spruce Gum. North Americans now spend more than $2 billion per year on chewing gum.

Clothespins

Fasten holiday lights

Keep your outdoor holiday lights in place and ready to withstand the elements. As you affix your lights to gutters, trees, bushes (or even your spouse!) fasten them securely with clip-on clothespins.

Keep snacks fresh

Tired of biting into stale potato chips from a previously opened bag? Use clip-on clothespins to reseal bags of chips and other snacks, cereal, crackers, and seeds. The foods will stay fresh longer and you won't have as many spills in the pantry, either. Use a clothespin for added freshness when you store food in a freezer bag too.

Prevent vacuum cord "snapback"

Whoops! You're vacuuming the living room floor when suddenly the machine stops. You've accidentally pulled out the plug and the cord is automatically retracting and snapping back into the machine. To avoid similar annoyance in the future, simply clip a clothespin to the cord at the length you want.

Organize your closet

Okay, you found one shoe. Now, where the heck is the other one? Use clip-on clothespins to hold together pairs of shoes, boots, or sneakers, and put an end to those unscheduled hunting expeditions in your closets. It's a good idea for gloves, too.

Hold leaf bag open

Ever try filling a large leaf bag all by your lonesome, only to see half the leaves fall to the ground because the bag won't stay open? Next time enlist a couple of clip-on clothespins as helpers. After you shake open the bag and spread it wide, use the clothespins to clip one side of the bag to a chain-link fence or other convenient site. The bag will stay open for easy filling.

Keep gloves in shape

After washing wool gloves, insert a straight wooden clothespin into each finger. The clothespins will keep the gloves in their proper shape.

Clamp thin objects

Use clip-on clothespins as clamps when you're gluing two thin objects together. Let the clothespin hold them in place until the glue sets.

Make clothespin puppets

Traditional straight clothespins without the metal springs are ideal for making little puppets. Using the knob as a head, have kids paste on bits of yarn for hair, and scraps of cloth or colored paper for clothes to give each one its own personality.

Mark a bulb spot

What to do when a flower that blooms in the spring...doesn't? Just push a straight clothespin into the soil at the spot where it didn't grow. In the fall you will know exactly where to plant new bulbs to avoid gaps.

Grip a nail

Hammer the nail and not your fingers. Just remember to use a clip-on clothespin to hold nails when hammering in hard-to-reach places.

The Vanishing Clothespin Makers

Between 1852 and 1857 the U.S. Patent Office granted patents for **146 different clothespins.** Today wood clothespin makers have practically disappeared. "The small family-owned...companies are dying off," says **Richard Penley,** who closed his family's clothespin plant in Maine in 2002. The company founded by Penley's grandfather and two brothers in 1923 survives, importing and distributing clothespins made overseas. Only two wood clothespin manufacturers are left in the United States.

Club Soda

Make pancakes and waffles fluffier

If you like your pancakes and waffles on the fluffy side, substitute club soda for the liquid called for in the recipes. You'll be amazed at how light and fluffy your breakfast treats turn out.

Give your plants a mineral bath

Don't throw out that leftover club soda. Use it to water your indoor and outdoor plants. The minerals in the soda water help green plants grow. For maximum benefit, try to water your plants with club soda about once a week.

Remove fabric stains

Clean grease stains from double-knit fabrics. Pour club soda on the stain and scrub gently. Scrub more vigorously to remove stains on carpets or less delicate articles of clothing.

Help shuck oysters

If you love oysters but find shucking them to be a near-impossible chore, try soaking them in club soda before you shuck. The oysters won't exactly jump out of their shells, but they will be much easier to open.

Clean precious gems

Soak your diamonds, rubies, sapphires, and emeralds in club soda to give them a bright sheen. Simply place them in a glass full of club soda and let them soak overnight.

Clean your car windshield

Keep a spray bottle filled with club soda in the trunk of your car. Use it to help remove bird droppings and greasy stains from the windshield. The fizzy water speeds the cleaning process.

Restore hair color

If your blond hair turns green when you swim in a pool with too much chlorine, don't panic. Rinse your hair with club soda and it will change back to its original color.

Tame your tummy

Cold club soda with a dash of bitters will work wonders on an upset stomach caused by indigestion or a hangover.

Clean countertops and fixtures

Pour club soda directly on stainless steel countertops, ranges, and sinks. Wipe with a soft cloth, rinse with warm water, and wipe dry. To clean porcelain fixtures, simply pour club soda over them and wipe with a soft cloth. There's no need for soap or rinsing, and the soda will not mar the finish. Give the inside of your refrigerator a good cleaning with a weak solution of club soda and a little bit of salt.

Remove rust

To loosen rusty nuts and bolts, pour some club soda over them. The carbonation helps to bubble the rust away.

Eliminate urine stains

Did someone have an accident? After blotting up as much urine as possible, pour club soda over the stained area and immediately blot again. The club soda will get rid of the stain and help reduce the foul smell.

Ease cast-iron cleanup

Food tastes delicious when it's cooked in cast iron, but cleaning those heavy pots and pans with the sticky mess inside is no fun at all. You can make the cleanup a lot easier by pouring some club soda in the pan while it's still warm. The bubbly soda will keep the mess from sticking.

Have a seltzer for your health

Bubbling water has been associated with good health since the time of the **ancient Romans,** who enjoyed drinking mineral water almost as much as they liked bathing in it. The first club soda was sold in North America at the end of the 1700s. That's when pharmacists figured out how to **infuse plain water** with carbon dioxide, which they believed was responsible for  giving natural bubbling water health-inducing qualities. Club soda and seltzer are essentially the same. However, seltzer is a natural effervescent water (named for a region in **Germany** where it is plentiful) whereas club soda is manufactured.

Coat Hangers

Stop caulk-tube ooze

To prevent caulk from oozing from the tube once the job is done, cut a 3-inch (7.5-cm) piece of coat hanger wire; shape one end into a hook and insert the other, straight end into the tube. Now you can easily pull out the stopper as needed.

Secure a soldering iron

Keeping a hot soldering iron from rolling away and burning something on your workbench is a real problem. To solve this, just twist a wire coat hanger into a holder for the iron to rest in. To make the holder, simply bend an ordinary coat hanger in half to form a large V. Then bend each half in half so that the entire piece is shaped like a W.

Extend your reach

Can't reach that utensil that has fallen behind the refrigerator or stove? Try straightening a wire coat hanger (except for the hook at the end), and use it to fish for the object.

Make a giant bubble wand

Kids will love to make giant bubbles with a homemade bubble wand fashioned from a wire coat hanger. Shape the hanger into a hoop with a handle and dip it into a bucket filled with 1 part liquid dishwashing detergent in 2 parts water. Add a few drops of food coloring to make the bubbles more visible.

The Unsung Creator of the Wire Coat Hanger

All **Albert J. Parkhouse** wanted to do when he arrived at work was to hang up his coat and get busy doing his job. It was 1903, and Albert worked at Timberlake Wire and Novelty Company in Jackson, Michigan. But when he went to hang his clothes on the hooks the company provided for workers, all were in use. Frustrated, Albert picked up a piece of wire, bent it into two large oblong hoops opposite each other, and twisted both ends at the center into a hook. He hung his coat on it and went to work. The company thought so much of the idea they patented it and made a fortune. Alas, Albert **never got a penny** for inventing the wire coat hanger.

Create arts and crafts

Make mobiles for the kids' room using wire coat hangers; paint them in bright colors. Or use hangers to make wings and other accessories for costumes.

Unclog toilets and vacuum cleaners

If your toilet is clogged by a foreign object, fish out the culprit with a straightened wire coat hanger. Use a straightened hanger to unclog a jammed vacuum cleaner hose.

Make plant markers

Need some waterproof markers for your outdoor plants? Cut up little signs from a milk jug or similar rigid but easy-to-cut plastic. Write the name of the plant with an indelible marker. Cut short stakes from wire hangers. Make two small slits in each marker and pass the wire stakes through the slits. Neither rain nor sprinkler will obscure your signs.

Hang a plant

Wrap a straightened wire coat hanger around a 6- to 8-inch (15- to 20-cm) flowerpot, just below the lip; twist it back on itself to secure it, then hang.

Make a mini-greenhouse

To convert a window box into a mini-greenhouse, bend three or four lengths of coat hanger wire into U's and place the ends into the soil. Punch small holes in a dry-cleaning bag and wrap it around the box before putting it back in the window.

Make a paint can holder

When you are up on a ladder painting your house, one hand is holding on while the other is painting. How do you hold the paint can? Grab a pair of wire snips and cut the hook plus 1 inch (2.5 cm) of wire from a wire hanger. Use a pair of pliers to twist the 1-inch section firmly around the handle of your paint can. Now you have a handy hanger.

Coffee Cans

Bake perfectly round bread

Use small coffee cans to bake perfectly cylindrical loaves of bread. Use your favorite recipe but put the dough in a well-greased coffee can instead of a loaf pan. For yeast breads use two cans and fill each only half full. Grease the inside of the lids and place them on the cans. For yeast breads, you will know when it is time to bake when the rising dough pushes the lids off. Place the cans—without the lids—upright in the oven to bake.

Separate hamburgers

Before you put those hamburger patties in the freezer, stack them with a coffee-can lid between each and put them in a plastic bag. Now, when the patties are frozen, you'll be able to easily peel off as many as you need.

Hold kitchen scraps

Line a coffee can with a small plastic bag and keep it near the sink to hold kitchen scraps and peelings. Instead of walking back and forth to the garbage can, you'll make one trip to dump all the scraps at the same time.

Make a bank

To make a bank for the kids or a collection can for a favorite charity, use a utility knife to cut a 1/8-inch (3-mm) slit in the center of the plastic lid of a coffee can. Tape decorative paper or adhesive plastic to the sides of the kids' bank; for a collection can, use the sides of the can to highlight the charity you are helping.

Create a toy holder

Make a decorative container for kids' miniature books and small toys. Wash and dry a coffee can and file off any sharp edges. Sponge on two coats of white acrylic paint, letting it dry between coats. Cut out a design from an old sheet or pillowcase to wrap around the can. Mix 4 tablespoons of white glue with enough water to the consistency of paint. Paint on the glue mixture and gently press the fabric onto the can. Trim the bottom and tuck top edges inside the can. Apply two coats of glue mixture over the fabric overlay, letting it dry between coats.

Make a dehumidifier

If your basement is too damp, try this easy-to-make dehumidifier. Fill an empty coffee can with salt and leave it in a corner where it will be undisturbed. Replace the salt at monthly intervals or as needed.

Keep carpets dry

Place plastic coffee-can lids under houseplants as saucers. They will protect carpets or wood floors and catch any excess water.

Keep toilet paper dry when camping

Bring a few empty coffee cans with you on your next camping trip. Use them to keep toilet paper dry in rainy weather or when you're carrying supplies in a canoe or boat.

Gauge rainfall or sprinkler coverage

Find out if your garden is getting enough water from the rain. Next time it starts to rain, place empty coffee cans in several places around the garden. When the rain stops, measure the depth of the water in the cans. If they measure at least an inch, there's no need for additional watering. This is also a good way to test if your sprinkler is getting sufficient water to the areas it is supposed to cover.

Make a coffee-can bird feeder

To fashion a coffee can into a sturdy bird feeder, begin with a full can and open the top only halfway. (Pour the coffee into an airtight container.) Then open the bottom of the can halfway the same way. Carefully bend the cut ends down inside the can so the edges are not exposed to cut you. Punch a hole in the side of the can at both ends, where it will be the "top" of the feeder, and put some wire through each end to make a hanger.

Soak a paintbrush

An empty coffee can is perfect for briefly soaking a paintbrush in thinner before continuing a job the next day. Cut an X into the lid and insert the brush handles so the bristles clear the bottom of the can by about 1/2 inch (13 mm). If the can has no lid, attach a stick to the brush handle with a rubber band to keep the bristles off the bottom of the can.

Catch paint drips

Turn the plastic lids from old coffee cans into drip catchers under paint cans and under furniture legs when you're painting. Protect cupboard shelves by putting them under jars of cooking oil and syrup too.

SOME FACTS ABOUT COFFEE AND COFFEE CANS

Ground coffee loses its flavor immediately unless it is specially packaged or brewed. Freshly roasted and ground coffee is often sealed in combination plastic-and-paper bags, but the coffee can is by far the most common container in North America. **Vacuum-sealed** cans keep coffee fresh for up to three years. The U.S. is the world's largest consumer of coffee, importing up to 2.5 million pounds (1.1 million km) each year. More than half the U.S. population consumes coffee. The typical coffee drinker has **3.4 cups of coffee per day**. That translates into 350 million cups of coffee guzzled daily.

Cooking Spray

Prevent rice and pasta from sticking

Most cooks know that a little cooking oil in the boiling water will keep rice or pasta from sticking together when you drain it. If you run out of cooking oil, however, a spritz of cooking oil spray will do the job just as well.

Grating cheese

Put less elbow grease into grating cheese by using a nonstick cooking spray on your cheese grater for smoother grating. The spray also makes for easier and faster cleanup.

Prevent tomato sauce stains

Sick of those hard-to-clean tomato sauce stains on your plastic containers? To prevent them, apply a light coating of nonstick cooking spray on the inside of the container before you pour in the tomato sauce.

Lubricate your bicycle chain

Is your bike chain a bit creaky and you don't have any lubricating oil handy? Give it a shot of nonstick cooking spray instead. Don't use too much—the chain shouldn't look wet. Wipe off the excess with a clean rag.

Keep car wheels clean

You know that fine black stuff that collects on the wheels of your car and is so hard to clean off? That's brake dust—it's produced every time you apply your brakes and the pads wear against the brake disks or cylinders. The next time you invest the elbow grease to get your wheels shiny, give them a light coating of cooking spray. The brake dust will wipe right off.

Cure door squeak

Heard that door squeak just one time too many? Hit the hinge with some nonstick cooking spray. Have paper towels handy to wipe up the drips.

Remove paint and grease

Forget smelly solvents to remove paint and grease from your hands. Instead, use cooking spray to do the job. Work it in well and rinse. Wash again with soap and water.

Dry nail polish

Need your nail polish to dry in a hurry? Spray it with a coat of cooking spray and let dry. The spray is also a great moisturizer for your hands.

Quick casting

Pack a can of cooking spray when you go fishing. Spray it on your fishing line and the line will cast easier and farther.

Prevent grass from sticking

Mowing the lawn should be easy, but cleaning stuck grass from the mower is tedious. Prevent grass from sticking on mower blades and the underside of the housing by spraying them with cooking oil before you begin mowing.

Pam—the First Cooking Spray

Ever wondered where **PAM,** the name of the popular cooking spray, comes from? It stands for **"Product of Arthur Meyerhoff."** The first patent for a nonstick cooking spray was issued in 1957 to Arthur and his partner, Leon Rubin, who began marketing PAM All Natural Cooking Spray in 1959. After appearing on local Chicago **TV cooking shows** in the early '60s, the product developed a loyal following, and it quickly became a household word. By the way, PAM is pretty durable stuff—it has a shelf life of two years.

Cornstarch

paste yourself. Mix 3 teaspoons of cornstarch for every 4 teaspoons of cold water. Stir until you reach a paste consistency. This is especially great for applying with fingers or a wooden tongue depressor or Popsicle stick. If you add food coloring, the paste can be used for painting objects.

Separate marshmallows

Ever buy a bag of marshmallows only to find them stuck together? Here's how to get them apart: Add at least 1 teaspoon of cornstarch to the bag and shake. The cornstarch will absorb the extra moisture and force most of the marshmallows apart. Repackage the remaining marshmallows in a container and freeze them to avoid sticking in the future.

Lift a scorch mark from clothing

You moved the iron a little too slowly and now you have a scorch mark on your favorite shirt. Wet the scorched area and cover it with cornstarch. Let the cornstarch dry, then brush it away along with the scorch mark.

Remove grease spatters from walls

Even the most careful cook cannot avoid an occasional spatter. A busy kitchen takes some wear and tear but here's a handy remedy for that unsightly grease spot. Sprinkle cornstarch onto a soft cloth. Rub the grease spot gently until it disappears.

furniture after polishing. Wipe up the oil and cornstarch, then buff the surface.

Remove ink stains from carpet

Oh no, ink on the carpet! In this case a little spilt milk might save you from crying. Mix the milk with cornstarch to make a paste. Apply the paste to the ink stain. Allow the concoction to dry on the carpet for a few hours, then brush off the dried residue and vacuum it up.

Give carpets a fresh scent

Before vacuuming a room, sprinkle a little cornstarch on your carpeting. Wait about half an hour and then vacuum normally.

Make your own paste

The next time the kids want to go wild with construction paper and paste, save money by making the

Dry shampoo

Fido needs a bath, but you just don't have time. Rub cornstarch into his coat and brush it out. The dry bath will fluff up his coat until it's tub time.

Untangle knots

Knots in string or shoelaces can be stubborn to undo, but the solution is easy. Sprinkle the knot with a little cornstarch. It will then be easy to work the segments apart.

Soak up furniture polish residue

You've finished polishing your furniture, but there's still a bit left on the surface. Sprinkle cornstarch lightly on

Make finger paints

This simple recipe will keep the kids happy for hours. Mix together 1/4 cup of cornstarch and 2 cups of cold water. Bring to a boil and continue boiling until the mixture becomes thick. Pour your product into several small containers and add food coloring to each container. You've created a collection of homemade finger paints.

Clean stuffed animals

To clean a stuffed animal toy, rub a little cornstarch onto the toy, wait about 5 minutes, and then brush it clean. Or place the stuffed animal (or a few small ones) into a bag. Sprinkle cornstarch into the bag, close it tightly, and shake. Now brush the pretend pets clean.

Get rid of bloodstains

The quicker you act, the better. Whether it's on clothing or table linens, you can remove or reduce a bloodstain with this method. Make a paste of cornstarch mixed with cold water. Cover the spot with the cornstarch paste and rub it gently into the fabric. Now put the cloth in a sunny location to dry. Once dry, brush off the remaining residue. If the stain is not completely gone, repeat the process.

Polish silver

Is the sparkle gone from your good silverware? Make a simple paste by mixing cornstarch with water. Use a damp cloth to apply this to your silver-ware. Let it dry, then rub it off with cheesecloth or another soft cloth to reveal that old shine.

Make windows sparkle

Create your own streak-free window cleaning solution by mixing 2 tablespoons of cornstarch with 1/2 cup of ammonia and 1/2 cup of white vinegar in a bucket containing 3 or 4 quarts (3 or 4 liters) of warm water. Don't be put off by the milky concoction you create. Mix well and put the solution in a trigger spray bottle. Spray on the windows, then wipe with a warm-water rinse. Now rub with a dry paper towel or lint-free cloth. Voilà!

Say good riddance to roaches

There's no delicate way to manage this problem. Make a mixture that is 50 percent plaster of Paris and 50 percent cornstarch. Spread this in the crevices where roaches appear. It's a killer recipe.

EARTH-SAVING PACKING PEANUTS

Cornstarch has been made into **biodegradable** packing "peanuts" sold in bulk. If you receive an item shipped in this material, you can toss the peanuts on the lawn. They'll dissolve with water, leaving no toxic waste. To test if the peanuts are made from cornstarch, wet one in the sink to see if it dissolves.

Cotton Balls

Scent the room

Saturate a cotton ball with your favorite cologne and drop it into your vacuum cleaner bag. Now, as you vacuum, the scent will be expressed and gently permeate the room.

Deodorize the refrigerator

Sometimes the refrigerator just doesn't smell fresh. Dampen a cotton ball with vanilla extract and place it out of the way on a shelf. You'll find it acts as a deodorizer, offering its own pleasant scent.

Protect little fingers

Pad the ends of drawer runners with a cotton ball. This will prevent the drawer from closing completely and keep children from catching their fingers as the drawer slides shut.

Fight mildew

There are always hard-to-reach spots in the bathroom, usually around the fixtures, where mildew may breed in the grout between tiles. Forget about becoming a contortionist to return the sparkle to those areas. Soak a few cotton balls in bleach and place them in those difficult spots. Leave them to work their magic for a few hours. When you remove them, you'll find your job has been done. Finish by rinsing with a warm-water wash.

Rescue your rubber gloves

If your long, manicured nails sometimes puncture the fingertips of your rubber dishwashing gloves, here's a solution you'll appreciate. Push a cotton ball into the fingers of your gloves. The soft barrier should prolong the gloves' life.

Cream of Tartar

Tub scrubber

Let this simple solution of cream of tartar and hydrogen peroxide do the hard work of removing a bathtub stain for you. Fill a small, shallow cup or dish with cream of tartar and add hydrogen peroxide drop by drop until you have a thick paste. Apply to the stain and let it dry. When you remove the dried paste, you'll find that the stain is gone too.

Brighten cookware

Discolored aluminum pots will sparkle again if you clean them with a mixture of 2 tablespoons of cream of tartar dissolved into 1 quart (1 liter) of water. Bring the mixture to a boil inside the pot and boil for 10 minutes.

MAKE PLAY CLAY FOR KIDS

Here's a recipe for fun dough that's like the store-bought stuff:

Ingredients
- 2 tablespoons cream of tartar
- 1 cup salt
- 4 cups plain flour (without rising agents)
- 1 to 2 tablespoons cooking oil
- 4 cups of water
- Food coloring

1 Mix the cream of tartar, salt, flour, and oil together with a wooden spoon, then slowly stir while adding water.

2 Cook in a saucepan over a medium flame, stirring occasionally until it thickens. It's ready when it forms a ball that is not sticky.

3 Work in food coloring. Let it cool, then let the kids get creative. It dries out quicker than the commercial variety, so store it in an airtight container in the fridge.

Dental Floss

Remove a stuck ring

Here's a simple way to slip off a ring that's stuck on your finger. Wrap the length of your finger from the ring to the nail tightly with dental floss. Now you can slide the ring off over the floss "carpet."

Lift cookies off baking tray

Ever fought with a freshly baked cookie that wouldn't come off the pan? Crumbled cookies may taste just as good as those in one piece, but they sure don't look as nice on the serving plate. Use dental floss to easily remove cookies from the baking tray. Hold a length of dental floss taut and slide it neatly between the cookie bottom and the pan.

Slice cake and cheese

Use dental floss to cut cakes, especially delicate and sticky ones that tend to adhere to a knife. Just hold a length of the floss taut over the cake and then slice away, moving it slightly side to side as you cut through the cake. You can also use dental floss to cut small blocks of cheese cleanly.

Repair outdoor gear

Because dental floss is strong and resilient but slender, it's the ideal replacement for thread when you are repairing an umbrella, tent, or backpack. These items take a beating and sometimes get pinhole nicks. Sew up the small holes with floss. To fix larger gouges, sew back and forth over the holes until you have covered the space with a floss patch.

Extra-strong string for hanging things

Considering how thin it is, dental floss is strong stuff. Use it instead of string or wire to securely hang pictures, sun catchers, or wind chimes. Use it with a needle to thread together papers you want to attach or those you want to display, in clothesline fashion.

Secure a button permanently

Did that button fall off again? This time, sew it back on with dental floss—it's much stronger than thread, which makes it perfect for reinstalling buttons on coats, jackets, and heavy shirts.

Separate photos

Sometimes photos get stuck to each other and it seems the only way to separate them is to ruin them. Try working a length of dental floss between the pictures to gently pry them apart.

123

Denture Tablets

Clean a coffeemaker

Hard water leaves mineral deposits in the tank of your electric drip coffeemaker that not only slows the perking but also affects the taste of your brew. Denture tablets will fizz away these deposits and give the tank a bacterial clean-out too. The tablets were designed to clean and disinfect dentures, and they'll do the same job on your coffeemaker. Drop two denture tablets in the tank and fill it with water. Run the coffeemaker. Discard that potful of water and follow up with one or two rinse cycles with clean water.

Re-ignite your diamond's sparkle

Has your diamond ring lost its sparkle? Drop a denture tablet into a glass containing a cup of water. Follow that with your ring or diamond earrings. Let it sit for a few minutes. Remove your jewelry and rinse to reveal the old sparkle and shine.

Vanish mineral deposits on glass

Fresh flowers often leave a ring on your glass vases that seems impossible to remove no matter how hard you scrub. Here's the answer. Fill the vase with water and drop in a denture tablet. When the fizzing has stopped, all of the mineral deposits will be gone. Use the same method to clean thermos bottles, cruets, glasses, and coffee decanters.

Clean your toilet

Looking for a way to make the toilet sparkle again? Porcelain fixtures respond to the cleaning agent in denture tablets. Here's a solution that does the job in the twinkling of an eye. Drop a denture tablet in the bowl. Wait about 20 minutes and flush. That's it!

Clean enamel cookware

Stains on enamel cookware are a natural for the denture tablet cleaning solution. Fill the pot or pan with warm water and drop in a tablet or two, depending on its size. Wait a bit—once the fizzing has stopped, your cookware will be clean.

Unclog a drain

Slow drain got you down? Reach for the denture tablets. Drop a couple of tablets into the drain and run water until the problem clears. For a more stubborn clog, drop 3 tablets down the sink, follow that with 1 cup of white vinegar, and wait a few minutes. Now run hot water in the drain until the clog is gone.

WHY DENTURE TABLETS ARE GOOD POT-BRIGHTENERS

Bleaching agents are a common component of denture cleaner tablets, providing the chemical action that helps the tablets to remove plaque and to whiten and bleach away stains. This is what makes them surprisingly useful for cleaning **toilets, coffeemakers, jewelry,** and **enamel cookware,** among other things.

Epsom Salt

Get rid of raccoons

Are the masked night marauders poking around your trash can, creating a mess and raising a din? A few tablespoons of Epsom salt spread around your garbage cans will deter the raccoons, who don't like the taste of the stuff. Don't forget to reapply after it rains.

Deter slugs

Are you tired of visiting your yard at night only to find the place crawling with slimy slugs? Sprinkle Epsom salt where they glide and say good-bye to the slugs.

Fertilize tomatoes and other plants

Want those Big Boys to be big? Add Epsom salt as a foolproof fertilizer. Every week, for every foot of height of your tomato plant, add one tablespoon. Your tomatoes will be the envy of the neighborhood. Epsom salt is also a good fertilizer for houseplants, roses and other flowers, and trees.

Make your grass greener

How green is your valley? Not green enough, you say? Epsom salt, which adds needed magnesium and iron to your soil, may be the answer. Add 2 tablespoons to 1 gallon (3.8 liters) of water. Spread on your lawn and then water it with plain water to make sure it soaks into the grass.

Clean bathroom tiles

Is the tile in your bathroom getting that grungy look? Time to bring in the Epsom salt. Mix it in equal parts with liquid dish detergent, then dab it onto the offending area and start scrubbing. The Epsom salt works with the detergent to scrub and dissolve the grime.

Get rid of blackheads

Here's a surefire way to dislodge blackheads: Mix 1 teaspoon of Epsom salt and 3 drops iodine in 1/2 cup of boiling water. When the mixture cools enough to stick your finger in it, apply it to the blackhead with a cotton ball. Repeat this three or four times, reheating the solution if necessary. Gently remove the blackhead and then dab the area with an alcohol-based astringent.

Frost your windows for Christmas

If you are dreaming of a white Christmas, but the weather won't cooperate, at least you can make your windows look frosty. Mix Epsom salt with stale beer until the salt stops dissolving. Apply the mixture to your windows with a sponge—for a realistic look, sweep the sponge in an arc at the bottom corners. When the mixture dries, the windows will look frosted.

Regenerate a car battery

Is your car battery starting to sound as if it won't turn over? Worried that you'll be stuck the next time you try to start your car? Give your battery a little more life with this potion. Dissolve about an ounce of Epsom salt in warm water and add it to each battery cell.

Fabric Softener

Using liquid fabric softener

End clinging dust on your TV

Are you frustrated to see dust fly back onto your television screen, or other plastic surfaces, right after cleaning them? To eliminate the static cling that attracts dust, simply dampen your dust cloth with fabric softener straight from the bottle and dust as usual.

Remove old wallpaper

Removing old wallpaper is a snap with fabric softener. Just stir 1 capful of liquid softener into 1 quart (1 liter) of water and sponge the solution onto the wallpaper. Let it soak in for 20 minutes, then scrape the paper from the wall. If the wallpaper has a water-resistant coating, score it with a wire-bristle brush before treating with the fabric softener solution.

Remove hair-spray residue

Dried-on overspray from hair spray can be tough to remove from walls and vanities, but even a buildup of residue is no match for a solution of 1 part liquid fabric softener to 2 parts water. Stir to blend, pour into a spray bottle, spritz the surface, and polish it with a dry cloth.

Abolish carpet shock

To eliminate static shock when you walk across your carpet, spray the carpet with a fabric softener solution. Dilute 1 cup of softener with 2 1/2 quarts (2.5 liters) of water; fill a spray bottle and lightly spritz the carpet. Take care not to saturate it and damage the carpet backing. Spray in the evening and let the carpet dry overnight before walking on it. The effect should last for several weeks.

Clean now, not later

Clean glass tables, shower doors, and other hard surfaces, and repel dust with liquid fabric softener. Mix 1 part softener into 4 parts water and store in a squirt bottle, such as an empty dishwashing liquid bottle. Apply a little solution to a clean cloth, wipe the surface, and then polish with a dry cloth.

Float away baked-on grime

Forget scrubbing. Instead, soak burned-on foods from casseroles with liquid fabric softener. Fill the casserole with water, add a squirt of liquid fabric softener, and soak for an hour, or until residue wipes easily away.

Untangle and condition hair

Liquid fabric softener diluted in water and applied after shampooing can untangle and condition fine, flyaway hair, as well as curly, coarse hair. Experiment with the amount of conditioner to match it to the texture of your hair, using a weaker solution for fine hair and a stronger solution for coarse, curly hair. Comb through your hair and rinse.

Keep paintbrushes pliable

After using a paintbrush, clean the bristles thoroughly and rinse them in a coffee can full of water with a drop of liquid fabric softener mixed in. After rinsing, wipe the bristles dry and store the brush as usual.

Remove hard-water stains

Hard-water stains on windows can be difficult to remove. To speed up the process, dab full-strength liquid fabric softener onto the stains and let it soak for 10 minutes. Then wipe the softener and stain off the glass with a damp cloth and rinse.

Make your own fabric softener sheets

Fabric softener sheets are convenient to use, but they're no bargain when compared to the price of liquid softeners. You can make your own dryer sheets and save money. Just moisten an old washcloth with 1 teaspoon of liquid softener and toss it into the dryer with your next load.

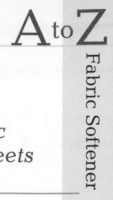
Using fabric softener sheets

Pick up pet hair

Pet hair can get a pretty tenacious grip on furniture and clothing. But a used fabric softener sheet will suck that fur right off the fabric with a couple of swipes. Just toss the fuzzy wipe into the trash.

End car odors

Has that new-car smell gradually turned into that old-car stench? Tuck a new dryer fabric softener sheet under each car seat to counteract musty odors and cigarette smells.

Lift burned-on casserole residue

Those sheets will soften more than fabric. The next time food gets burned onto your casserole dish, save the elbow grease. Instead fill the dish with hot water and toss in three or four used softener sheets. Soak overnight, remove the sheets, and you'll have no trouble washing away the residue. Be sure to rinse well.

Freshen drawers

There's no need to buy scented drawer-liner paper; give your dresser drawers a fresh-air fragrance by tucking a new dryer fabric softener sheet under existing drawer liners, or tape one to the back of each drawer.

THE SECRET BEHIND FABRIC SOFTENERS

How does fabric softener reduce cling as well as soften clothes? The secret is in the electrical charges. Positively charged chemical lubricants in the fabric softener are attracted to your load of negatively charged clothes, softening the fabric. The softened fabrics create less friction, and less static, as they rub against each other in the dryer, and because fabric softener attracts moisture, the slightly damp surface of the fabrics makes them electrical conductors. As a result, the electrical charges travel through them instead of staying on the surface to cause static cling and sparks as you pull the clothing from the dryer.

Wipe soap scum from shower door

Tired of scrubbing scummy shower doors? It's easy to wipe the soap scum off the glass with a used dryer fabric softener sheet.

Repel dust from electrical appliances

Because television and PC screens are electrically charged, they actually attract dust, making dusting them a never-ending chore, but not if you dust them with used dryer softener sheets. These sheets are designed to reduce static cling, so they remove the dust,

and keep it from resettling for several days or more.

Do away with doggy odor

If your best friend comes in from the rain and smells like a...well...wet dog, wipe him down with a used dryer softener sheet, and he'll smell as fresh as a daisy.

Freshen laundry hampers and wastebaskets

There's still plenty of life left in used dryer fabric softener sheets. Toss one into the bottom of a laundry hamper or wastebasket to counteract odors.

Tame locker-room and sneaker smells

Deodorizing sneakers and gym bags calls for strong stuff. Tuck a new dryer fabric softener sheet into each sneaker and leave overnight to neutralize odors (just remember to pull them out before wearing the sneaks). Drop a dryer sheet into the bottom of a gym bag and leave it there until your nose lets you know it's time to renew it.

Prevent musty odors in suitcases

Place a single, unused dryer fabric softener sheet into an empty suitcase

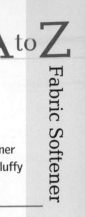

⊕ TAKE CARE People with allergies or chemical sensitivities may develop rashes or skin irritations when they come into contact with laundry treated with some commercial fabric softeners or fabric softener sheets. If you are sensitive to softeners, you can still soften your laundry by substituting 1/4 cup of white vinegar or the same amount of your favorite hair conditioner to your washer's last rinse cycle for softer, fresher-smelling washables.

tennis shoes and a fabric softener sheet, and they will come out fluffy and with silky-soft fur.

Substitute a dryer sheet for a tack cloth

Sticky tack cloths are designed to pick up all traces of sawdust on a woodworking project before you paint or varnish it, but they are expensive and not always easy to find at the hardware store. If you find yourself in the middle of a project without a tack cloth, substitute an unused dryer fabric softener sheet; it will attract sawdust and hold it like a magnet.

or other piece of luggage before storing. The bag will smell great the next time you use it.

Buff chrome to a brilliant shine

After chrome is cleaned, it can still look streaky and dull, but whether it's your toaster or your hubcaps, you can easily buff up the shine with a used dryer softener sheet.

Use as a safe mosquito repellent

For a safe mosquito repellent, look no farther than your laundry room. Save used dryer fabric softener sheets and pin or tie one to your clothing when you go outdoors to help repel mosquitoes.

Use an inconspicuous air freshener

Don't spend hard-earned money on those plug-in air fresheners. Just tuck a few sheets of dryer fabric softener

into closets, behind curtains, and under chairs.

Do away with static cling

You'll never be embarrassed by static cling again if you keep a used fabric softener sheet in your purse or dresser drawer. When faced with static, dampen the sheet and rub it over your pantyhose to put an end to clinging skirts.

Keep dust off blinds

Cleaning Venetian blinds is a tedious chore, so make the results last by wiping them down with a used dryer fabric softener sheet to repel dust. Wipe them with another sheet whenever the effect wears off.

Renew grubby stuffed toys

Wash fake-fur stuffed animals in the washing machine set on gentle cycle, then put the stuffed animals into the clothes dryer along with a pair of old

Consolidate sheets and make them smell pretty

To improve sheet storage, store the sheet set in one of the matching pillowcases, and tuck a new dryer fabric softener sheet into the packet for a fresh fragrance.

Abolish tangled sewing thread

To put an end to tangled thread, keep an unused dryer fabric softener sheet in your sewing kit. After threading the needle, insert it into the sheet and pull all of the thread through to give it a nonstick coating.

Film Canisters

Rattle toy for the cat

Cats are amused by small objects that rattle and shake, and they really don't care what they look like. To provide endless entertainment for your cat, drop a few dried beans, a spoonful of dry rice, or other small objects that can't harm a cat, into an empty film canister, snap on the lid, and watch the fun begin.

Handy stamp dispenser

To keep a roll of stamps from being damaged, make a stamp dispenser from an empty film canister. Hold the canister steady by taping it to a counter with duct tape, and use a utility knife to carefully cut a slit into the side of the canister. Drop the roll of stamps in, feed it out through the slit, snap the cap on, and it's ready to use.

Use as hair rollers

You can collect all the hair rollers you'll ever need if you save your empty plastic film canisters. To use, pop the top off, roll damp hair around the canister, and hold it in place by fastening a hair clip over the open end of the canister and your hair.

Emergency sewing kit

You'll never be at a loss if you pop a button or your hem unravels if you fill an empty film canister with buttons, pins, and a pre-threaded needle. Make several; tuck one into each travel bag, purse, or gym bag, and hit the road.

On-the-road pill dispensers

Use empty film canisters as travel-size pill bottles for your purse or overnight bag. If you take more than one medication, use a separate canister for each. Write the medication and dosage on a peel-and-stick label and attach to each canister. For at-a-glance identification, color the labels with different-colored highlighter pens.

Store fishing flies

You can save a lot of money and grief by storing fishing flies and hooks in film canisters. They don't take up much room in a fishing vest, and if you do drop one in a stream, the airtight lid will keep it floating long enough for you to...well...fish it out.

Carry spices for camp cooking

Just because you are roughing it, doesn't mean that you have to eat bland food. You can store a multitude of seasonings in individual film canisters to take along when you go camping, and you'll still have plenty of room for the food itself in your backpack or car trunk. It's a good idea for your RV or vacation cabin too.

Carry small change for laundry and tolls

Film canisters are just the right size to hold quarters and smaller change. Tuck a canister of change into your laundry bag or your car's glove compartment, and you'll never have to hunt for change when you're at a self-service laundry or a tollbooth.

THE VANISHING FILM CANISTER

Plastic film canisters have myriad uses, from emergency ashtrays to spice bottles. But with the rise of digital cameras, these small wonders are rapidly going the way of the rotary dial phone or the phonograph needle. A good source for free film canisters has always been the neighborhood one-hour photo shop. But these days you may find that even they have a canister shortage. If so, check the yellow pages for a **professional film developer,** because most high-quality, professional photographers still use film—and film canisters.

Bring your own diet aids

If you are on a special diet, you can easily and discreetly transport your favorite salad dressings, artificial sweetener, or other condiments to restaurants in plastic film canisters. Clean, empty canisters hold single-sized servings, have snap-on, leakproof lids, and are small enough to tuck into a purse.

Keep jewelry close at hand

An empty film canister doesn't take up much room in your gym bag, and it'll come in handy for keeping your rings and earrings from being misplaced while you work out.

Emergency nail polish remover

Create a small, spillproof carry case for nail polish remover by tucking a small piece of sponge into a plastic film canister. Saturate the sponge with polish remover and snap on the lid. For an emergency repair, simply insert a finger and rub the nail against the fluid-soaked sponge to remove the polish.

Flour

Safe paste for children's crafts

Look no farther than your kitchen canister for an inexpensive, nontoxic paste that is ideal for children's papercraft projects, such as papier-mâché and scrap-booking. To make the paste, add 3 cups of cold water to a saucepan and blend in 1 cup of all-purpose flour. Stirring constantly, bring the mixture to a boil. Reduce heat and simmer, stirring until smooth and thick. Cool and pour into a plastic squeeze bottle to use. This simple paste will keep for weeks in the refrigerator, and cleans up easily with soap and water.

Freshen playing cards

After a few games, cards can accumulate a patina of snack residue and hand oil, but you can restore them with some all-purpose flour in a paper bag.

Drop the cards into the bag with enough flour to cover, shake vigorously, and remove the cards. The flour will absorb the oils, and it can be easily knocked off the cards by giving them a vigorous shuffle.

Repel ants with flour

Sprinkle a line of flour along the backs of pantry shelves and wherever you see ants entering the house. Repelled by the flour, ants won't cross over the line.

Make modeling clay

Keep the kids busy on a rainy day with modeling clay—they can even help you make the stuff. Knead together 3 cups of all-purpose flour, 1/4 cup of salt, 1 cup of water, 1 tablespoon of vegetable oil, and 1 or 2 drops food coloring. If the mixture is sticky, add more flour; if it's too stiff, add more water. When the "clay" is a workable consistency, store it until needed in a self-sealing plastic bag.

Polish brass and copper

No need to go out and buy cleaner for your brass and silver. You can whip up your own at much less cost. Just combine equal parts of flour, salt, and vinegar, and mix into a paste. Spread the paste onto the metal, let it dry, and buff it off with a clean, dry cloth.

Bring back luster to a dull sink

To buff your stainless steel sink back to a warm glow, sprinkle flour over it and rub lightly with a soft, dry cloth. Then rinse the sink to restore its shine.

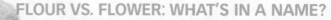

FLOUR VS. FLOWER: WHAT'S IN A NAME?

Ever wondered why the word flour is pronounced exactly like the word flower? Well, you may be surprised to learn that flour is actually derived from the **French word** for flower, which is fleur. The French use the word to describe the most desirable, or floury (flowery) and protein-rich, part of a grain after processing removes the hull. And, because much of our food terminology comes from the French, we still bake and make sauces with the **flower of grains,** such as wheat, which we call flour.

Hair Conditioner

Take off makeup

Put your face first. Why buy expensive makeup removers when a perfectly good substitute sits in your shower stall? Hair conditioner quickly and easily removes makeup for much less money than name-brand makeup removers.

Unstick a ring

Grandma's antique ring just got stuck on your middle finger. Now what? Grab a bottle of hair conditioner and slick down the finger. The ring should slide right off.

Protect your shoes in foul weather

Here's a way to keep salt and chemicals off your shoes during the winter: Lather your shoes or boots with hair conditioner to protect them from winter's harsh elements. It's a good leather conditioner too.

Lubricate a zipper

You're racing out the door, throwing on your jacket, and dang! Your zipper's stuck, so you yank and pull until it finally zips up. A dab of hair conditioner rubbed along the zipper teeth can help you avoid this bother next time.

Smooth shave-irritated legs

After you shave your legs, they may feel rough and irritated. Rub on hair conditioner; it acts like a lotion and can soothe the hurt away.

SOME FACTS ABOUT HAIR AND HAIR CONDITIONER

Hair conditioner has been around for about 50 years. While researching ways to help World War II **burn victims,** Swiss chemists developed a compound that improved the health of hair. In the 1950s other scientists developing **fabric softeners** found that the same material could soften hair.

Despite our efforts to keep hair healthy with hair conditioner, we still lose on average between 50 and 100 strands a day. For most of us, thankfully, there are still many more strands left: People with blond hair have an average of 140,000 strands of hair, brown-haired people, 100,000, and redheads, 90,000.

Smooth-sliding shower curtain

Tired of yanking on the shower curtain? Instead of closing smoothly, does it stutter along the curtain rod, letting the shower spray water onto the floor? Rub the rod with hair conditioner, and the curtain will glide across it.

Prevent rust on tools

Every good do-it-yourselfer knows how important it is to take care of the tools in your toolbox. One way to condition them and keep rust from invading is to rub them down with hair conditioner.

Oil skate wheels

Do your child's skateboard wheels whine? Or are the kids complaining about their in-line and roller skates sticking? Try this trick: Rub hair conditioner on the axles of the wheels, and they'll be down the block with their rehabilitated equipment in no time.

Shine stainless steel

Forget expensive stainless steel polishers. Apply hair conditioner to your faucets, golf clubs, chrome fixtures, or anything else that needs a shine. Rub it off with a soft cloth, and you'll be impressed with the gleam.

Clean silk garments

Do you dare to ignore that "dry clean only" label in your silk shirt? Here's a low-cost alternative to sending it out. Fill the sink with water (warm water for whites and cold water for colors). Add a tablespoon of hair conditioner. Immerse the shirt in the water and let it sit for a few minutes. Then pull it out, rinse, and hang it up to dry. The conditioner keeps the shirt feeling silky smooth.

Hair Spray

Exterminate houseflies

An annoying, buzzing housefly has been bobbing and weaving around your house for two days. Make it bite the dust with a squirt of hair spray. Take aim and fire. Watch the fly drop. But make sure the hair spray is water-soluble so that if any spray hits the walls, you'll be able to wipe it clean. Works on wasps and bees too.

Reduce runs in pantyhose

Often those bothersome runs in your pantyhose or stockings start at the toes. Head off a running disaster by spraying hair spray on the toes of a new pair of pantyhose. The spray strengthens the threads and makes them last longer.

Remove lipstick from fabric

Has someone been kissing your shirts? Apply hair spray to the lipstick stain and let it sit for a few minutes. Wipe off the hair spray and the stain should come off with it. Then wash your shirts as usual.

Preserve a Christmas wreath

When you buy a wreath at your local Christmas tree lot, it's fresh, green, and lush. By the time a week has gone by, it's starting to shed needles and look a little dry. To make the wreath last longer, grab your can of hair spray and spritz it all over as soon as you get the fresh wreath home. The hair spray traps the moisture in the needles.

Preserve your shoes' shine

After you've lovingly polished your shoes to give them the just-from-the-store look, lightly spray them with hair spray. The shoe polish won't rub off so easily with this coat of protection.

Keep recipe cards splatter-free

Don't let the spaghetti sauce on the stove splatter on your favorite recipe card. A good coating of hair spray will prevent the card from being ruined by kitchen eruptions. With the protection, they wipe off easily.

Keep drapes dirt-free

Did you just buy new drapes or have your old ones cleaned? Want to keep that like-new look for a while? The trick is to apply several coats of hair spray, letting each coat dry thoroughly before the next one.

Remove ink marks on garments

Your toddler just went wild with a ballpoint pen on your white upholstery and your new shirt. Squirt the stain with hair spray and the pen marks should come right off.

Extend the life of cut flowers

A bouquet of cut flowers is such a beautiful thing, you want to do whatever you can to postpone wilting. Just as it preserves your hairstyle, a spritz of hair spray can preserve your cut flowers. Stand a foot away from the bouquet and give them a quick spray, just on the undersides of the leaves and petals.

Protect children's artwork

Picture this: Your preschooler has just returned home with a priceless work of art, demanding that it find a place on the refrigerator door. Before you stick it up, preserve the creation with hair spray. This works especially well on chalk pictures, keeping them from being smudged so easily.

Great Moments in Hair-Spray History

- **L'Oréal** introduced its hair spray, called Elnett, in 1960. The next year **Alberto VO5** introduced its version.

- In 1964 hair spray surpassed lipstick as women's most popular cosmetic aid. Must have been all those beehive hairdos.

- In 1984 the hair spray on **Michael Jackson's** hair ignited while he was rehearsing a commercial for **Pepsi**.

Ice Cubes

Water hanging plants and Christmas trees

If you're constantly reaching for the step stool to water hard-to-reach hanging plants, ice cubes can help. Just toss several cubes into the pots. The ice melts and waters the plants and does it without causing a sudden downpour from the drain hole. This is also a good way to water your Christmas tree, whose base may be hard to reach with a watering can.

Remove dents in carpeting

If you've recently rearranged the furniture in your living room, you know that heavy pieces can leave ugly indents in your carpet. Use ice cubes to remove them. Put an ice cube, for example, on the spot where the chair leg stood. Let it melt, then brush up the dent. Rug rehab completed.

Smooth caulk seams

You're caulking around the bathtub, but the sticky caulk compound keeps adhering to your finger as you try to smooth it. If you don't do something about it, the finished job will look pretty awful. Solve the problem by running an ice cube along the caulk line. This forms the caulk into a nice even bead and the caulk will never stick to the ice cube.

Help iron out wrinkles

So your ready-to-wear shirt is full of wrinkles and there's no time to wash it again. Turn on the iron and wrap an ice cube in a soft cloth. Rub over the wrinkle just before you iron and the shirt will smooth out.

Mask the taste of medicine

No matter what flavor your local pharmacist offers in children's medicine, kids can still turn up their noses at the taste. Have them suck on an ice cube before taking the medicine. This numbs the taste buds and allows the medicine to go down, without the spoonful of sugar.

Pluck a splinter

Parental challenge #573: removing a splinter from the hand of a screaming, squirming toddler. Before you start jabbing with that needle, grab an ice cube and numb the area. This should make splinter removal more painless and quicker.

Prevent a blister from a burn

Have you burned yourself? An ice cube applied to the burn will stop it from blistering.

Cool water for your pets

Imagine what it's like to wear a fur coat in the middle of summer. Your rabbits, hamsters, and gerbils will love your thoughtfulness if you place a few cubes in their water dish to cool down. This is also a good tip for your cat, who's spent the hot morning lounging on your bed, or your dog, who's just had a long romp in the park.

Unstick a sluggish disposal

If your garbage disposal is not working at its optimum because of grease buildup (not something stuck inside), ice cubes may help. Throw some down the disposal and grind them up. The grease will cling to the ice, making the disposal residue-free.

Make creamy salad dressing

Do you want to make your homemade salad dressing as smooth and even as the bottled variety? Try this: Put all the dressing ingredients in a jar with a lid, then add a single ice cube. Close the lid and shake vigorously. Spoon out the ice cube and serve. Your guests will be impressed by how creamy your salad dressing is.

Stop sauces from curdling

Imagine this: Your snooty neighbors are over for a Sunday brunch featuring eggs Benedict. But when you mixed butter and egg yolks with lemon juice to make hollandaise sauce for the dish, it curdled. What do you do? Place an ice cube in the saucepan, stir, and watch the sauce turn back into a silky masterpiece.

De-fat soup and stews

Want to get as much fat as possible out of your homemade soup or stew as quickly as possible? Fill a metal ladle with ice cubes and skim the bottom of the ladle over the top of the liquid in the soup pot. Fat will collect on the ladle.

Reheat rice

Does your leftover rice dry out when you reheat it in the microwave? Try this: Put an ice cube on top of the rice when you put it in the microwave. The ice cube will melt as the rice reheats, giving the rice much-needed moisture.

Remove gum from clothing

You're just about to walk out the door when Junior points to the gum stuck to his pants. Keep your cool and grab an ice cube. Rub the ice on the gum to harden it, then scrape it off with a spoon.

SOME COLD, HARD FACTS ABOUT ICE CUBES

■ To make **clear ice cubes,** use distilled water and boil it first. It's the air in the water that causes ice cubes to turn cloudy.

■ A British Columbian company sells **fake ice cubes** that glow and blink in your drink.

■ Those aren't ice cubes in that inviting drink in the **print advertisement,** because they'd never last under hot studio lights. They're plastic or glass.

■ The **word ice cube** has been commercially co-opted over the years. To name two examples: a vintage candy (the chocolate pat wrapped in silver paper) and a well-known rapper/actor.

Keys

Weigh down drapery

Need to keep your draperies hanging properly? Just slip a few old keys in the hems. If you are worried about them falling out, tack them in place with a few stitches going through the holes in the keys. You can also keep blind cords from tangling by using keys as weights on their bottoms.

Make fishing sinkers

Old unused keys make great weights for your fishing line. Since they already have a hole in them, attaching them to the line is a cinch. Whenever you come across an unidentified key, toss it into your tackle box.

Create an instant plumb bob

You are getting ready to hang wallpaper and you need to draw a perfectly vertical line on the wall to get you started. Take a length of cord or string and tie a key or two to one end. You've got a plumb bob that will give you a true vertical. You can do the same with a pair of scissors too.

Kool-Aid

Color wall paints

Mix any flavor of unsweetened Kool-Aid into water-based latex paint to alter its color. Or mix unsweetened Kool-Aid with water to create your own watercolors, but don't give them to the kids—Kool-Aid stains can be tough to remove.

Make play makeup lip gloss

Make some tasty lip gloss for little girls playing dress-up. Let the girls pick their favorite presweetened Kool-Aid flavor. Blend a package of the drink mix with 3 tablespoons of vegetable shortening, then microwave for one minute. Transfer to a 35mm film canister and refrigerate overnight.

Clean your dishwasher

Is the inside of your dishwasher rusty brown? The cause is a high iron content in your water. Dump a packet of unsweetened lemonade Kool-Aid into the soap drawer and run the washer through a hot-water cycle. When you open the door, the inside will be as white as the day you bought the machine.

Clean rust from concrete

Nasty rust stains on your concrete? Mix unsweetened lemonade Kool-Aid with hot water. Scrub and the rust stain should come right out.

Lemons

Using lemons around the house

Eliminate fireplace odor

There's nothing cozier on a cold winter night than a warm fire burning in the fireplace—unless the fire happens to smell horrible. Next time you have a fire that sends a stench into the room, try throwing a few lemon peels into the flames. Or simply burn some lemon peels along with your firewood as a preventive measure.

Get rid of tough stains on marble

You probably think of marble as stone, but it is really petrified calcium (also known as old seashells). That explains why it is so porous and easily stained and damaged. Those stains can be hard to remove, but here is a simple method that should do the trick: Cut a lemon in half, dip the exposed flesh into some table salt, and rub it vigorously on the stain. You will be amazed how well it works!

Make a room scent/humidifier

Freshen and moisturize the air in your home on dry winter days. Make your own room scent that also doubles as a humidifier. If you have a wood-burning stove, place an enameled cast-iron pot or bowl on top, fill with water, and add lemon (and/or orange) peels, cinnamon sticks, cloves, and apple skins. No wood-burning stove? Use your stovetop instead and just simmer the water periodically.

Neutralize cat-box odor

You don't have to use an aerosol spray to neutralize foul-smelling cat-box odors or freshen the air in your bathroom. Just cut a couple of lemons in half. Then place them, cut side up, in a dish in the room, and the air will soon smell lemon-fresh.

Deodorize a humidifier

When your humidifier starts to smell funky, deodorize it with ease: Just pour 3 or 4 teaspoons of lemon juice into the water. It will not only remove the off odor but will replace it with a lemon-fresh fragrance. Repeat every couple of weeks to keep the odor from returning.

Polish chrome

Get rid of mineral deposits and polish chrome faucets and other tarnished chrome. Simply rub lemon rind over the chrome and watch it shine! Rinse well and dry with a soft cloth.

Using lemons in the kitchen

Brighten dull aluminum

Make those dull pots and pans sparkle, inside and out. Just rub the cut side of half a lemon all over them and buff with a soft cloth.

Deodorize your garbage disposal

If your garbage disposal is beginning to make your sink smell yucky, here's an easy way to deodorize it: Save leftover lemon and orange peels and toss them down the drain. To keep it smelling fresh, repeat once every month.

Refresh cutting boards

No wonder your kitchen cutting board smells! After all, you use it to chop onions, crush garlic, cut raw and cooked meat and chicken, and prepare fish. To get rid of the smell and help sanitize the cutting board, rub it all over with the cut side of half a lemon or wash it in undiluted juice straight from the bottle.

Keep guacamole green

You've been making guacamole all day long for the big party, and you don't want it to turn brown on top before the guests arrive. The solution: Sprinkle a liberal amount of fresh lemon juice over it and it will stay fresh and green. The flavor of the

BEFORE YOU SQUEEZE THAT LEMON

To get the most juice out of fresh lemons, bring them to room temperature and **roll them** under your palm against the kitchen counter before squeezing. This will break down the connective tissue and juice-cell walls, allowing the lemon to release more liquid when you squeeze it. This also works well for getting the most out of oranges and grapefruits.

lemon juice is a natural complement to the avocados in the guacamole. Make the fruit salad hours in advance too. Just squeeze some lemon juice onto the apple slices, and they'll stay snowy white.

Using lemons in the laundry

Bleach delicate fabrics

Ordinary household chlorine bleach can cause the iron in water to precipitate out into fabrics, leaving additional stains. For a mild, stain-free bleach, soak your delicates in a mixture of lemon juice and baking soda for at least half an hour before washing.

Remove unsightly underarm stains

Avoid expensive dry-cleaning bills. You can remove unsightly underarm stains from shirts and blouses simply by scrubbing them with a mixture of equal parts lemon juice (or white vinegar) and water.

Boost laundry detergent

To remove rust and mineral discolorations from cotton T-shirts and briefs, pour 1 cup of lemon juice into the washer during the wash cycle. The natural bleaching action of the juice will zap the stains and leave the clothes smelling fresh.

Rid clothes of mildew

You unpack the clothes you've stored for the season and discover that some of the garments are stained with mildew. To get rid of mildew on clothes, make a paste of lemon juice and salt and rub it on the affected area, then dry the clothes in sunlight. Repeat the process until the stain is gone. This works well for rust stains on clothes too.

Whiten clothes

Diluted or straight, lemon juice is a safe and effective fabric whitener when added to your wash water. Your clothes will also come out smelling lemon-fresh.

Using lemons for health and beauty

Lighten age spots

Before buying expensive medicated creams to lighten unsightly liver spots and freckles, try this: Apply lemon juice directly to the area, let sit for 15 minutes, and then rinse your skin clean. Lemon juice is a safe and effective skin-lightening agent.

Create blond highlights

For blond highlights worthy of the finest beauty salon, add 1/4 cup of lemon juice to 3/4 cup of water and rinse your hair with the mixture. Then sit in the sun until your hair dries. Lemon juice is a natural bleach. Don't forget to put on plenty of sunscreen before you sit out in the sun. To maximize the effect, repeat once daily for up to a week.

Clean and whiten nails

Pamper your fingernails without the help of a manicurist. Add the juice of 1/2 lemon to 1 cup of warm water and soak your fingertips in the mixture for

THE POOR LEMON TREE AND ITS AMAZING FRUIT

With all due respect to **Trini Lopez** and his rendition of "Lemon Tree," a lemon tree actually isn't very pretty—and its flower isn't sweet either. The tree's **straggly branches** bear little resemblance to an orange tree's dense foliage, and its **purplish flowers** lack the pleasant fragrance of orange blossoms. Yes, the fruit of the "poor lemon" is sour—thanks to its high citric acid content—but it is hardly "impossible to eat." Sailors have been sucking on vitamin C-rich lemons for hundreds of years to prevent scurvy. To this day, the British navy requires ships to carry enough lemons so that every sailor can have one ounce of juice daily.

5 minutes. After pushing back the cuticles, rub some lemon peel back and forth against the nail.

Cleanse your face

Clean and exfoliate your face by washing it with lemon juice. You can also dab lemon juice on blackheads to draw them out during the day. Your skin should improve after several days of treatment.

Freshen your breath

Make an impromptu mouthwash using lemon juice straight from the bottle. Rinse with the juice and then swallow it for longer-lasting fresh breath. The citric acid in the juice alters the pH level in your mouth, killing the bacteria that cause bad breath. Rinse after a few minutes, because long-term exposure to the acid in the lemon can harm tooth enamel.

Treat flaky dandruff

If itchy, scaly dandruff has you scratching your head, relief may be no farther away than your refrigerator. Just massage 2 tablespoons of lemon juice into your scalp and rinse with water. Then stir 1 teaspoon of lemon juice into 1 cup of water and rinse your hair with it. Repeat this daily until your dandruff disappears. No more itchy scalp, and your hair will smell lemon-fresh.

Soften dry, scaly elbows

It's bad enough that your elbows are dry and itchy, but they look terrible too. Your elbows will look and feel better after a few treatments with this regimen: Mix baking soda and lemon juice to make an abrasive paste. Then rub the paste into your elbows for a soothing, smoothing, and exfoliating treatment.

Remove berry stains

Sure it was fun to pick your own berries, but now your fingers are stained with berry juice that won't come off with soap and water. Try washing your hands with undiluted lemon juice. Wait a few minutes and wash with warm, soapy water. Repeat if necessary until the stain is completely gone.

Soothe poison ivy rash

You won't need an ocean of calamine lotion the next time poison ivy comes a-creeping around. Just apply lemon juice full-strength directly to the affected area to soothe itching and alleviate the rash.

Relieve rough hands and sore feet

You don't have to take extreme measures to soothe your extremities. If you have rough hands or sore feet, rinse them in a mixture of equal parts lemon juice and water, then massage with olive oil and dab dry with a soft cloth.

Remove warts

You've tried countless remedies to get rid of your warts, and nothing seems to work. Next time, try this: Apply a dab of lemon juice directly to the wart, using a cotton swab. Repeat for several days until the acids in the lemon juice dissolve the wart completely.

Magnets

Clean up a nail spill

Keep a strong magnet on your workbench. Next time you spill a jar of small items like nails, screws, tacks, or washers, save time and energy and let the magnet help pick them up for you.

Prevent a frozen car lock

Here's a great way to use refrigerator magnets during the bitter cold of winter. Place them over the outside door locks of your car overnight and they will keep the locks from freezing.

Keep your desk drawer neat

Are your paper clips all over the place? Place a magnet in your office desk drawer to keep the paper clips together.

Don't lose your gas cap

If your car's gas cap isn't attached, mount a magnet near the opening to the gas tank to hold the cap while you are filling up.

Replace your pincushion

In your sewing box, use a small magnet to keep your straight pins from flying all over the place.

THE AMAZING, EVER-PUZZLING MAGNET

Ancient Chinese and Greeks discovered that certain rare stones, called **lodestones,** seem to magically attract bits of iron and always pointed in the same direction when allowed to swing freely. Manmade magnets come in many shapes and sizes, but every magnet has a **north pole** and a **south pole.** If you break a magnet into pieces, each piece, no matter how small, will have a north and south pole. The magnetic field, which every magnet creates, has long been used to harness energy, although scientists still don't know for sure what it is!

Mayonnaise

Condition your hair

Hold the mayo...and massage it into your hair and scalp just as you would any fine conditioner! Cover your head with a shower cap, wait several minutes, and shampoo. The mayonnaise will moisturize your hair and give it a lustrous sheen.

Give yourself a facial

Why waste money on expensive creams when you can treat yourself to a soothing facial with whole-egg mayonnaise from your own refrigerator? Gently spread the mayonnaise over your face and leave it on for about 20 minutes. Then wipe it off and rinse with cool water. Your face will feel clean and smooth.

Strengthen your fingernails

To add some oomph to your fingernails, just plunge them into a bowl of mayonnaise every so often. Keep them bathed in the mayo for about 5 minutes and then wash with warm water.

Relieve sunburn pain

Did someone forget to put on sunscreen? To treat dry, sunburned skin, slather mayonnaise liberally over the affected area. The mayonnaise will relieve the pain and moisturize the skin.

Remove dead skin

Soften and remove dead skin from elbows and feet. Rub mayonnaise over the dry, rough tissue, leave it on for 10 minutes, and wipe it away with a damp cloth.

Safe way to kill head lice

Many dermatologists now recommend using mayonnaise to kill and remove head lice from kids instead of toxic prescription drugs and over-the-counter preparations. What's more, lice are becoming more resistant to such chemical treatments. To treat head lice with mayonnaise, massage a liberal amount of mayonnaise into the hair and scalp before bedtime. Cover with a shower cap to maximize the effect. Shampoo in the morning and then use a fine-tooth comb to remove any remaining lice and nits. To completely eradicate the infestation, repeat the treatment in 7 to 10 days.

Remove crayon marks

Did the kids leave crayon marks on your wood furniture? Here's a simple way to remove them that requires hardly any elbow grease: Simply rub some mayonnaise on the crayon marks and let it soak in for several minutes. Then wipe the surface clean with a damp cloth.

Clean piano keys

If the keys to your piano are starting to yellow, just tickle the ivories with a little mayonnaise applied with a soft cloth. Wait a few minutes, wipe with a damp cloth, and buff. The piano keys will look like new.

Remove bumper stickers

Time to get rid of that **"Nixon for President"** bumper sticker on your car? Instead of attacking it with a razor and risk scratching the bumper, rub some mayonnaise over the entire sticker. Let it sit for several minutes and wipe it off. The mayonnaise will dissolve the glue.

Get tar off your car

To get road tar or pine sap off your car with ease, slather some mayonnaise over the affected area, let it sit for several minutes, and wipe it away with a clean, soft rag.

Meat Tenderizer

Ease backache

To relieve your aching back, mix sufficient water with meat tenderizer to make a paste and rub it on your back where it hurts. The enzymes in the tenderizer will help soothe those aching back muscles.

Relieve wasp-sting pain

Make a paste of meat tenderizer and water and apply it directly to the sting from a bee or wasp. Be careful not to push any remaining part of the stinger deeper into your skin. The enzymes in the meat tenderizer will break down the proteins in the insect venom.

Remove protein-based stains

Try a little tenderness to remove any protein-based stains like milk, chocolate, and blood from clothes. For fresh wet stains, sprinkle on enough meat tenderizer to cover the area and let it sit for an hour. Then brush off the dried tenderizer and launder as usual. For stains that are already set, mix water and meat tenderizer to make a paste and rub it into the stain. Wait an hour before laundering as usual.

"Tenderize" tough perspiration stains

Tenderize away hard-to-remove perspiration stains. Before you wash that sweat-stained sweatshirt (or any other perspiration-stained garment), dampen the stain and then sprinkle some meat tenderizer on it. Then just wash as usual.

The Dinner That Lead to Adolph's Tenderizer

When **Lloyd Rigler** and **Lawrence Deutsch** dined at **Adolph Rempp's** Los Angeles restaurant one night in 1949, they had no clue that their fortunes were about to change forever. But the two partners were so impressed with the **tender, flavorful meat** they were served that they soon bought the rights to the product now known as Adolph's Meat Tenderizer.

Rigler toured the country—visiting 63 cities in 60 days—demonstrating the product, winning over skeptical food critics by sending them home with tenderized meat to cook themselves. Rave reviews led to windfall sales and profits, allowing the partners to sell the business in 1974 and turn their attention to philanthropy and the arts for the rest of their lives.

Milk

Make frozen fish taste fresh

If you want fish from your freezer to taste like it was fresh caught, try this trick: Place the frozen fish in a bath of milk until it thaws. The milk will make it taste fresher.

Boost corn-on-the-cob flavor

Here's a simple way to make corn on the cob taste sweeter and fresher. Just add 1/4 cup of powdered milk to the pot of boiling water before you toss in the corn.

Soothe sunburn and bug bites

If your skin feels like it's burning up from too much sun exposure or if itchy bug bites are driving you crazy, try using a little milk paste for soothing relief. Mix one part powdered milk with two parts water and add a pinch or two of salt. Dab it on the burn or bite. The enzymes in the milk powder will help neutralize the insect-bite venom and help relieve sunburn pain.

Impromptu makeup remover

When you run out of makeup remover and you can't get to the store, use powdered milk instead. Just mix 3 tablespoons of powdered milk with 1/3 cup of warm water in a jar and shake well. Add more water or powder as necessary to achieve the consistency of heavy cream. Now you are ready to apply your makeshift makeup remover with a facecloth. When you're done, wipe it off and rinse with water.

Give yourself a facial

Here's another way to give yourself a fancy spa facial at home. Make a mask by mixing 1/4 cup of powdered milk with enough water to form a thick paste. Thoroughly coat your face with the mixture, let dry completely, then rinse with warm water. Your face will feel fresh and rejuvenated.

Soften skin

Treat yourself to a luxurious foamy milk bath. Toss 1/2 cup or so of powdered milk into the tub as it fills. Milk acts as a natural skin softener.

Clean and soften dirty hands

You come back from the garden with stained and gritty hands. Regular soap just won't do, but this will: Make a paste of oatmeal and milk and rub it vigorously on your hands. The stains will be gone and the oatmeal-and-milk mixture will soften and soothe your skin.

Clean patent leather

Make your patent-leather purses or shoes look like new again. Just dab on a little milk, let it dry, and buff with a soft cloth.

Remove ink stains from clothes

To remove ink stains from colored clothes, an overnight milk bath will often do the trick. Just soak the affected garment in milk overnight and launder as usual the next day.

Mouthwash

Clean computer monitor screen

Out of glass cleaner? A strong, alcohol-based mouthwash will work as well as, or better than, glass cleaner on your computer monitor or TV screen. Apply with a damp, soft cloth and buff dry. Remember to use only on glass screens, not liquid crystal displays! The alcohol can damage the material used in LCDs.

Cleanse your face

An antiseptic mouthwash makes a wonderful astringent for cleansing your face. Check the ingredients to make sure it does not contain sugar, then use as follows. Wash your face with warm, soapy water and rinse. Dab a cotton ball with mouthwash and gently wipe your face as you would with any astringent. You should feel a pleasant, tingling sensation. Rinse with warm water followed by a splash of cold water. Your face will look and feel clean and refreshed.

Treat athlete's foot

A sugarless antiseptic mouthwash may be all you need to treat mild cases of athlete's foot or toenail

MAKE YOUR OWN MOUTHWASH

Freshen your breath with your own **alcohol-free** mouthwash. Place 1 ounce (30 grams) whole **cloves** and/or 3 ounces (85 grams) fresh **rosemary** in a pint-size (half-liter) **jar** and pour in 2 cups of boiling water. Cover the jar tightly and let it steep overnight before straining. Need a mouthwash immediately? Dissolve 1/2 teaspoon of **baking soda** in 1/2 cup of warm water.

fungus. Use a cotton ball soaked in mouthwash to apply to the affected area several times a day. Be prepared: It will sting a bit! Athlete's foot should respond after a few days. Toenail fungus may take up to several months. If you do not see a response by then, make an appointment with a dermatologist or podiatrist.

Add to wash water

Smelly gym socks are often full of bacteria and fungi that may not all come out in the wash—unless you add a cup of alcohol-based, sugarless mouthwash during the regular wash cycle.

Cure underarm odor

Regular deodorants mask unpleasant underarm odors with a heavy perfume smell but do little to attack the cause of the problem. To get rid of the bacteria that cause perspiration odor, dampen a cotton ball with a sugarless, alcohol-based mouthwash and swab your armpits. If you've just shaved your armpits, it's best to wait for another day to try this.

Get rid of dandruff

To treat a bad case of dandruff, wash your hair with your regular shampoo; then rinse with an alcohol-based mouthwash. You can follow with your regular conditioner.

Clean your toilet

All out of your regular toilet bowl cleaner? Try pouring 1/4 cup of alcohol-based mouthwash into the bowl. Let it stand in the water for 1/2 hour, then swish with a toilet brush before flushing. The mouthwash will disinfect germs as it leaves your toilet bowl sparkling and clean.

Mustard

Relieve congestion

Relieve congestion with a mustard plaster just like Grandma used to make. Rub your chest with prepared mustard, soak a washcloth in hot water, wring it out, and place it over the mustard.

Make a facial mask

Pat your face with mild yellow mustard for a bracing facial that will soothe and stimulate your skin. Try it on a small test area first to make sure it will not be irritating.

Soothe an aching back

Take a bath in yellow mustard to relieve an aching back or arthritis pain. Simply pour a regular 6- to 8-ounce (175- to 240-ml) bottle of mustard into the hot water as the tub fills. Mix well and soak yourself for 15 minutes.

If you don't have time for a bath, you can rub some mustard directly on the affected areas. Use only mild yellow mustard and make sure to apply it to a small test area first. Undiluted mustard may irritate your skin.

Relax stiff muscles

Next time you take a bath in Epsom salt, throw in a few tablespoons of yellow mustard too. The mustard will enhance the soothing effects of the Epsom salt and also help to relax stiff, sore muscles.

Remove skunk smell from car

You didn't see the skunk in the road until it was too late, and now your car exudes that foul aroma. Use mustard powder to get rid of those awful skunk odors. Pour 1 cup of dry mustard into

a bucket of warm water, mix well, and splash it on the tires, wheels, and underbody of the car. Your passengers will thank you.

Remove odor from bottles

You've got some nice bottles you'd like to keep, but after washing them, they still smell like whatever came in them. Mustard is a sure way to kill the smell. After washing, just squirt a little mustard into the bottle, fill with warm water, and shake it up. Rinse well, and the smell will be gone.

A Condensed History of Mustard

Ancient Romans brought mustard back from Egypt and used the seeds to flavor unfermented grape juice, called **must.** This is believed to be how the mustard plant got its name. The Romans also made a paste from the ground seeds for **medicinal purposes** and may have used it as a condiment. But the mustard we use today was first prepared in **Dijon, France,** in the 13th century. Dijon-style mustard is made from darker seeds than yellow mustard.

Nail Polish

Using nail polish around the house

Make buttons glow in the dark

It happens all the time. The lights are dimmed, you grab the remote control to increase the TV volume, and darn, you hit the wrong button and change the channel instead. To put an end to video flubs, dab glow-in-the-dark nail polish onto frequently used remote buttons. You can also use phosphorescent polish to mark keys and keyholes and other hard-to-spot items.

Mark your thermostat setting

When you wake up with a chill and don't have your glasses, it's easy to return to your comfort zone if you've marked your dial-type thermostat. Simply set it to your preferred temperature and then make a thin mark with colored nail polish from the dial into the outside ring.

Mark temperature settings on shower knobs

Don't waste precious shower time fiddling with the water temperature. With the shower on, select your ideal settings, then turn off the flow to the shower and make a small mark with bright nail

polish onto the stationary lip of both the hot and cold knob indicating the handle position that's best. Once it's set, no sweat!

Make cup measurements legible

Find your measuring cup markings faster, especially if you like to measure "on the fly" while cooking. Use a very visible color of nail polish to trace over the basic measurement levels. This also works great for those dimly lit, late-night bottle feedings, when you need to see how well Junior has tanked up. And you won't have to squint to find the correct dosage on little plastic medicine cups if you first mark them with a thin line of dark polish.

Mark levels inside a bucket

When you're mixing in a big bucket, you don't typically have the opportunity to lift the bucket to check the quantity. Besides, the bucket you use for mixing might not have the measurements clearly marked at all. Make sure you know you're using the right amounts by marking pint, quart, and gallon (or half, full, and other liter) levels with lines of nail polish. Use a color that stands out against the bucket's color.

Label your sports gear

You share a lot of interests with your golf partner, including the same brand of golf balls. Make it clear who got on the green first, by putting a dot of bright nail polish on your ball supply. This also works well with batting gloves and other items that don't have enough room to fit your name.

Label poison containers

If everyone in your home has easy access to your cupboard, prevent someone from grabbing dangerous items in haste. Use dark red or other easily visible nail polish to label the poisons. Draw an unmistakable X on the label as well as the lid or spout.

Seal an envelope

Do you have a mild distrust of those self-sealing envelopes? Brush a little nail polish along the underside of the flap, seal it, and it won't even open over a teakettle! Add some flair to a special card by brushing your initial (or any design) in nail polish over the sealed flap tip, as a modern type of sealing wax that doesn't need to be melted first.

Smudge-proof important drug labels

Preserve the important information on your prescription medicine and other important medicine labels with a coat of clear polish, and they won't be smudged as you grab them after getting your glass of water.

Waterproof address labels

When you're sending a parcel on a rainy day, a little clear polish brushed over the address information will make sure your package goes to the right place.

Prevent rust rings from metal containers

If your guests are going to peek into your medicine cabinet, you don't want them to see rust rings on your shelves. Brush nail polish around the bottom of shaving cream cans and other metal containers to avoid those unsightly stains.

Make a gleaming paperweight

To create paperweights that look like gemstones, or interesting rocks for the base of your potted cactus, try this:

Find some palm-size, smooth clean rocks. Put about 1/2 inch (13 mm) of water into a pie pan, and put 1 drop of clear nail polish onto the water. The polish will spread out over the water surface. Holding a rock with your fingertips, slowly roll it in the water to coat it with the polish. Set the rock on newspaper to dry.

Prevent rusty toilet seat screws

If you're installing a new toilet seat, keep those screws from quickly rusting. Paint them with a coat or two of clear nail polish; it will also help prevent seat wobble by keeping the screws in place.

HOW TO KEEP YOUR NAIL POLISH AT ITS BEST

- To keep nail polishes fresh and easy to use, store them in the **refrigerator.** Keep them together in a little square plastic container.
- Shaking a polish bottle to mix the color can cause **bubbles.** Roll the bottle between your palms instead.
- Wipe the **inside threads** of your nail polish bottle and cap with a cotton swab dipped in polish remover before closing them. It'll open more easily.

Paint shaker holes to restrict salt

If your favorite saltshaker dispenses a little too generously, paint a few of the holes shut with nail polish. It is a good idea for those watching their salt.

Tarnish-proof costume jewelry

Inexpensive costume jewelry can add sparkle and color to an everyday outfit, but not if it tarnishes and the tarnish rubs off the jewelry and onto your skin. To keep your fake jewelry and your skin sparkling clean, brush clear nail polish onto the back of each piece and allow it to dry before wearing.

Protect your belt buckle's shine

Cover new or just-shined belt buckles with a coat of clear polish. You'll prevent oxidation and guarantee a gleaming first impression.

Seal out scuffs on shoes

On leather shoes, it's the back and toes that really take the brunt of the wear and tear that leaves scratches on the surface. Next time you buy a new pair of shoes—especially ones for a kid or an active adult—give these areas the extra measure of protection they need. Paint a little clear nail polish on the outside of the back seam and over the toes. Rub the polish in a little to

Nail Polish's Long History

Nail polish is certainly not a recent concept. As early as 3000 B.C., ancient **Chinese nobility** are believed to have colored their long nails with polishes, made from gum arabic, beeswax, gelatin, and pigments. The nobility wore shades of gold, silver, red, or black, while lesser classes were restricted to pastel shades. Colored nails were also popular with **ancient Egyptians,** who often dyed their nails with henna or stained them with berries. Polish wasn't just for women. In Egypt and Rome, **military commanders** painted their nails red before going into battle.

feather out the shine of the polish. After it dries, you'll be a step ahead of those perennial shoe problems "driver's heel" and "jump rope toe."

Keep laces from unraveling

Neaten the appearance of frayed shoelaces, and extend their life. Dip the ends in clear nail polish and twist the raveled ends together. Repair laces in the evening so that the polish will dry overnight.

Get rid of a wart

Warts are unsightly, embarrassing, and infectious. In order to get rid of warts and prevent spreading the virus to others, cover them with nail polish. The wart should be gone or greatly diminished in one week.

Using nail polish for repairs

Mend a fingernail

You just split a nail, but don't have a nail repair kit handy? Grab an unused tea bag instead. Cut the bag open, dump the tea, cut a piece of the bag into the shape of your nail, and cover it with clear nail polish. Press it onto your nail, then apply colored nail polish. You'll be good to go until the break grows out.

Temporarily repair eyeglasses

So you sat on your glasses and one lens has a small crack, but you can't get to the optometrist right away? Seal the crack on both sides with a thin coat of clear nail polish. That will hold it together until you can see your way to the doctor's office.

Fill small nicks on floors and glass

Have the children been playing hockey on your hardwood floors? Fill those little nicks by dabbing them with some clear nail polish. It will dry shiny, so sand the spot gently with some 600-grit sandpaper. A thick coat of clear nail polish also helps to soften the sharp edge of a nicked mirror or glass pane.

Reset loose jewelry stones

If your jewelry has popped a stone or two, you don't have to put it in the "play dress-up" box yet. The stone can be reset using a little drop of clear nail polish as the "glue." It dries quickly, and the repair will be invisible.

Repair lacquered items

Did you chip a favorite lacquered vase or other lacquered item? Try mixing colors of nail polish to match the piece. Paint over the chipped area to make it less noticeable. Caution: You may lower the value of an antique by doing this, so you probably only want to try this with inexpensive items.

Plug a hole in your cooler

A small hole inside your cooler doesn't make it trash-worthy yet. Seal the hole with two coats of nail polish to hold in ice and other melted substances.

Fill washtub nicks

It's a mystery how they got there, but your washing machine tub has one or two nicks near the holes, and now you're concerned about snags in your clothes or even rust spots. Seal those nicks with some nail polish, feathering the edges so there is no lip.

Keep chipped car paint from rusting

If your car suffers small dings and chips, you can keep them from rusting or enlarging by dabbing clear nail polish onto the damaged areas.

Smooth wooden hangers

If you've noticed a few splinters or nicks in your wooden hangers, no need to toss them out. Brush some nail polish over the rough edges to smooth the surface again and keep your coat linings safe.

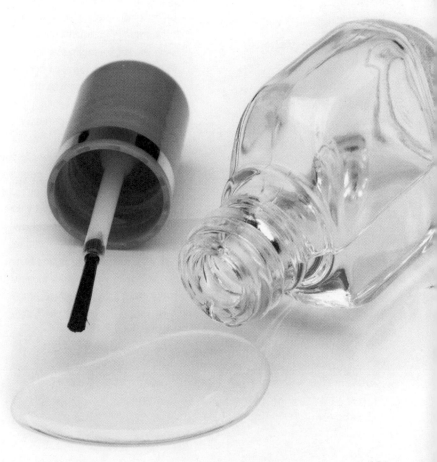

Tighten loose screws

You're not rough with your drawers and cabinets, but you find yourself tightening certain pull screws once too often. Keep them in place by brushing a little clear polish on the screw threads, insert the screws, and let dry before using again. This is also a great solution if you've been keeping a Phillips screwdriver in the kitchen for loose pot handles. You can also use clear nail polish to keep nuts on machine screws or bolts from coming loose, and if you need to take the nuts off, a twist with a wrench will break the seal.

Fix torn window shades

Got a little tear in your window shade? Don't worry. You can usually seal it with a dab of clear nail polish.

Using nail polish when sewing

Protect pearl buttons

Delicate pearl buttons will keep their brand-new sparkle with a protective coat of clear nail polish. It will keep costume pearl buttons from peeling as well.

Prevent loss of buttons

Keep that brand-new shirt in good shape by putting a drop of clear nail polish on the thread in the buttons. It prevents the thread from fraying, so taking this precaution in advance could save you some embarrassment later. Put a dab on just-repaired buttons also to keep them from coming off.

Make needle threading easier

Do you fumble with your needle and thread, licking and re-licking the frayed thread end until it's too floppy to go through the eye? Try dragging the cut thread end through the application brush of nail polish once or twice, and then roll the thread end between your thumb and forefinger. It will dry in a second, and your thread end stays stiff enough to thread in a flash. Your sewing box is a great retirement home for a nail color you no longer use.

Prevent frayed fabric from unraveling

Do you have wisps peeking out from the bottom of your skirt? Is the nylon lining of your jacket fraying at the cuffs? You can tame those fraying strays by brushing them into place with some clear nail polish.

Keep ribbons from fraying

The gift is perfect, so make sure the wrapping is just as nice. Brush the cut ends of ribbon with a little clear nail polish to stop them from unraveling. This is also the perfect solution for your little girl's hair ribbons on special occasions; at least one part of her will stay together all day!

Stop a run in your hose

It's a helpless feeling, realizing that a small run in your stocking is about to turn into a big embarrassment. Happily you can stop runs permanently and prolong the life of fragile stockings with a dab of clear nail polish. Simply apply polish to each end of a run (no need to remove hose), and let it dry. This invisible fix stops runs, and lasts through many hand launderings.

NAIL POLISH UNDER THE MICROSCOPE

Unless you work in a lab, you probably don't know that clear nail polish is the respected workhorse used in mounting **microscopic slides**. Officially referred to as NPM (nail polish mountant), it is the preferred and inexpensive substance used around a cover glass to seal it onto a slide, protecting the specimen from air and moisture.

Oatmeal

Treat itchy poison ivy or chicken pox

Take the itch out of a case of chicken pox or a poison ivy rash with a relaxing, warm oatmeal bath. Simply grind 1 cup of oatmeal in your blender until it is a fine powder, then pour it into a piece of cheesecloth, the foot section of a clean nylon stocking, or the leg of an old pantyhose. Knot the material, and tie it around the faucet of your bathtub so the bag is suspended under the running water. Fill the tub with lukewarm water and soak in it for 30 minutes. You may find additional relief by applying the oatmeal pouch directly to the rash or pox.

Add luxury to a regular bath

You don't have to have itchy skin to make a luxurious bath mix with oatmeal. And it beats buying expensive bath oils. All you need is 1 cup of oatmeal and your favorite scented oil, such as rose or lavender. Grind the oatmeal in a blender, put it in a cheesecloth bag, add a few drops of the scented oil, and suspend the bag under the running water as you fill your bathtub. You'll not only find it sweetly soothing, you can also use the oatmeal bag as a washcloth to exfoliate your skin.

Make a facial mask

If you're looking for a quick pick-me-up that will leave you feeling and looking better, give yourself an oatmeal facial. Combine

WHY OATMEAL COOKING TIMES VARY SO MUCH

Thirty minutes. Five minutes. One minute! Oatmeal cooking times depend on **how the oats were made** into oatmeal. After the inedible hull is removed, the oat is called a groat. If the groats are just cut into about four pieces, the oatmeal takes up to 30 minutes to cook. If the groats are steamed and rolled but not cut, it takes about five minutes. If they are steamed, rolled, and cut, the cooking time drops to a minute or so. Steaming, rolling, and cooking breaks down the fiber, so if you want a lot of fiber, use 30-minute oatmeal and cook it until it is chewy, not mushy.

1/2 cup of hot—not boiling—water and 1/3 cup of oatmeal. After the water and oatmeal have settled for two or three minutes, mix in 2 tablespoons of plain yogurt, 2 tablespoons of honey, and 1 small egg white. Apply a thin layer of the mixture to your face, and let it sit for 10 to 15 minutes. Then rinse with warm water. (Be sure to place a metal or plastic strainer in your sink to avoid clogging the drain with the granules.)

Make a dry shampoo

Do you sometimes need to skip washing your hair in order to get to work on time? Keep a batch of dry shampoo on hand in an airtight container specifically for those occasions when your alarm clock "malfunctions." Put 1 cup of oatmeal

in the blender and grind it into a fine powder. Add 1 cup of baking soda, and mix well. Rub a bit of the mixture into your hair. Give it a minute or two to soak up the oils, then brush or shake it out of your hair (preferably over a towel or bag to avoid getting it all over). This dry shampoo mixture is also ideal for cleaning the hair of bedridden people who are unable to get into a shower or bathtub. Plus, it's equally effective for deodorizing that big ol' bath-hating mutt of yours.

Olive Oil

Remove paint from hair

Did you get almost as much paint in your hair as you did on the walls in your last paint job? You can easily remove that undesirable tint by moistening a cotton ball with some olive oil and gently rubbing it into your hair. The same approach is also effective for removing mascara—just be sure to wipe your eyes with a tissue when done.

Make your own furniture polish

Restore the lost luster of your wooden furniture by whipping up some serious homemade furniture polish that's just as good as any of the commercial stuff. Combine 2 parts olive oil and 1 part lemon juice or white vinegar in a clean recycled spray bottle, shake it up, and spritz on. Leave on the mixture for a minute or two, then wipe off with a clean terry-cloth or paper towel. In a hurry? Get fast results by applying olive oil straight from the bottle onto a paper towel. Wipe off the excess with another paper towel or an absorbent cloth.

Use as hair conditioner

Is your hair as dry and brittle as sagebrush in the desert? Put the moisture back into it by heating 1/2 cup of olive oil (don't boil it), and then liberally applying it to your hair. Cover your hair with a plastic grocery bag, then wrap it in a towel. Let it set for 45 minutes, then shampoo and thoroughly rinse.

Clear up acne

Okay, the notion of applying oil to your face to treat acne does sound a bit wacky. Still, many folks swear this works: Make a paste by mixing 4 tablespoons of salt with 3 tablespoons of olive oil. Pour the mixture onto your hands and fingers and work it around your face. Leave it on for a minute or two, then rinse it off with warm, soapy water. Apply daily for one week, then cut back to two or three times weekly. You should see a noticeable improvement in your condition. (The principle is that the salt cleanses the pores by exfoliation, while the olive oil restores the skin's natural moisture.)

Substitute for shaving cream

If you run out of shaving cream, don't waste your time trying to make do with soap—it could be rough on your skin. Olive oil, on the other hand, is a dandy substitute for shaving cream. It not only makes it easier for the blade to glide over your face or legs, but it will moisturize your skin as well. In fact, after trying this, you may swear off shaving cream altogether.

Clean your greasy hands

To remove car grease or paint from your hands, pour 1 teaspoon of olive oil and 1 teaspoon of salt or sugar into your palms. Vigorously rub the mixture into your hands and between your fingers for several minutes; then wash it off with soap and water. Not only will your hands be cleaner, they'll be softer as well.

Recondition an old baseball mitt

If your beloved, aging baseball glove is showing signs of wear and tear—cracking and hardening of the leather—you can give it a second lease on life with an occasional olive oil rubdown. Just work the oil into the dry areas of your mitt with a soft cloth, let it set for 30 minutes, then wipe off any excess. Your game may not improve, but at least it won't be your glove's fault. Some folks prefer to use bath oil to recondition their mitts.

WHAT KIND OF OLIVE OIL TO BUY?

Expensive extra virgin olive oil is made from olives crushed soon after harvest and processed without excessive heat. It's great for culinary uses where the taste of the oil is important. But for **everyday cooking** and **nonfood applications,** lower grades of olive oil—light, extra light, or just plain olive oil—work fine and save you money.

Oven Cleaner

Clean ovenproof glass cookware

You've tried everything to scrub those baked-on stains off your Pyrex or CorningWare cookware. Now try this: Put on rubber gloves and cover the cookware with oven cleaner. Then place the cookware in a heavy-duty garbage bag, close it tightly with twist ties, and leave overnight. Open the bag outdoors, keeping your face away from the dangerous fumes. Use rubber gloves to remove and wash the cookware.

Clean a cast-iron pot

If you need to clean and re-season that encrusted secondhand cast-iron skillet you found at a yard sale, start by giving it a good spraying with oven cleaner and placing it in a sealed plastic bag overnight. (This keeps the cleaner working by preventing it from drying.) The next day, remove the pot and scrub it with a stiff wire brush. Then, wash it thoroughly with soap and water, rinse well, and immediately dry it with a couple of clean, dry cloths. Note: This technique eliminates built-up gunk and grease, but not rust. For that, you'll need to use vinegar. Don't leave it on too long, though. Prolonged exposure to vinegar can damage your cast-iron utensil.

Put the style back in your curling iron

Is your curling iron buried under a layer of caked-on styling gel or conditioner? Before the next time you use it,

➕ **TAKE CARE** Most oven cleaners contain highly caustic lye, which can burn the skin and damage the eyes. Always wear long rubber gloves and protective eyewear when using oven cleaner. The mist from oven cleaner spray can irritate nasal membranes. Ingestion can cause corrosive burns to the mouth, throat, and stomach that require immediate medical attention. Store oven cleaner well out of children's reach.

spray on a light coating of oven cleaner. Let it sit for one hour, then wipe it off with a damp rag, and dry with a clean cloth. Warning: Do not use iron until it is thoroughly dry.

Wipe away bathtub ring

Got a stubborn stain or ring around your white porcelain tub that refuses to come clean? Call out the big guns by spraying it with oven cleaner. Let it sit for a few hours, then give it a thorough rinsing. Warning: Do not apply oven cleaner to colored porcelain tubs; it could cause fading. And be careful not to get the oven cleaner on your shower curtain; it can ruin both plastic and fabric.

Remove stains from concrete

Get those unsightly grease, oil, and transmission fluid stains off your concrete driveway or garage floor. Spray them with oven cleaner. Let it settle for 5 to 10 minutes, then scrub with a stiff brush and rinse it off with your garden hose at its highest pressure. Severe stains may require a second application.

Clean grimy tile grout lines

Ready for an all-out attack on grout grunge? First, make sure you have plenty of ventilation—it's a good idea to use your exhaust fan to suck air out of a small bathroom. Put on your rubber gloves and spray oven cleaner into the grout lines. Wipe the cleaner off with a sponge within five seconds. Rinse thoroughly with water to reveal sparkling grout lines.

Strip paint or varnish

For an easy way to remove paint or varnish from wooden or metal furniture, try using a can of oven cleaner; it costs less than commercial paint strippers and is easier to apply (that is, if you spray rather than brush it on). After applying, scrub off the old paint with a wire brush. Neutralize the stripped surface by coating it with vinegar, and then wash it off with clean water. Allow the wood or metal to thoroughly dry before repainting. Don't use oven cleaner to strip antiques or expensive furnishings; it can darken the wood or discolor the metal.

Pantyhose

Using pantyhose around the house

Find lost small objects

Have you ever spent hours on your hands and knees searching through a carpet for a lost gemstone, contact lens, or some other tiny, precious item? If not, count yourself among the lucky few. Should you ever be faced with this situation, try this: Cut a leg off an old pair of pantyhose, make sure the toe section is intact, and pull it up over the nozzle of your vacuum cleaner hose. (If you want additional security, you can even cut off the other leg and slip that over as well.) Secure the stocking in place with a tightly wound rubber band. Turn on the vacuum, carefully move the nozzle over the carpet, and you'll soon find your lost valuable attached to the pantyhose filter.

Vacuum your fish tank

If you have a wet-dry shop vacuum, you can change the water in your fish tank without disturbing the gravel and tank accessories. (You'll still have to relocate the fish, of course.) Just pull the foot of an old nylon stocking over the end of the vacuum's nozzle, secure it with a rubber band, and you are ready to suck out the water.

Buff your shoes

Bring out the shine in your freshly pol-ished shoes by buffing them with a medium-length strip of pantyhose. It works so well, you may retire that chamois cloth for good.

Keep your hairbrush clean

If you dread the prospect of cleaning out your hair-brush, here's a way to make the job much easier. Cut a 2-inch (50-mm) strip from the leg section of a pair of panty-hose, and stretch it over and around the bristles of your new (or newly cleaned) hairbrush. If necessary, use a bobby pin or a comb to push the hose down over the bristles. The next time your brush needs cleaning, simply lift up and remove the pantyhose layer—along with all the dead hair, lint, etc. on top—and replace it with a fresh strip.

Remove nail polish

Can't find the cotton balls? Moisten strips of recycled pantyhose with nail polish remover to take off your old nail polish. Cut the material into 3-inch (75-mm) squares, and store a stack of them in an old bandage container or makeup case.

Keep spray bottles clog-free

If you recycle your spray bottles to use with homemade cleaners or furniture polishes, you can prevent any potential clogs by covering the open end of the tube—the part that goes inside the bottle— with a small, square-cut piece of pantyhose held in place with a small rubber band. This works especially well for filtering garden sprays that are mixed from concentrates.

Substitute for stuffing

Is your kid's teddy bear or doll losing its stuffing? Get out a needle and thread and prepare the patient for an emergency "stuffing transplant." Replace the lost filler with narrow strips of clean, worn-out pantyhose (ball them up, if possible). Stitch the hole up well, and a complete recovery is guaranteed. This works well with throw pillows and seat cushions too.

Organize your suitcase

As any seasoned traveler knows, you can squeeze more of your belongings into any piece of luggage by rolling up your clothes. To keep your bulkier rolls from unwrapping, cover them in flexible nylon tubes. Simply cut the legs off a pair of old pantyhose, snip off the foot sections, and stretch the stockings over your rolled-up garments. Happy travels!

Hold mothballs or potpourri

Looking for an easy way to store mothballs in your closet or to make sachets of potpourri to keep in your dresser drawers? Pour either ingredient into the toe section of your recycled nylons. Knot off the contents, then cut off the remaining hose. If you plan to hang up the mothballs, leave several inches of material before cutting.

Make a ponytail scrunchy

Why buy a scrunchy for your ponytail when you can easily make one for nothing? Just cut a horizontal strip about 3inches (75 mm) wide across a pantyhose leg, wrap it a few times around your ponytail, and you're done.

The Introduction of Nylon

Nylon, the world's first synthetic fiber, was invented at **E. I. DuPont de Nemours, Inc.,** and unveiled on October 28, 1938. Instead of calling a press conference, company vice president **Charles Stine** chose to make the landmark announcement to 3,000 women's club members at the **New York World's Fair,** introducing it with live models wearing nylon stockings. Stine's instincts were right on the money: By the end of 1940, DuPont had sold 64 million pairs of stockings. Nylon actually made its big-screen debut a year earlier, when it was used to create the tornado that lifted Dorothy out of Kansas in *The Wizard of Oz.*

Take a citrus bath

Make your own scented bath oil by drying and grinding up orange and/or lemon peels and then pouring them into the foot section of a recycled pantyhose. Put a knot about 1 inch (25 mm) above the peels, and leave another 6 inches (15 cm) or so of hose above that before cutting off the remainder. Tie the stocking to the bathtub faucet with the peels suspended below the running water. In addition to giving your bath a fresh citrus fragrance, you can use the stocking to exfoliate your skin.

Use to hang-dry sweaters

Avoid getting clothespin marks on your newly washed sweaters by putting an old pair of pantyhose through the neck of the sweater and running the legs out through the arms. Then hang the sweater to dry on your clothesline by clipping the clothespins onto the pantyhose instead of the wool.

Tie up boxes, newspapers, magazines

If you run out of twine (or need something stronger—say, for a large stack of glossy magazines), tie up your bundles of boxes, newspapers, and other types of recyclable paper goods using an old pair of pantyhose. Cut off the legs and waistband, and you'll be able to get everything curbside without any snags.

Cover a kids' bug jar

What child doesn't like to catch fireflies—and hopefully release them—on a warm summer night? When making a bug jar for your youngster, don't bother using a hammer and nail to punch holes in the jar's metal lid (in fact, save the lids for other projects). It's much easier to just cut a 5- or 6-inch (15-cm) square from an old pair of pantyhose and affix it to the jar with a rubber band. The nylon cover lets plenty of air enter the jar, and makes it easier to get the bugs in and out.

Using pantyhose in the kitchen

Make a pot or dish scrubber

Clean those stains off your nonstick cookware by making a do-it-yourself scrub pad. Crumple up a pair of clean old pantyhose, moisten it with a bit of warm water, add a couple of drops of liquid dishwashing detergent, and you're good to go. You can also make terrific scrubbers for dishes—as well as walls and other nonporous surfaces—by cutting off the foot or toe section, fitting it over a sponge, and knotting off the end.

Make a flour duster

Looking for a simple way to dust baking pans and surfaces with exactly the right amount of flour? Just cut the foot section off a clean old pantyhose leg, fill it with flour, tie a knot in it, and keep it in your flour jar. Give your new flour dispenser a few gentle shakes whenever you need to dust flour onto a baking pan or prepare a surface for rolling out dough for breads or pastries.

Keep a rolling pin from sticking

Getting pie dough to the perfect consistency is an art form in itself. Although you can always add water to dough that's too dry, it often results in a gluey consistency that winds up sticking to your rolling pin. Avoid the hassle of scraping clean your rolling pin by covering it with a piece of pantyhose. It will hold enough flour to keep even the wettest pie dough from sticking to the pin.

Secure trash bags

How many times have you opened your kitchen trash can only to discover that the liner has slipped down (and that someone in your house has covered it over with fresh garbage anyway)? You can prevent such "accidents" by firmly securing the garbage bag or liner to your trash can with the elastic waistband from a recycled pair of pantyhose; tie a knot in the band to keep it tight. You can also use this method to keep garbage bags from slipping off the edge of your outdoor garbage bins.

Dust under the fridge

Having trouble catching those dust bunnies residing underneath and alongside your refrigerator? Round them up by balling up a pair of old pantyhose and attaching it with a rubber band to a coat hanger or yardstick. The dust and dirt will cling to the nylon, which can easily be washed off before being called back for dusting duty.

Using pantyhose for house and garden jobs

Keep deer out of your garden

If you've been catching Bambi and her friends nibbling on your crops, put up a "No Trespassing" sign they will easily understand. Simply fill the foot sections of some old pantyhose with human hair clippings collected from hairbrushes or your local barbershop— or, even better, use Rover's fur after a good brushing. Tie up the ends, and hang up the nylon satchels where the deer tend to snack. They won't be back for seconds. The hair or fur will lose its scent after a while, so replace every four or five days as needed.

Clean up after gardening

Here are two recycling tips in one: Save up your leftover slivers of soap, and place them in the foot section of an old nylon stocking. Knot it off, and hang it next to your outdoor faucet. Use the soap-filled stocking to quickly wash off your hands after gardening and other outdoor work without worrying about getting dirt on door handles or bathroom fixtures inside your house.

Apply stain to wood crevices

Getting wood stain or varnish into the tight corners and crevices of that unfinished bookcase or table that you just bought can be a maddening task. Your brush just won't fit into them and

PANTYHOSE IS NOT AN EMERGENCY FAN BELT

You have probably heard that you can temporarily replace **a broken fan belt** with pantyhose in an emergency. Well, don't believe it—**it won't work!** Jim Kerr, automotive technician instructor at the Saskatchewan Institute of Applied Arts and Sciences and "Tech Talk" columnist for CanadianDriver.com, says, "Pulleys in most vehicles require flat belts, not the rounded shape pantyhose would present. Even on a V-belt pulley, **they fly off** as soon as the engine starts. We know; we've tried it." A much better idea is to replace the belts before they get in bad condition.

give them an even coating. But there's really nothing to it once you know the secret. Just cut a strip from an old pair of pantyhose, fold it over a few times, and use a rubber band to affix it to the tip of a wooden Popsicle stick. Dip your homemade applicator into the stain or varnish, and you'll have no trouble getting it into those hard-to-reach spots.

Test a sanded surface for snags

Think you did a pretty good job sanding down that woodworking project? Put it to the pantyhose test. Wrap a long piece of pantyhose around the palm of your hand and rub it over the wood. If the pantyhose snags onto any spots, sand them until you're able to freely move the nylon over the surface without any catches.

Clean your pool

Want a more effective way to skim the debris off the surface of your pool water? Cut a leg off a pair of pantyhose and fit it over your pool's skimmer basket. It will catch a lot of tiny dirt particles and hairs that would otherwise make their way into—and possibly clog—your pool's filter unit.

Make a paint strainer

Strain your paint like the pros: Use a pantyhose filter to remove the lumps of paint from an old can of paint. First, cut a leg off a pair of old pantyhose, clip the foot off the leg, and make a cut along the leg's length so that you have a flat piece of nylon. Then cut the leg into 12- to 14-inch (30- to 32-cm) sections to make the filters. Stretch the nylon over a clean bucket or other receptacle and hold it in place with a rubber band or perhaps even the waistband from that pair of pantyhose. Now slowly pour the paint into the bucket.

Some Stretchable Facts About Pantyhose

According to the Toy Industry Association, legendary doll maker **Madame Alexander** came up with the concept for pantyhose in the early 1950s, when she started sewing tiny pairs of silk stockings onto her dolls' underpants to keep them from slipping down. But **Allen Gant, Sr.,** of Burlington, North Carolina, invented pantyhose as we know them, and they were first produced in 1959 by Glen Raven Mills, his family's textile business. Another pantyhose pioneer is Hollywood actress **Julie Newmar,** best known as the original Catwoman on the old Batman TV series in the late 1960s, who holds a patent for "ultra-sheer, ultra-snug" pantyhose.

Paper Clips

Open shrink-wrapped CDs

Opening shrink-wrap, especially on CDs, can be a test of skill and patience! Save your fingernails and teeth from destruction. Twist out the end of a paper clip and slice the wrap. To prevent scratches, slip the clip under the folded section of wrap and lift up.

Use as hooks for hanging

Paper clips make great impromptu hooks. Making a hanging ceramic plaque? Insert a large, sturdy paper clip on the back before the clay hardens.

Use as zipper pull

Don't throw away your jacket or pocketbook just because the zipper pull broke. Untwist a small paper clip enough to slip it through the hole. Twist it closed and zip! For a more decorative look, thread beads over the paper clip or glue on sequins before closing.

Hold the end of transparent tape

Got a roll of transparent tape without a dispenser? Don't drive yourself nuts trying to locate and lift the end of the tape. Stick a paper clip under the end the next time you use the roll.

Make a bookmark

Paper clips make great bookmarks because they don't fall out. A piece of ribbon or colorful string attached to the clip will make it even easier to use and find.

Pit cherries

Need a seedless cherry for a recipe? Don't like to pit the cherry while you're eating it? Clip it to pit it! Over a bowl or sink, unfold a clean paper clip at the center and, depending on cherry size, insert either the clip's large or small end through the top. Loosen pit and pull. To de-pit cherries but leave stems intact, insert the clip in the bottom. Cherry juice stains, so watch your clothing.

Extend a ceiling fan chain

Put away the step stool and put an end to your ballet routine while trying to reach a broken or too-short ceiling fan chain. To extend the chain, just fasten a chain of paper clips to its end.

Potatoes

Remove stains on hands

Your family's favorite carrot soup is simmering on the stove, and you've got the orange hands to show for it. Otherwise hard-to-remove stains on hands from peeling carrots or handling pumpkin come right off if you rub your hands with a potato.

Remove a broken lightbulb

You're changing a lightbulb in the night-stand lamp, and it breaks off in your hand. So now the glass is off, but the stem's still inside. Unplug the lamp. Cut a potato widthwise and place it over the broken bulb. Twist, and the rest of the lightbulb should come out easily.

Remove tarnish on silverware

High tea is being served at your house later today, and you're out of silver polish. Grab a bunch of potatoes and boil them up. Remove them from the water and save them for another use. Place your silverware in the remaining water and let it sit for an hour. Then remove the silverware and wash. The tarnish should be gone.

Keep ski goggles clear

You can't keep a good lookout for trees and other skiers through snow goggles that fog up during your downhill descent. Rub raw potato over the goggles before you get on the ski lift, and the ride down should be crystal clear.

End puffy morning eyes

We all hate waking up in the morning and looking at our mug in the mirror. What are those puffy spots on your face? Oh yeah, those are your eyes. A little morning TLC is what you need. Apply slices of raw, cold potatoes to your peepers to make the puffiness go away.

Lure worms in houseplants

The worms crawl in and the worms crawl out of the roots of your favorite houseplant. The roots are suffering. What to do? Slice raw potato around the base of the plant to act as a lure for the worms. They'll crawl up to eat, and you can grab them and toss them out.

Feed new geraniums

A raw potato can give a fledgling geranium all the nutrients it could desire. Carve a small hole in a potato. Slip a geranium stem into the hole. Plant the whole thing, potato and all.

Hold a floral arrangement in place

If you have a small arrangement of flowers that you'd like to stabilize but have none of that green floral foam on hand to stick the flower stems in, try a large baking potato. Cut it in half lengthwise and place it cut side down. Poke holes where you want the flowers and then insert the stems.

Restore old, beat-up shoes

Try as you might, your old shoes are just too scuffed to take a shine anymore. They don't have holes, and they are so nice and comfy that you hate to throw them away. Before you give them the brush-off, cut a potato in half and rub those old shoes with the raw potato. After that, polish them; they should come out nice and shiny.

Make a hot or cold compress

Potatoes retain heat and cold well. The next time you need a hot compress, boil a potato, wrap it in a towel, and apply to the area. Refrigerate the boiled potato if you need a cold compress.

MAKE A DECORATIVE STAMP

Forget those expensive rubber stamps that go for up to $10 or more apiece. A potato can provide the right medium for making your own stamp for decorating **holiday cards** and envelopes. Here's how:

1 Cut a potato in half widthwise.

2 Use a **ballpoint pen** to draw a design on the cut surface of one potato half. Start with something simple—a square, triangle, star, or a Christmas tree. Or even easier, use a **cookie cutter** to press a shape into the potato.

3 Using a **sharp knife**—utility, craft, and paring knives all work well—cut around the design along the lines. Trim away the surrounding potato flesh to a depth of about 1/4 inch (6 mm). *Note:* Make sure that this knife wielding is done by an adult. If you want children to do the carving, give them a plastic knife or a spoon.

4 Pour a little **poster paint** in a shallow dish or old **pie pan,** dip the stamp in the paint, and start stamping as you would with a rubber version. Experiment with clusters, repeating patterns, overlaps, and other colors using the same and different designs.

Rubber Bands

Get a grip on twist-off tops

Ouch! The tops on most beer bottles these days are supposed to be twist-off, but for some reason they still have those sharp little crimps from the bottle-opener days. And those little crimps can really dig into your hand. Wrap the top in a rubber band to save the pain. The same trick works great for smooth, tough-to-grip soda bottle tops too.

Get a grip on drinking glasses

Does arthritis make it tough for you to grasp a drinking glass securely, especially when it is wet with condensation? Wrap a couple of rubber bands around the glass to make it easier to grip. Works great for kids, too, whose small hands sometimes have a hard time holding a glass.

Reshape your broom

No need to toss out that broom because the bristles have become splayed with use. Wrap a rubber band around the broom a few inches from the bottom. Leave it for a day or so to get the bristles back in line.

Childproof kitchen and bath cabinets

The grandkids are coming! Time to get out the rubber bands and temporarily childproof the bathroom and kitchen cabinets you don't want them to get into. Just wrap the bands tightly around pairs of handles.

Keep thread from tangling

Tired of tangled thread in your sewing box? Just wrap a rubber band around the spools to keep the thread from unraveling.

Make a holder for your car visor

Snap a couple of rubber bands around the sun visors of your car. Now you have a handy spot to slip toll receipts, directions, maybe even your favorite CD.

Thumb through papers with ease

Stop licking your finger. Just wrap a rubber band around your index finger a few times the next time you need to

The Birth of the Rubber Band

The first rubber band was patented in 1845 by **Stephen Perry,** who owned a manufacturing company in London.

shuffle papers. Not too tight, though! You don't want to cut off circulation to your fingertip.

Extend a button

Having trouble breathing? Maybe that top shirt button is a tad too tight. Stick a small rubber band through the buttonhole, then loop the ends over the button. Put on your tie and breathe easy.

Use as a bookmark

Paper bookmarks work fine, until they slip out of the book. Instead, wrap a rubber band from top to bottom around the part of the book you've already read. You won't lose your place, even if you drop the book.

Cushion your remote control

To protect your fine furniture from scratches and nicks, wrap a wide rubber band around both ends of the television remote control. You'll be protecting the remote too—it will be less likely to slide off a table and be damaged.

Secure bed slats

Do the slats under your mattress sometimes slip out? Wrap rubber bands around their ends to make them stay in place.

Tighten furniture casters

Furniture leg casters can become loose with wear. To tighten up a caster,

AN INTERESTING FACT ABOUT RUBBER

A key ingredient in making rubber bands is **sulfur.** When it is added to the rubber and heated—a process known as **vulcanization**—it makes the rubber strong and stretchy and prevents it from rotting. The process of making rubber bands is surprisingly similar to making a loaf of bread. First the dry ingredients are mixed with natural rubber. The resulting friction and chemical reaction heats and partially vulcanizes the rubber. The rubber is cooled, then rolled out like bread dough. It's extruded into a long tube, and the tube is heated to finish the vulcanization. Then it's rinsed, cooled, and sliced into bands.

wrap a rubber band around the stem and reinsert.

Gauge your liquids

Hm, just how much finish is left in that can up on the shelf anyway? Snap a band around the liquid containers in your workshop to indicate how much is left and you'll always know at a glance.

Wipe your paintbrush

Every time you dip your paintbrush, you wipe the excess against the side of the can. Before you know it, paint is dripping off the side of the can and the little groove around the rim is so full of paint that it splatters everywhere when you go to hammer the lid back on. Avoiding all this mess is easy. Just wrap a rubber band around the can

from top to bottom, going across the middle of the can opening. Now, when you fill your brush, you can just tap it against the rubber band and the excess paint will fall back into the can.

Rubbing Alcohol

Remove hair spray from mirrors

When you are spritzing your head with hair spray, some of it inevitably winds up on the mirror. A quick wipe with rubbing alcohol will whisk away that sticky residue and leave your mirror sparkling clean.

Clean Venetian blinds

Rubbing alcohol does a terrific job of cleaning the slats of Venetian blinds. To make quick work of the job, wrap a flat tool—a spatula or maybe a 6-inch (15-cm) drywall knife—in cloth and secure with a rubber band. Dip in alcohol and go to work.

Keep windows sparkling and frost-free

Do your windows frost up in the wintertime? Wash them with a solution of 1/2 cup of rubbing alcohol to 1 quart (1 liter) of water to prevent the frost. Polish the windows with newspaper after you wash them to make them shine.

Dissolve windshield frost

Wouldn't you rather be inside savoring your morning coffee a little longer instead of scrape, scrape, scraping frost off your car windows? Fill a spray bottle with rubbing alcohol and spritz the car glass. You'll be able to wipe the frost right off. Ah, good to the last drop!

Prevent ring around the collar

To prevent your neck from staining your shirt collar, wipe your neck with rubbing alcohol each morning before you dress. Feels good too.

Clean your phone

Is your phone getting a bit grubby? Wipe it down with rubbing alcohol. It'll remove the grime and disinfect the phone at the same time.

Remove ink stains

Did you get ink on your favorite shirt or dress? Try soaking the spot in rubbing alcohol for a few minutes before putting the garment in the wash.

Erase permanent markers.

Did Junior decide to decorate your countertop with a permanent marker? Don't worry, most countertops are made of a nonpermeable material such as plastic laminate or marble. Rubbing alcohol will dissolve the marker back to a liquid state so you can wipe it right off.

Remove dog ticks

Ticks hate the taste of rubbing alcohol as much as they love the taste of your dog. Before you pull a tick off Fido, dab the critter with rubbing alcohol to make it loosen its grip. Then grab the tick as close to the dog's skin as you can and pull it straight out. Dab again with alcohol to disinfect the wound. This works on people too.

Get rid of fruit flies

The next time you see fruit flies hovering in the kitchen, get out a fine-misting spray bottle and fill it with rubbing alcohol. Spraying the little flies knocks them out and makes them fall to the floor, where you can sweep them up. The alcohol is less effective than insecticide, but it's a lot safer than spraying poison around your kitchen.

Make a shapeable ice pack

The problem with ice packs is they won't conform to the shape of the injured body part. Make a slushy, conformable pack by mixing 1 part rubbing alcohol with 3 parts water in a self-closing plastic bag. The next time that sore knee acts up, wrap the bag of slush in a cloth and apply it to the area. Ahhh!

Stretch tight-fitting new shoes

This doesn't always work, but it sure is worth a try: If your new leather shoes are pinching your feet, try swabbing the tight spot with a cotton ball soaked in rubbing alcohol. Walk around in the shoes for a few minutes to see if they stretch enough to be comfortable. If not, the next step is to take them back to the shoe store.

➕ **TAKE CARE** Don't confuse denatured alcohol with rubbing alcohol. Denatured alcohol is ethanol (drinking alcohol) to which poisonous and foul-tasting chemicals have been added to render it unfit for drinking. Often, the chemicals used in denatured alcohol are not ones you should put on your skin. Rubbing alcohol is made of chemicals that are safe for skin contact—most often it's 70 percent isopropyl alcohol and 30 percent water.

Sandpaper

Sharpen sewing needles

Think twice before throwing out a used piece of fine-grit sandpaper; the unused edges or corners are perfect for tucking into your sewing box. Poking your sewing needles through sandpaper a few times, or twisting them inside a folded piece of sandpaper, will make them sharper than ever.

Sharpen your scissors

Are your scissor cuts less than crisp? Try cutting through a sheet of fine-grit sandpaper to finish off the edge and keep your cuts clean.

Remove fuzzy pills on sweaters

If you're fighting a losing battle with the fuzz balls on your sweaters, a little sandpaper will handle them. Use any grit, and rub lightly in one direction.

Remove scorches on wool

Take some medium-grit sandpaper to any small scorch spots on your woolen clothing. The mark left by a careless spark will be less noticeable with some light sanding around the edges.

Hold pleats while ironing

If you're a pleat perfectionist, keep some fine- or medium-grit sandpaper handy with your iron. Put the sandpaper under the pleat to hold it in place while you iron a nice sharp fold.

Roughen slippery leather soles

New shoes with slippery soles can send you flying, so take a little sandpaper and a little time to sand across the width of the soles and roughen up the slick surface. It's thriftier and easier than taking your new shoes to a repair shop to have new rubber soles put on.

Remove ink stains and scuff marks from suede

A little fine-grit sandpaper and a gentle touch are great for removing or at least minimizing an ink stain or small scuff mark on suede clothing or shoes. Afterward, bring up the nap with a toothbrush or nailbrush. You might avoid an expensive trip to the dry cleaner!

Use to deter slugs

Slugs are truly the unwelcome guests that will never leave, but you can stop them from getting into your potted plants in the first place. Put those used sanding disks to work under the bases of your pots, making sure the sandpaper is wider than the pot base.

Remove stubborn grout stains

Sometimes your bathroom abrasive cleaner is just not abrasive enough. Get tough on grout stains with fine-grit sandpaper. Fold the sandpaper and use the folded edge to sand in the grout seam. Be careful not to sand the tile and scratch the finish.

Open a stuck jar

Having a tough time opening a jar? Grab a piece of sandpaper and place it grit side down on the lid. The sandpaper should improve your grip enough to do the job.

Make an emery board

If you don't have an emery board handy the next time you need to smooth your nails, just raid the sandpaper stash in the garage workshop. Look for a piece marked 120 grit or 150 grit on the back.

Shampoo

Revitalize leather shoes and purses

You don't need expensive mink oil to bring life back to your leather shoes and purses. A little shampoo and a clean rag will do the job. Rub shampoo into worn areas in circles to clean and bring back the color of your accessories. It will protect your shoes from salt stains as well.

Lubricate a zipper

If your zipper gets stuck, don't yank on it until it breaks. Put a drop of shampoo on a cotton swab and dab it onto the zipper. The shampoo will help the zipper to slide free, and any residue will come out in the next wash.

Resize a shrunken sweater

Oh no, you've shrunk your favorite sweater! Don't panic, you can bring it back to full size again with baby shampoo and warm water. Fill a basin with warm water, squirt in some baby shampoo, and swish once with your hand. Lay the sweater on top of the water and let it sink on its own and soak for 15 minutes. Gently take your sweater out without wringing it and put it in a container, then fill the sink again with clean water. Lay the sweater on top and let it sink again to rinse. Take the sweater out, place it on a towel, and roll the towel to take out most of the moisture. Lay the sweater on a dry towel on a flat surface and gently start to reshape it. Come back to the sweater while it's drying to

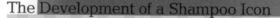

The Development of a Shampoo Icon

One of the longest-running advertising campaigns in history, **"the Breck Girl,"** was the brainchild of Edward Breck, a member of the family that started Breck Shampoo Co. The ads, featuring wholesome, beautiful girls with gorgeous hair, began in 1936, during the Great Depression, although they didn't go national until 1947. Only two artists were used during the 40-year campaign. The best known was Ralph William Williams, who took over the job in 1957. Among the models for Williams's Breck girls were **Cybill Shepherd, Kim Basinger,** and **Brooke Shields**—all unknowns at the time. The campaign ceased soon after Williams's death in 1976.

reshape a little more each time. Your patience will be rewarded!

Remove sticky gunk from pet fur

Did Rex or Fluffy step on tar or roll in what you hope is gum? Rub a tiny amount of shampoo on the spot and gently draw out the sticky stuff toward the end of the fur. Rinse with a wet cloth.

Revitalize your feet

Give your feet a pick-me-up while you sleep. Rub a little shampoo all over your feet and put on a light pair of cotton socks. When you wake up, your feet will feel smooth and silky.

Clean your car

The grease-cutting power of shampoo works on the family grease monkey's baby as well. Use about 1/4 cup shampoo to a bucket of water and sponge up the car as usual. Use a dab of shampoo directly on a rag or sponge for hard-to-remove tar spots.

Lubricate stubborn nuts and bolts

Got a nut and bolt that won't come apart? If your spot lubricant isn't handy or you've run out, try a drop of shampoo. Let the shampoo seep into the threads and the bolt will be much more cooperative.

Remove your eye makeup

You can't beat no-tears baby shampoo for a thrifty eye makeup remover. Put a drop on a damp cotton pad to gently remove the makeup, then rinse clear. No frills, no tears!

Remove bandages painlessly

Now you don't have to say "Ready?" when removing a bandage. Rub just a drop of shampoo on and around the bandage to let it seep through the air holes. It will come off with no muss and definitely no fuss.

Give yourself a bubble bath

Shampoo makes a nice and sudsy bubble bath. It's especially relaxing if

The Lean-Back Chair for Shampooing

In the early 1900s, **Martha Matilda Harper** invented the reclining chair used when shampooing hair at beauty salons—unfortunately, she never patented it. But Harper was still a success. She emigrated from Canada to the United States as a young girl, bringing her own recipe for a hair "tonic" (shampoo). Eventually she went from making her tonic in a shed to opening her own shop, where she offered the **Harper Method.** She enticed wealthy women to leave their homes for a health-conscious salon experience, where they would be shampooed and pampered by professionals. She was her own best advertisement, with hair that reached down past her feet.

you love the scent of your favorite shampoo, and the tub will rinse cleaner.

Substitute for shaving cream

You're on the road and discover you forgot to bring your shaving cream. Don't use soap to lather up. With its softening agents, shampoo is a much better alternative.

Clean grimy hands

In place of soap, some straight shampoo works wonders for cleaning stubborn or sticky grime from your hands. It even works well to remove water-based paint.

Remove hair spray from walls

If you've been using hair spray to kill flies, or you've just noticed hair spray buildup on your bathroom walls, reach for the shampoo. Put some on a wet sponge to clean, and wipe off suds with a clean, wet sponge. Shampoo is tailor-made to handle hair product buildup.

Clean the tub and faucets

Need to do a quick tub cleanup before guests arrive? Grab the handiest item—your shampoo! It does a great job on soap scum because it rinses clean. You can use it to buff a shine into your chrome faucets as well.

Use to wash delicates

Shampoo makes a great cleanser for your delicates. It suds up well with just a drop, and you get two cleaning products for the price of one!

Clean brushes and combs

Skin oils can build up on your combs and brushes faster than you realize. And if you're tucking them into your purse or pocket, they're accumulating dust and dirt as well. Give them a fresh start in a shampoo bath. First comb any loose hair out of the brush, then rub a little shampoo around the bristles or along the teeth of the comb. Put a small squirt of shampoo in a tall glass of water, let the comb and brush sit for a few minutes, swish, and rinse clean.

Shortening

Clean ink stains

Next time a leaky pen leaves your hands full of ink, reach for a can of shortening. To remove ink stains from your hands and also from vinyl surfaces, rub on a dollop of shortening and wipe the stains away with a rag or paper towel.

Remove sticky adhesives

Don't wear down your fingernails trying to scratch off resistant sticky labels and price tags. Instead use shortening to remove them (and their dried glue and gum residue) from glass, metals, and most plastics. Simply coat the area with shortening, wait 10 minutes, and scrub clean with a gentle scrub-sponge.

Soothe and prevent diaper rash

Next time the baby is fussing from a painful case of diaper rash, rub some shortening on his bottom for fast relief. It will soothe and moisturize his sensitive skin.

Remove tar from fabric

Tar stains on clothing are icky and tough to remove, but you can make the job easier with a little help from some shortening. After scraping off as much of the tar as you can, put a small glob of shortening over the remaining spot. Wait 3 hours, and then launder as usual.

TIPS ON USING SHORTENING

- Keep shortening away from **sunlight** to keep it from turning rancid.
- Never leave shortening **unattended** while frying.
- The most **efficient temperature** for frying with shortening is 325° to 350°F (165° to 180°C). Do not overheat shortening or it will burn. If shortening starts to smoke, turn off the heat and let it cool.
- If shortening catches **fire,** cover the pan with its lid, turn off the heat, and let it cool. Never put water on burning or hot shortening: It may splatter and burn you.

Keep snow from sticking to shovel

Before you dig out the car or shovel the driveway after a snowstorm, coat the blade of your snow shovel with shortening or liquid vegetable oil. It will not only keep snow from sticking but also make shoveling less tiring and more efficient.

Polish galoshes

To make dirty galoshes shine like new again, rub on some shortening and wipe with a clean rag or cloth.

Remove makeup

All out of your regular makeup remover? Don't fret: Just use a dab of shortening instead. Your face won't know the difference.

Moisturize dry skin

Why pay for fancy creams and lotions to moisturize your skin when ordinary shortening can do the trick at a fraction of the cost? Some hospitals even use shortening to keep skin soft and moist, and you can too. Next time your hands are feeling dry and scaly, just rub in a little shortening. It's natural and fragrance-free.

Repel squirrels

Keep pesky squirrels from getting at a bird feeder. Just grease the pole with a liberal amount of shortening and the rodents won't be able to get a claw hold to climb up.

Soap

Loosen stuck zippers

Zipper stuck? Rub it loose with a bar of soap along the zipper's teeth. The soap's lubrication will get it moving.

Unstick furniture drawers

If your cabinet or dresser drawers are sticking, rub the bottom of the drawer and the supports they rest on with a bar of soap.

Lubricate screws and saw blades

A little lube with soap makes metal move through wood much more easily. Twist a screw into a bar of soap before driving it and rub some on your handsaw blade.

Remove a broken lightbulb

If a bulb breaks while still screwed in, don't chance nicks and cuts trying to remove it. First, turn off the power. Insert the corner of a large, dry bar of soap into the socket. Give it a few turns and that base will unscrew.

Say farewell to fleas

Fed up with those doggone fleas? Put a few drops of dish soap and some water on a plate. Place the plate on the floor next to a lamp. Fleas love light—they will jump on the plate and drown.

Deodorize your car

Want your car to smell nice, but tired of those tree-shaped pine deodorizers? Place a little piece of your favorite-smelling soap in a mesh bag and hang it from your rearview mirror.

Mark a hem

Forget store-bought marking chalk. A thin sliver of soap, like the ones left when a bar is just about finished, works just as well when you are marking a hem, and the markings wash right out.

Make a pin holder

Here's an easy-to-make alternative to a pincushion. Wrap a bar of soap in fabric and tie the fabric in place with a ribbon. Stick in your pins. As a bonus, the soap lubricates the pins, making them easier to insert.

Prevent cast-iron marks

Nip cookout cleanup blues in the bud. Rub the bottom of your cast-iron pot with a bar of soap before cooking with it over a sooty open flame. Look, Ma! No black marks!

Keep stored clothes fresh

Pack a bar of your favorite scented soap when you store clothes or luggage. It will keep your clothes smelling fresh till next season and prevent musty odor in your luggage.

Save those soap slivers

When your soap slivers get too tiny to handle, don't throw them away. Just make a small slit in a sponge and put the slivers inside. The soap will last for several more washings. Or make a washcloth that's easy for little hands to hold by putting the soap slivers in a sock.

MAKE YOUR OWN SOAP FOR GIFT-GIVING

Handcrafted soap makes a great gift and is easy to make. You need a solid bar of **glycerin** (from a drugstore); **soap molds** (from a crafts store); a clean, dry can; a double boiler; food coloring; and **essential oil**. Place the glycerin in the can and put the can in a double boiler, which has water in the top as well as the bottom, and heat until the glycerin melts. For color, mix in food coloring. Spray a mold with nonstick cooking spray and fill it halfway with melted glycerin. Add a few drops of essential oil and fill the rest with glycerin. Let it harden.

Soda pop

Clean car battery terminals

Yes, it's true, the acidic properties of soda pop will help to eliminate corrosion from your car battery. Nearly all carbonated soft drinks contain carbonic acid, which helps to remove stains and dissolve rust deposits. Pour some soda pop over the battery terminals and let it sit. Remove the sticky residue with a wet sponge.

Loosen rusted-on nuts and bolts

Stop struggling with rusted-on nuts and bolts. Soda pop can help to loosen any rusted-on nuts and bolts. Soak a rag in the soda pop and wrap it around the bolt for several minutes.

Remove rust spots from chrome

Are you babying an older car—you know, one of those babies that has real chrome on the outside? If the chrome is developing small rust spots, you can remove them by rubbing the area with a crumpled piece of aluminum foil dipped in cola.

Make cut flowers last longer

Don't throw away those last drops of soda pop. Pour about 1/4 cup into the water in a vase full of cut flowers. The sugar in the soda will make the blossoms last longer. *Note:* If you have a clear vase and want the water to remain clear, use a clear soda pop, such as Sprite or 7-Up.

Clean your toilet

Eliminate dirt and odor with a simple can of soda. Pour into the toilet, let sit for an hour, then scrub and flush.

Keep drains from clogging

Slow drain and no drain cleaner in the house? Pour a 2-liter bottle of cola down the drain to help remove the clog.

Get gum out of hair

It's inevitable—kids get gum in their hair. Put the gummy hair section in a bowl with some cola. Let soak for a few minutes and rinse.

Make a roast ham moist

Want to make your ham juicier? Pour a can of cola over your traditional ham recipe and follow regular baking instructions. Yum!

Clean your coins

Who wants dirty money? If coin collecting is your hobby, use cola to clean your stash. Place the coins in a small dish and soak in cola for a shimmering shine. Of course, you don't want to do this with very rare and valuable coins.

Remove oil stains from concrete

Here's how to remove oil stains from concrete driveways and garage floors: Gather up a small bag of cat litter, a few cans of cola, a stiff bristle broom, bucket, laundry detergent, bleach, eye protection, and rubber gloves. Cover the stain with a thin layer of cat litter and brush it in. Sweep up the litter and pour cola to cover the area. Work the cola in with a bristle broom, and leave the cola for about twenty minutes. Mix 1/4 cup of laundry detergent with 1/4 cup of bleach in 1 gallon (3.8 liters) of warm water and use it to mop up the mess.

Sponges

An unwelcome mat for garden

Anyone who's ever cleaned a floor with ammonia knows that the smell of this strong, everyday household cleaner is overpowering. Throw browsing animals "off the scent" of ripening vegetables in your garden by soaking old sponges in your floor-cleaning solution and distributing them wherever you expect the next garden raid.

Keep your veggies fresh

Moisture that collects at the bottom of your refrigerator bins hastens the demise of healthful vegetables. Extend their life by lining bins with dry sponges. When you notice that they're wet, wring them out and let them dry before putting them back in the fridge. Every now and then, between uses, let them soak in some warm water with a splash of bleach to discourage the growth of mold.

Stretch the life of soap

A shower is so refreshing in the morning—until you reach for the soap and are treated to the slimy sensation of a bar that's been left to marinate in its own suds. You'll enjoy bathing more and your soap will last longer if you park a sponge on the soap dish. It'll absorb moisture so soap can dry out.

Sop up umbrella overrun

It's raining, and the family has been tramping in and out with umbrellas all day. Your umbrella stand has only a shallow receptacle to catch drips. Suddenly there's a waterfall coming out of it! Protect your flooring from umbrella stand overflow with a strategically placed sponge in its base. If you forget to squeeze it out, it'll dry on its own as soon as the weather clears.

Protect fragile items

If you're shipping or storing small, fragile valuables that won't be harmed by a little contact with water, sponges are a clever way to cushion them. Dampen a sponge, wrap it around the delicate item, and use a rubber band to secure it. As it dries, the sponge will conform to the contours of your crystal ashtray or porcelain figurine. To unpack it, just dip the item in water again. You'll even get your sponge back!

Lift lint from fabric

To quickly remove lint and pet fur from clothes and upholstery, give the fabric a quick wipe with a dampened and wrung-out sponge. Just run your fingers over the sponge and the unwanted fuzz will come off in a ball for easy disposal.

Steel Wool

Turn nasty sneakers nice

If your sneakers are looking so bad that the only thing you'd do in them is, well, sneak around, some steel wool may keep them from the trash can. Moisten a steel wool soap pad and gently scrub away at stains and stuck-on goo. Wipe them clean with a damp sponge or send them through the washer, and you may be able to enjoy many more months of wear.

Crayons begone

Your toddler just created a work of crayon art on paper. Unfortunately, it's on the wallpaper. Use a bit of steel wool soap pad to just skim the surface, making strokes in one direction instead of scrubbing in a circle, and your wall will be a fresh "canvas" in no time.

"Shoo" heel marks away

Those black marks that rubber soles leave behind just don't come off with a mop, no matter how long you try. To rid a vinyl floor of unsightly smudges, gently rub the surface with a moistened steel wool soap pad. When the heel mark is gone, wipe the floor clean with a damp sponge.

Sharpen your scissors

Sometimes you just want a small piece of a steel wool soap pad for a minor job. Cutting it in half with a pair of scissors will help keep the scissors sharp while giving you the pint-size pad you need for your project.

Rebuff rodents

Mice, squirrels, and bats are experts at finding every conceivable entry into a house. When you discover one of their entry points, stuff it full of steel wool. Steel wool is much more effective than foam or newspaper because even dedicated gnawers are unlikely to try to chew through such a sharp blockade.

Keep garden tools in good shape

Nothing will extend the life of your gardening tools like a good cleaning at the end of each growing season. Grab a wad of fine steel wool from your woodshop (000, or "three aught," would be a good choice), saturate it with the same ordinary household oil you use on squeaky door hinges, and rub rust off your shears, loppers, shovels, and anything else with metal parts. Wipe them clean with a dry rag, sharpen any blades, and reapply a bit of oil before storing them for the winter.

DON'T USE STEEL WOOL ON STAINLESS STEEL

An oft-repeated advice is to clean stainless steel with steel wool. Yet stainless steel manufacturers caution against using any abrasive on stainless steel. Steel wool may make stainless steel look better, but it **scratches the surface** and ultimately **hastens rusting**. The safest way to care for stainless steel is to wash with a sponge and mild soap and water.

Straws

Keep jewelry chains unknotted

You're dressing for dinner out, and you reach into your jewelry box for your best gold chain only to find that it's tangled and kinked. Next time, run it through a straw cut to the proper length and close the clasp before putting it away. It'll always be ready to wear.

Give flowers needed height

Your flower arrangement would be just perfect, except a few of the flowers aren't tall enough. You can improve on nature by sticking each of the too-short stems into plastic straws, trimming the straw to get the desired height, and inserting them into the vase.

Get slow ketchup flowing

Anticipation is great, but ketchup that comes out of the bottle while your burger and fries are still hot is even better. If your ketchup is recalcitrant, insert a straw all the way into the bottle and stir it around a little to get the flow started.

Improvise some foamy fun

To make enough cheap and easy toys for even a large group of children, cut the ends of some plastic straws at a sharp angle and set out a shallow pan of liquid dish soap diluted with a little bit of water. Dip a straw in the soap and blow through the other end.

The Invention of the Paper Straw

The quest for a perfectly cold **mint julep** led to the invention of the drinking straw. Mint juleps are served chilled, and their flavor diminishes as they warm up. Holding a glass heats the contents, so the custom was to drink mint juleps through natural straws made from a section of **hollow grass stem,** usually rye. But the rye imparted an undesirable "grassy" flavor. In 1888 **Marvin Stone,** a Washington, D.C., manufacturer of paper cigarette holders, fashioned a **paper tube** through which to sip his favorite libation. When other mint julep aficionados began clamoring for paper straws, he realized he had a hot new product on his hands.

Little kids love the piles of bubbles that result.

Make a pull-toy protector

Pull toys are perennial favorites of young children, but you can spend all day untying the knots that a toddler will inevitably put in the pull string. By running the string through a plastic straw (or a series of them), you can keep it untangled.

Have seasonings, will travel

Maybe you're on a low-sodium diet and need potassium salt that most restaurants don't keep on the table, or perhaps you want salt and pepper to season your brown-bag lunch just before you eat it. Straws provide an easy way to take along small amounts of dry seasonings. Fold one end over and tape it shut, fill it, and fold and tape the other end. If moisture is a concern, use a plastic straw.

Fix loose veneer

The veneer from a favorite piece of furniture has lost its grip near the edge of the piece. A bit of yellow carpenter's glue is the obvious solution for re-adhering the veneer, but how do you get the glue under there? Veneer can be very brittle, and you don't want to break off a piece by lifting it up. The solution: Cut a length of plastic drinking straw and press it to flatten it somewhat. Fold it in half and fill one half with glue, slowly dripping the glue in from the top. Slip the filled half under the veneer and gently blow in the glue. Wipe off any excess, cover the area with wax paper and a wood block, and clamp overnight.

Sugar

Keep cut flowers fresh

Make your own preservative to keep cut flowers fresh longer. Dissolve 3 tablespoons of sugar and 2 tablespoons of white vinegar per quart (liter) of warm water. When you fill the vase, make sure the cut stems are covered by 3 to 4 inches (7 to 10 cm) of the prepared water. The sugar nourishes the plants, while the vinegar inhibits bacterial growth. You'll be surprised how long the arrangement stays fresh!

Nix nematode worms in garden

If your outdoor plants look unhealthy, with ugly knots at the roots, chances are they've been victims of an attack of the nematodes! The nematode worm, nemesis of many an otherwise healthy garden, is a microscopic parasite that pierces the roots of plants and causes knots. You can prevent nematode attacks by using sugar to create an inhospitable environment for the tiny worms. Apply 5 pounds (2 kg) sugar for every 250 square feet (25 square meters) of garden. Microorganisms feeding on the sugar will increase the organic matter in the soil, thereby eliminating those nasty little nematodes.

Soothe a burned tongue

That slice of piping-hot pizza sure looked great, but ouch! You burned your tongue when you bit into it. To relieve a tongue burned by hot pizza, coffee, tea, or soup, reach for the sugar bowl and sprinkle a pinch or two of sugar over the affected area. The pain will begin to subside immediately.

Stop your hiccups

Nobody really knows what causes hiccups, but they sure can be disruptive, annoying—and sometimes embarrassing. Next time they happen to you, try this sweet solution: Stir 1 teaspoon of sugar in a little warm water and put the solution on the back of your tongue. A teaspoon of honey will work just as well.

Settle an upset tummy

If you are feeling queasy, make your own anti-nausea syrup. Put 1/2 cup of white sugar and 1/4 of water into a saucepan, turn the heat to medium, and stir until you have a clear syrup. After the syrup cools to room temperature, take 1 to 2 tablespoons as needed.

Pamper a smarting bee sting

If you get stung by a bee or a wasp or bit by any other insect, just dip your index finger in water and dab it in the sugar bowl; then touch the sting site with your sugar-coated finger. Of course, if you are allergic to bees or wasps, get prompt medical attention instead.

Tea

Using tea for health and beauty

Cool sunburned skin

What can you do when you forget to use sunscreen and have to pay the price with a painful burn? A few wet tea bags applied to the affected skin will take out the sting. This works well for other types of minor burns (i.e., from a teapot or steam iron) too. If the sunburn is too widespread to treat this way, put some tea bags in your bathwater and soak your whole body in the tub.

Relieve your tired eyes

Revitalize tired, achy, or puffy eyes. Soak two tea bags in warm water and place them over your closed eyes for 20 minutes. The tannins in the tea act to reduce puffiness and soothe tired eyes.

Reduce razor burn

Ouch! Why didn't you remember to replace that razor blade before you started to shave? To soothe razor burn and relieve painful nicks and cuts, apply a wet tea bag to the affected area. And don't forget to replace the blade before your next shave.

Get the gray out

Turn gray hair dark again without an expensive trip to the salon or the use of chemical hair dyes. Make your own natural dye using brewed tea and herbs: Steep 3 tea bags in 1 cup of boiling water. Add 1 tablespoon of each of rosemary and sage (either fresh or dried) and let it stand overnight before straining. To use, shampoo as usual, and then pour or spray the mixture on your hair, making sure to saturate it thoroughly. Take care not to stain clothes. Blot with a towel and do not rinse. It may take several treatments to achieve desired results.

Condition dry hair

To give a natural shine to dry hair, use a quart (liter) of warm, unsweetened tea (freshly brewed or instant) as a final rinse after your regular shampoo.

Tan your skin with tea

Give pale skin a healthy tan appearance without exposure to dangerous ultraviolet rays. Brew 2 cups of strong black tea, let it cool, and pour into a plastic spray bottle. Make sure your skin is clean and dry. Then spray the tea directly onto your skin and let it air-dry. Repeat as desired for a healthy-looking glowing tan. This will also work to give a man's face a more natural look after shaving off a beard.

Drain a boil

Drain a boil with a boiled tea bag! Cover a boil with a wet tea bag overnight and the boil should drain without pain by the time you wake up next morning.

Soothe nipples sore from nursing

When breast-feeding the baby leaves your nipples sore, treat them to an ice-cold bag of tea. Just brew a cup of tea, remove the bag, and place it in a cup of ice for about a minute. Then place the wet tea bag on the sore nipple and cover it with a nursing pad under your bra for several minutes while you enjoy a cup of tea. The tannic acid in the wet tea leaves will soothe and help heal the sore nipple.

Soothe those bleeding gums

The child may be all smiles later when the tooth fairy arrives, but right now those bleeding gums are no fun whatsoever. To stop the bleeding and soothe the pain from a lost or recently pulled tooth, wet a tea bag with cool water and press it directly onto the site.

Relieve baby's pain from injection

Is the baby still crying from that recent inoculation shot? Try wetting a tea bag and placing it over the site of the injection. Hold it gently in place until the crying stops. The tannic acid in the tea will soothe the soreness. You might try it on yourself the next time an injection leaves your arm sore.

Dry poison ivy rash

Dry a weepy poison ivy rash with strongly brewed tea. Simply dip a cotton ball into the tea, dab it on the affected area, and let it air-dry. Repeat as needed.

Stop foot odor

Put an end to smelly feet by giving them a daily tea bath. Just soak your tootsies in strongly brewed tea for 20 minutes a day and say good-bye to offensive odors.

Make soothing mouthwash

To ease toothache or other mouth pain, rinse your mouth with a cup of hot peppermint tea mixed with a pinch or two of salt. Peppermint is an antiseptic and contains menthol, which alleviates pain on contact with skin surfaces. To make peppermint tea, boil 1 tablespoon of fresh peppermint leaves in 1 cup of water and steep for several minutes.

Using tea around the house

Tenderize tough meat

Even the toughest cuts of meat will melt in your mouth after you marinate them in regular black tea. Here's how: Place 4 tablespoons of black tea leaves in a pot of warm (not boiling) water and steep for 5 minutes. Strain to remove the leaves and stir in 1/2 cup of brown sugar until it dissolves. Set aside. Season up to 3 pounds (1.5 kg) meat with salt, pepper, onion, and garlic powder, and place it in a Dutch oven. Pour the liquid over the seasoned meat and cook in a preheated 325°F (165°C) oven until the meat is fork tender, about 90 minutes.

Clean wood furniture and floors

Freshly brewed tea is great for cleaning wood furniture and floors. Just boil a couple of tea bags in a quart (liter) of water and let it cool. Dip a soft cloth in the tea, wring out the excess, and use it to wipe away dirt and grime. Buff dry with a clean, soft cloth.

Create "antique" fashions

Soak white lace or garments in a tea bath to create an antique beige, ecru, or ivory look. Use 3 tea bags for every 2 cups of boiling water and steep for 20 minutes. Let it cool for a few minutes before soaking the material for 10 minutes or more. The longer you let it soak, the darker the shade you will get.

Shine your mirrors

To make mirrors sparkle and shine, brew a pot of strong tea, let it cool, and then use it to clean the mirrors. Dampen a soft cloth in the tea and wipe it all over the surface of the mirrors. Then buff with a soft, dry cloth for a sparkly, streak-free shine.

DYEING WITH HERBAL TEAS

Using regular tea to dye fabrics has been around for a long time and was first used to hide stains on linens. But you can also use **herbal teas** to dye fabric different colors and subtle hues. Try using hibiscus to achieve red tones and darker herbal teas like licorice for soft brown tints. Always experiment using fabric scraps until you obtain the desired results.

How an Emperor Discovered Tea

Legend has it that tea originated some 5,000 years ago with the Chinese emperor **Shen Nung.** A wise ruler and creative scientist, the emperor insisted that all drinking water be boiled as a health precaution. One summer day, during a rest stop in a distant region, servants began to boil water for the royal entourage to drink when some **dried leaves** from a nearby bush fell into the pot. As the water boiled, it turned brown. The emperor's scientific curiosity was aroused, and he insisted on tasting the liquid. It was just his cup of tea.

Control dust from fireplace ash

Keep dust from rising from the ashes when you clean out your fireplace. Before you begin cleaning, sprinkle wet tea leaves over the area. The tea will keep the ashes from spreading all over as you lift them out.

Perfume a sachet

Next time you make a sachet, try perfuming it with the fragrant aroma of your favorite herbal tea. Just open a few used herbal tea bags and spread the wet tea on some old newspaper to dry. Then use the dry tea as stuffing for the sachet.

Using tea in the garden

Give roses a boost

Sprinkle new or used tea leaves (loose or in tea bags) around your rosebushes and cover with mulch to give them a midsummer boost. When you water the plants, the nutrients from the tea will be released into the soil, spurring growth. Roses love the tannic acid that occurs naturally in tea.

Feed your ferns

Schedule an occasional teatime for your ferns and other acid-loving house-plants. Substitute brewed tea when watering the plants. Or work wet tea leaves into the soil around the plants to give them a lush, luxuriant look.

Prepare planter for potting

For healthier potted plants, place a few used tea bags on top of the drainage layer at the bottom of the planter before potting. The tea bags will retain water and leach nutrients to the soil.

Enhance your compost pile

To speed up the decomposition process and enrich your compost, pour a few cups of strongly brewed tea into the heap. The liquid tea will hasten decomposition and draw acid-producing bacteria, creating desirable acid-rich compost.

Toothpaste

Remove scuffs from shoes

A little toothpaste does an amazing job of removing scuffs from leather shoes. Just squirt a dab on the scuffed area and rub with a soft cloth. Wipe clean with a damp cloth. The leather will look like new.

Spiff up your sneakers

Want to clean and whiten the rubber part of your sneakers? Get out the non-gel toothpaste and an old toothbrush. After scrubbing, clean off the toothpaste with a damp cloth.

Clean your clothes iron

The mild abrasive in non-gel toothpaste is just the ticket for scrubbing the gunk off the bottom plate of your clothes iron. Apply the toothpaste to the cool iron, scrub with a rag, then rinse clean.

Polish a diamond ring

Put a little toothpaste on an old toothbrush and use it to make your diamond ring sparkle instead of your teeth. Clean off the residue with a damp cloth.

Deodorize baby bottles

Baby bottles inevitably pick up a sour-milk smell. Toothpaste will remove the odor in a jiffy. Just put some on your bottle brush and scrub away. Be sure to rinse thoroughly.

Prevent fogged goggles

Whether you are doing woodworking or going skiing or scuba diving, nothing is more frustrating (and sometimes dangerous) than fogged goggles. Prevent the problem by coating the goggles with toothpaste and then wiping them off.

Prevent bathroom mirrors from fogging

Ouch! You cut yourself shaving and it's no wonder—you can't see your face clearly in that fogged-up bathroom mirror. Next time, coat the mirror with non-gel toothpaste and wipe it off before you get in the shower. When you get out, the mirror won't be fogged.

Clean the bathroom sink

Non-gel toothpaste works as well as anything else to clean the bathroom sink. The tube's sitting right there, so just squirt some in, scrub with a sponge, and rinse it out. Bonus: The toothpaste will kill any odors emanating from the drain trap.

Remove crayon from walls

Did crayon-toting kids get creative on your wall? Roll up your sleeves and grab a tube of non-gel toothpaste and a rag or—better yet—a scrub brush.

 TAKE CARE All toothpaste, including gels, contains abrasives. The amount varies, but too much can damage your tooth enamel. People with sensitive teeth in particular should use a low-abrasive toothpaste. Ask your dentist which toothpaste is best for you.

Squirt the toothpaste on the wall and start scrubbing. The fine abrasive in the toothpaste will rub away the crayon every time. Rinse the wall with water.

Remove ink or lipstick stains from fabric

Oh no, a pen opened up in the pocket of your favorite shirt! This may or may not work, depending on the fabric and the ink, but it is certainly worth a try before consigning the shirt to the scrap bin. Put non-gel toothpaste on the stain and rub the fabric vigorously together. Rinse with water. Did some of the ink come out? Great! Repeat the process a few more times until you get rid of all the ink. The same process works for lipstick.

Remove beach tar

Getting that black beach tar on your feet can put a small crimp in your vacation, but it is easy enough to remove. Just rub it with some non-gel toothpaste and rinse.

Clear up pimples

Your teenager is bemoaning a prominent pimple, and the day before the dance too! Tonight, have her or him dab a bit of non-gel, nonwhitening toothpaste on the offending spot, and it should be dried up by morning. The toothpaste dehydrates the pimple and absorbs the oil. This remedy works best on pimples that have come to a head. *Caution:* This remedy may be irritating to sensitive skin.

Clean smells from hands

The ingredients in toothpaste that deodorize your mouth will work on your hands as well. If you've gotten into something stinky, wash your hands with toothpaste, and they'll smell great.

A Brief History of Toothpaste

Ancient Egyptians used a mixture of ox-hoof ashes, burned eggshells, myrrh, pumice, and water to clean their teeth. And for most of history, tooth-cleaning concoctions were used mostly by the wealthy. That began to change in 1850, when **Dr. Washington Sheffield** of New London, Connecticut, developed a formula we would recognize as toothpaste. He called it Dr. Sheffield's Creme Dentifrice. It was his son, Dr. Lucius Tracy Sheffield, who observed **collapsible metal tubes** of paint and thought, Why not toothpaste? To this day, Sheffield Laboratories, the company Dr. Washington Sheffield founded in 1850, continues to make toothpaste and put it in tubes.

Yogurt

Make moss "paint" for the garden

Wouldn't it be nice to simply paint some moss between the cracks of your stone walkway, on the sides of flowerpots, or anywhere else you want it to grow? Well, you can. Just dump a cup of plain active-culture yogurt into your blender along with a handful of common lawn moss and about a cup of water. Blend for about 30 seconds. Use a paintbrush to spread the mixture wherever you want moss to grow—as long as the spot is cool and shady. Mist the moss occasionally until it gets established.

Relieve sunburn

For quick, temporary relief of mild sunburn, apply cold plain yogurt. The yogurt adds much needed moisture and, at the same time, its coldness soothes. Rinse with cool water.

Make play finger paint

Ready for some messy rainy-day fun? Mix food coloring with yogurt to make finger paints and let the little ones go wild. You can even turn it into a lesson about primary and secondary colors. For example, have the kids put a few drops of yellow food coloring and a few drops of blue in the yogurt to make green finger paint. Or mix red and blue to produce purple.

Cure dog or cat flatulence

If Bowser has been a bit odoriferous lately, the problem may be a lack of the friendly digestive bacteria that prevent gas and diarrhea. The active culture in plain yogurt can help restore the helpful bacteria. Add 2 teaspoons of yogurt to the food for cats or small dogs weighing up to 14 pounds (6 kg). Add 1 tablespoon for medium-size dogs weighing 15 to 34 pounds (7 to 15 kg). Add 2 tablespoons for large dogs weighing 35 to 84 pounds (16 to 38 kg). Add 3 tablespoons for dogs larger than that.

MAKE A FACIAL MASK

You don't have to go to a spa to give your face a quick assist:

■ To **cleanse your skin** and tighten the pores, slather some plain yogurt on your face and let it sit for about 20 minutes.

■ For a revitalizing **facial mask,** mix 1 teaspoon of plain yogurt with the juice from 1/4 slice of orange, some of the orange pulp, and 1 teaspoon of aloe. Leave the mixture on your face for at least five minutes before rinsing it off.

Index

index

Credits

Cover image courtesy of PictureQuest and Brand X Pictures.

Interior photography courtesy of RDA Australia, RDA USA, Brand X Pictures, Corbis, digitalStock, digitalVision, PhotoDisc, and Stockbyte.

How-to Illustrations, pages 50-65, © Bryon Thompson.